EDITH H. REINISCH, M.S., M.S. HYG., M.P.H.
Holyoke Community College
Holyoke, Massachusetts

RALPH E. MINEAR JR., M.D., M.P.H.
Roxbury Comprehensive Community Health Center, Inc.
Roxbury, Massachusetts

Health of the Preschool Child

JOHN WILEY & SONS
New York • Chichester • Brisbane • Toronto • Singapore

Copyright © 1978, by John Wiley & Sons, Inc.

All rights reserved. Published simultaneously in Canada.

Reproduction or translation of any part of
this work beyond that permitted by Sections
107 and 108 of the 1976 United States Copyright
Act without the permission of the copyright
owner is unlawful. Requests for permission
or further information should be addressed to
the Permissions Department, John Wiley & Sons.

Library of Congress Cataloging in Publication Data:

Reinisch, Edith H
   Health of the preschool child.

   Bibliography: p. 243
   Includes index.
   1. Children—Care and hygiene. 2. Children—
Diseases. 3. Education, Preschool—1965-
I. Minear, Ralph E., joint author. II. Title.
RJ101.R43   613′.04′32   78-8743
ISBN 0-471-60800-9

Printed in the United States of America

12 13 14 15 16 17 18 19

To our families

PREFACE

With the safeguarding of young children's health in places other than their homes, fast becoming a concern of people other than their parents, we felt a need to help provide those who are charged with overseeing the physical, social, emotional, and cognitive health of little children with accurate, practical, and comprehensive information

This need of personnel in all types of preschool settings came to us from almost opposite directions, as members of two different professions.

Professor Edith Reinisch, while instructing college students in early childhood education, found that child health information for students other than those in the health professions, was difficult to find. Information that was available dealt mostly with the health of older school age children. This was confirmed when she attended meetings for planning in-service educational programs for staffs of preschools. It was noted that locating sources of adequate health information and the need for education in child health was a constant concern among preschool personnel.

Dr. Ralph Minear, a pediatrician, engaged in giving care to children in an urban neighborhood health center, found that teachers and parents of young children often do not know many important health facts. The type of telephone calls in which teachers requested information about a child with a particular medical problem demonstrated this. It was difficult to be completely helpful because the teachers were unable to give useful health information based on their knowledge and observations. Parents continued to bring their child to the health center for preadmission health examinations with little understanding of the purpose of such an evaluation. This led to inaccurate and missing information that affected the ability of teachers and health professionals to share information that would benefit the health of that child. Because of these deficiencies, Dr. Minear began inservice instructions in several preschool centers.

Knowing of each other's interests, the two authors joined forces to help a large group of preschool personnel fulfill their role in the young child's health program, resulting in this book. It is the first one written specifically to aid those enrolled in early childhood education studies, as well as individuals already working in preschool programs. The unique blend of both of these professionals' perspectives will instruct and stimulate those who participate in the protection and improvement of the health of preschool children. This textbook helps the preschool teacher to distinguish between what is normal and what is unusual in the appearance, behavior, and characteristic reactions of a child; to know what to do in an emergency to protect the child's life and health; and to provide a healthful and safe environment while preserving the personal dignity of each child.

This textbook can be the basis of a formal course on child health. Such a course should be included in every early childhood curriculum. It may also be used for in-service education and as a reference for teachers and parents.

A note on avoiding sex bias: students, teachers, and health professionals are men and women; children are girls and boys. In order to avoid sex bias the use of *he* and *she* is alternated in this book.

We take pleasure in expressing our appreciation to Dr. Edith M. Dowley for her encouragement and many suggestions about content and style, to Sabina Minear for suggesting ways to present concepts more clearly, to Dr. Frances A Hellebrandt and Professor Constance D'Elia for many corrections and editorial changes, and to Louise Landry for unlimited patience in typing the manuscript.

We also thank the American National Red Cross, Washington, D.C. and Springfield, Mass., for reviewing and commenting on Chapter 8, First Aid.

Finally, we would like to thank Bill Sullivan for his patience and the many suggestions during the writing of this book.

Edith H. Reinisch
Dr. Ralph E. Minear Jr.

CONTENTS

List of Illustrations	xi
1. Child Health—Whose Concern?	1
2. Preschool Health Program—An Overview	7
3. Nutrition	61
4. The Infectious Process	79
5. Health Assessment: Health Observations and Sharing Information with Parents	103
6. Care of the Child Who Is Ill and the Child Who Needs Specialized Attention	127
7. Behavioral Problems	157
8. First Aid	169
9. Accident Prevention and Safety	215
Glossary	235
Bibliography	243
Films	247
Guide to Sources of Selected Publications and Films	249
Index	251

ILLUSTRATIONS

Figure 2-1	Preadmission child health record	*11-15*
Figure 2-2	Application for admission	*16*
Figure 2-3	Admission information	*17*
Figure 2-4	Permission forms	*19*
Figure 2-5	Parent's agreement with goals and philosophy of health program	*20*
Figure 2-6	Checklist for daily health observations	*21*
Figure 2-7	Attendance record—continuing health supervision	*22*
Figure 2-8	Day care staff health observations	*23*
Figure 2-9	Report of child alleged to be suffering from serious physical or emotional injury by abuse or neglect	*25-26*
Figure 2-10	Special procedures; physician's instructions; parent's permission	*27*
Figure 2-11	Dental health record	*29*
Figure 2-12	Periodic health evaluation record	*30-31*
Figure 2-13	Care and follow-up of child's health problems	*32*
Figure 2-14	Daily food plan and serving portions	*35*
Figure 2-15	Employee pre-employment health evaluation	*38*
Figure 2-16	Teacher evaluation	*40-42*
Figure 2-17	Responsibility for the administration of the health program	*45*
Figure 2-18	Contract for health services	*45*
Figure 2-19	Letter of invitation to serve on the advisory committee to the health program	*47*
Figure 2-20	Functions and organization of the advisory committee to the health program	*48*
Figure 2-21	Budget guide for health program	*49*
Figure 2-22	Authorization to release health information	*50*
Figure 2-23	Record of health conferences with parents	*52*
Figure 4-1	Transmission of immunity from mother to newborn	*91*

xi

Figure 4-2	Recommended schedule for active immunization and tuberculin testing of normal infants and children	93
Figure 5-1	Growth chart	*116-117*
Figure 5-2	Denver Developmental Screening Test	*120-121*
Figure 6-1	Record of acute illnesses	*130*
Figure 6-2	Physician's certification that a child may return to preschool after an absence due to a medical reason	*131*
Figure 8-1	List of important phone numbers to be posted near the telephone	*171*
Figure 8-2	Emergency file card	*173*
Figure 8-3	Accident report form	*175-176*
Figure 8-4	Immobilization of lower leg	*191*
Figure 8-5	Immobilization of collarbone	*192*
Figure 8-6	Tilt head back	*196*
Figure 8-7	Abdominal thrust	*200*
Figure 8-8	What school personnel should know about the student with diabetes	*204-206*
Figure 8-9	To the babysitter	*207*
Figure 9-1	Official safety inspections	*219*
Figure 9-2	Safety checklist for building and grounds	*220*
Figure 9-3	Location of safety control	*227*
Figure 9-4	Emergency evacuation plan	*228*
Figure 9-5	Record of safety education activities	*231*

HEALTH OF THE PRESCHOOL CHILD

Credit: *Cynthia Barrett Hodges*

CHAPTER 1

Child Health— Whose Concern?

The preschool child has his whole life before him. But he must be healthy if he is to have a life that permits him to benefit from all of his abilities. A disease, an abnormal condition, an injury, or emotional and physical abuse or neglect may damage the young child's health. Early detection, good treatment, prevention, and support may reduce the damage. The maintenance of health, then, becomes an important endeavor of those who surround the preschool child.

What is health if it is so important? Health is a complex concept that is difficult to define. Yet many individuals and professional groups have offered definitions. A useful definition of health is the following one issued by the American Academy of Pediatrics. "Good health is a dynamic state of physical, mental, and social well-being which is influenced by many environmental and hereditary factors over which an individual exercises varying degrees of control. It is a constantly changing entity, and acquisition of good health should never be left to chance."

Why is the general public so concerned about the health of the preschool child? Cultures have always had a strong interest in their future generations. Assuring health has been part of that concern. Because of recent scientific achievements more people have come to expect that health will be an important factor in producing a better next generation. In the past the focus of concern rested primarily with parents. Now a very large number of young children no longer remains exclusively within the care of their parents but is enrolled in a variety of preschool programs. Therefore, the direct concern for children of this age group has broadened to include all individuals who care for them.

Who is likely to be watching over the health of preschool children? Besides parents there are health professionals who watch a child's growth and development. The health professionals wait for the child to come to them. They include physicians, medical specialists, pediatric nurse practioners, nurses, physician's assistants, and a large number of other persons whose primary work is in the field of health. We are aware of the different levels of training and experience in this group and we will specify the type of professional when it becomes necessary. It may also be volunteers, aides, student teachers, assistant teachers, teachers, or preschool directors who watch the child's health. For the sake of simplicity, and because preschool programs are learning experiences for children, we refer to all people in this category as teachers. We are quite aware of the differences in educational background and levels of responsibility among such personnel. Where a distinction is necessary it will be made. All nursery schools, day care programs, Head Start programs and other projects for young children will be referred to as preschool programs.

Since health is influenced by environmental factors, what is a healthful preschool environment? It is a well-designed physical facility with proper ventilation, heat, light, and a low noise level. It is a good playground with safe equipment. It is safe toys and materials for learning experiences. In addition to these physical aspects, a healthful environment also includes well-planned activities in the preschool, conducted by a well-trained staff who have proper attitudes toward children. In a good environment the children's health is protected, maintained, and improved at the same time that growth and development are promoted. This means the preschool will have a well-planned health program. Thus a healthful environment is more than a good physical environment; it is also a good psychological, cultural, and social environment. This leads us to the comprehensive concept of health expressed in the above statement and throughout this book. The term environment is used here in its broadest sense. A healthful environment then is the result of integration of many components.

Who of those watching over the young child's health is in the best position to carry out that task? It is the teacher in the preschool program. She is the one who knows almost as much about each child as the parent, because she sees him every day. The teacher has the advantage of seeing each child as one of a group of children of the same age, rather than as a single individual. She is likely to make more diverse demands than a parent on the child. Thus, health may be watched differently than it would be by a parent. The teacher's sole responsibility in the preschool situation is the child, whereas at home, the child competes for parental attention with many other activities. Such a focus sharpens the teacher's observational skills as the program progresses. The teacher serves the parents and is accountable to them for the child's health during a specific time. A parent does not have this type of obligation. His only obligation under law concerns harm, neglect or abuse. All of these reasons give the teacher an advantage in listening to, watching over, observing and caring for a young child's health needs. The importance of this role cannot be stressed enough.

How does the teacher watch a child's health? The teacher may be called on to do many things. Some of these are:

1. Interview parents about their child's health and about family health.
2. Recognize ill children and act in case of an emergency.
3. Make judgments when to consult a parent or a health professional.
4. Assist in the health evaluation of the children in the program and keep records of health information.
5. Include health education in the child's learning experiences.
6. Make the environment of the program safe and healthy.
7. Support essential health needs of some children.
8. Become the link between the child and the health professional.

Though these demands appear to be overpowering it does not mean the teacher must be a health expert. For example, he does not have to diagnose a case of measles or chicken pox. The teacher is a member of the health team, therefore he does not act alone. Instead, he helps the health professionals make the diagnosis and assists in restoring the child to good health. He does not have to treat a child who has had an accident. All he needs to do is give first aid until a health professional gives care. He does not and should not make any final decisions about the physical and mental development of a child. The specialist in each area will do that.

How does the teacher acquire the knowledge to perform all those tasks related to the care of a young child's health? What should the teacher know? The teacher acquires the knowledge through education and experience. The education may be a formal one or it may be acquired on the job. Experience may come from work in preschool programs or from being a parent. Regardless of how the teacher acquires knowledge it will be broadened by frequent consultations with health professionals and health-oriented literature.

The purpose of this book is to strengthen the knowledge of those who already work in preschool programs and to offer information to those who are preparing to enter this challenging field. The aim throughout the book is to include enough theoretical background material to insure an intelligent application of broadly conceived principles and practices. The focus, however, is on the efficient management of the day-by-day problems of preschool facilities cognizant of their unique place in modern society.

CONTENTS

2.1.0 HEALTH PROGRAM FOR CHILDREN
    2.1.1 A Preadmission Health Evaluation
        Comprehensive Medical Evaluation
        Preadmission Interview with Parents
    2.1.2 Continuous Health Supervision
        Daily Health Observations
        Care of the Child Who Becomes Ill
        Care of Injuries and Other Emergencies
        Management of Cases of Suspected Child Neglect and Abuse
        Specialized Care for Children
    2.1.3 Periodic Health Evaluation: Care and Followup of Health Problems
        Periodic Health Evaluation
        Periodic Review
        Care and Follow-up
    2.1.4 A Cumulative Health Record
    2.1.5 A Nutrition and Food Service
    2.1.6 A Safety and Accident Prevention Program
    2.1.7 Healthful Activities
2.2.0 HEALTH PROGRAM FOR THE PRESCHOOL STAFF
    2.2.1 Preemployment Health Evaluation
    2.2.2 Continuous Health Supervision and Evaluation
    2.2.3 Health Record for Personnel
2.3.0 EDUCATION OF THE PRESCHOOL STAFF ABOUT CHILD HEALTH
    2.3.1 Preemployment Education
    2.3.2 In-service Education
2.4.0 ADMINISTRATION OF THE PRESCHOOL HEALTH PROGRAM
    2.4.1 Responsibility for Administration
    2.4.2 Financial Management of the Health Program
    2.4.3 Health Program Record Keeping
        Individual Records
        Administrative Records
    2.4.4 Communication with Parents about Their Child's Health
    2.4.5 Evaluation of the Health Program
2.5.0 LAWS, RULES, AND REGULATIONS
    2.5.1 How Is Preschool Child Care Controlled?
    2.5.2 Why Were Laws Concerned with Child Care Enacted?
    2.5.3 Who Makes the Rules and Regulations for Preschools?
    2.5.4 What is the Purpose of Rules and Regulations?
    2.5.5 Licensing
    2.5.6 Examples of Rules and Regulations

Consultants	*Building and Grounds*
Admission Procedures	*Equipment*
Continuing Health Supervision	*Healthful Activities*
Child's Cumulative Health Record	*Staff of the Preschool*
Nutrition and Food Service	*Parent Involvement*

… CHAPTER 2

Preschool Health Program— An Overview

Health programs for preschools vary according to the needs of the children and families who use them. Also these programs are limited by available resources. However, goals of preschool programs ought to be the same regardless of the circumstances. These goals should be to protect, maintain, and improve the health of children.

The health program presented here is built on the concept of a healthy environment as discussed in the previous chapter. For instructional purposes the program presented here is a comprehensive and ideal one. Some of its components may not be necessary for your program and others do not have to be provided because they are available through other community agencies. What is needed in your program will be determined during its planning.

This chapter presents an overview of the total health program and discusses laws, rules, and regulations. Those functions of the health program that must be explained in greater detail are presented in later chapters. Examples of forms and records are offered to assist you in implementing the health program.

Planning the Health Program.

The goals, policies, and procedures of a health program should be stated in writing. As interpreted here, *goals* are what one intends to attain. A *policy* is an adopted or commonly agreed-on statement to regulate, standardize, or govern a course of action. A procedure is a method to carry out a statement of policy; it will include when an activity is to be done, how it will be done, and by whom. For example, a policy will be established for the activity of recording and reporting accidents. The procedure would specify who is to make a report, when an accident occurs, the type of form to be used, how to complete the form, and who should receive copies of the accident report. Policies and procedures are based on experience and expert knowledge. They should be realistic, workable, and contain a statement of goals. They should also be flexible and adjustable to suit changing goals or needs.

The goals, policies, and procedures for the health program will be determined by a planning committee. Because these aspects of the program ought to be broad, the committee should be composed of the director of the preschool program, the program's medical consultant, other professionals from the community, and parents. In case of a need for revision of policies in the future, a mechanism to do so quickly and simply should be established. Minutes or a record of all meetings including names of persons who attended should be kept. All staff and parents should see the statements prepared by the planning committee.

The complete program consists of a health program for children as well as one for the staff. The health program for children includes preadmission health evaluation, continuous health supervision, periodic health evaluation, care and follow-up, cumulative health record, nutrition and food service, first aid, safety and accident prevention program, and healthful activities.

The health program for the preschool staff consists of preemployment health evaluation and continuous health supervision and evaluation. It also includes education of the staff about child health.

The administrative aspects necessary to implement the health program are administrative responsibilities, financial management, record keeping, communication with parents, and program evaluation.

2.1.0 HEALTH PROGRAM FOR CHILDREN

The health of the child is the primary responsibility of his parent. However, while the child is in a preschool program his good health should be assured and the activities of the preschool should reflect this concern.

The program should be planned by a medical consultant and a planning committee. The medical consultant should be a pediatrician (a specialist in child health care) or another physician who has demonstrated special interest in child health and preschool programs. The physician should understand the objectives of a preschool program and recognize both potentials and problems for the child in such a program. The advice of a nurse, nutritionist, social worker and other specialists, when needed, should be used. One staff member should be assigned the responsibility for supervising the program. The health program begins with an evaluation of the child's health before admission into the preschool.

2.1.1 A Preadmission Health Evaluation

Policy

The purpose of a health evaluation of each child before admission to preschool is to accomplish several objectives:

1. To detect any health problem that requires care before the child enters preschool.
2. To determine if the child's health and developmental maturity is such that preschool would be appropriate.
3. To establish the current state of the child's health and development. The status on admission will be used as a baseline for comparison in the future.
4. To determine that the child is free from communicable disease that would endanger other children.
5. To determine that the child received all age-appropriate immunizations.
6. To see if the child has any special conditions that may require attention while the child is in preschool. It should be specified in writing if the child's activities are to be restricted or the child is to be placed in unique circumstances.
7. To determine if a child with a handicap can be accepted into the preschool program without causing harm.
8. To learn if a child's handicap is such that a special program could be offered but without neglecting the care of other children.
9. To give a comprehensive view of the previous health history of both the child and his family (parents, grandparents, brothers, and sisters). If a significant condition is found in the child's family, then the condition should be noted and also who is affected by it.
10. To list in the health history any foods or substances to which the child is known to be allergic.

11. To present a concise description of the child's habits, such as sleeping, use of the toilet, and eating preferences and dislikes. This information is important in order to understand the child's needs and help him adjust to preschool.

Procedure

To obtain the data for the evaluation, a physician's examination and interview with the child and her parents by the preschool director or other staff member are necessary.

Comprehensive Medical Evaluation.

To guarantee that the intent of the preadmission health evaluation is met the child should be examined by a physician not earlier than one month before admission to preschool. The physician should complete the health information form.

The *health information form* should include the following:

1. Statement by the physician that the child is in good health (physically and mentally) and is emotionally ready to enter a preschool program.
2. Types and dates of all immunizations received and those not completed to date.
3. Statements about the child's hearing and sight.
4. Results of blood test for anemia and when appropriate, sickle cell or other blood deficiencies, and result of urine analysis.
5. Special problems and needs.
6. Health history of the child and his family.

In order to standardize this information obtained from the physician's examination of the child you may design your own form or use the sample *physician's preadmission examination form* (Figure 2-1).

Preadmission Interview with Parents.

The child's parent should be interviewed by the preschool director or a staff member. During this interview the goals and philosophy of the health program should be explained. The interviewer should obtain and record general information about the child's family and the child's habits such as napping and eating

Health Program For Children

PREADMISSION CHILD HEALTH RECORD	NAME OF CHILD (LAST, FIRST, MIDDLE)		
IDENTIFICATION OF PROGRAM OR AGENCY	HOME ADDRESS (USE PENCIL AND KEEP CURRENT)		TELEPHONE NO.
	DATE OF BIRTH	PLACE OF BIRTH (CITY AND STATE)	
NAME OF MOTHER (LAST, FIRST, MIDDLE)	YEAR OF BIRTH	SCHOOL GRADE COMPLETED	
OCCUPATION OF MOTHER	WHAT LANGUAGE IS USUALLY SPOKEN IN THE HOME? ☐ ENGLISH ☐ OTHER		
NAME OF FATHER (LAST, FIRST, MIDDLE)	YEAR OF BIRTH	SCHOOL GRADE COMPLETED	
USUAL OCCUPATION OF FATHER	NO. WEEKS UNEMPLOYED IN PAST YEAR	EMPLOYER	
HEAD OF HOUSEHOLD IS ☐ FATHER ☐ MOTHER ☐ OTHER (SPECIFY)	DURING THE DAY, THIS CHILD IS USUALLY CARED FOR BY: ☐ MOTHER ☐ OTHER PERSON (GIVE NAME)		

FAMILY AND HOUSEHOLD

NAME	DATE OF BIRTH	LIVES WITH PATIENT YES / NO	HEALTH PROBLEMS AND PROGRESS
FATHER			
MOTHER			
CHILDREN IN ORDER OF BIRTH (LIST ALL PREGNANCIES INCLUDING PATIENT)			
1.			
2.			
3.			
4.			
5.			
6.			
OTHERS IN HOUSEHOLD (SHOW RELATIONSHIP)			
1.			
2.			
3.			
4.			

ARE THERE ANY DISEASES WHICH "RUN IN THE FAMILY"?
☐ NO ☐ YES (DESCRIBE)

IN CASE OF AN EMERGENCY PARENT OR GUARDIAN MAY BE CONTACTED AT: ☐ HOME ☐ OTHER	TELEPHONE NO.	IF AN ILLNESS OR INJURY REQUIRES A DOCTOR'S ATTENTION, CALL (NAME OF DOCTOR OR CLINIC)	TELEPHONE NO.
IF PARENT CANNOT BE REACHED, CONTACT: ☐ NEIGHBOR ☐ RELATIVE ☐ FRIEND NAME	TELEPHONE NO.	THIS FAMILY IS ELIGIBLE FOR MEDICAL PAYMENTS UNDER ☐ BLUE CROSS - BLUE SHIELD ☐ PRIVATE HEALTH INS. ☐ PUBLIC FUNDS (TITLE XIX, WELFARE, CRIPPLED CHILDREN) ☐ NONE	

Figure 2-1, p. 1

12 Preschool Health Program—An Overview

PREADMISSION CHILD HEALTH RECORD

PREGNANCY AND BIRTH HISTORY

PLACE OF DELIVERY (NAME OF HOSPITAL)	DELIVERED BY

PREVIOUS PREGNANCIES
TOTAL NO. | MISCARRIAGES | STILL BIRTHS

MOTHER'S HEALTH DURING THIS PREGNANCY ☐ EXCELLENT ☐ OTHER (DESCRIBE)

DELIVERY ☐ NORMAL SPONTANEOUS VERTEX ☐ OTHER (DESCRIBE)

BABY'S BIRTHWEIGHT | DID BABY ARRIVE ☐ ON TIME ☐ EARLY BY ___ WEEKS ☐ LATE BY ___ WEEKS

ILLNESS OR COMPLICATION IN NEWBORN PERIOD ☐ NONE ☐ OTHER (DESCRIBE)

ILLNESS HISTORY

HAS CHILD HAD OR DOES HE HAVE:	YES	NO	DATE	DESCRIBE DETAILS OF ANY ITEM CHECKED "YES"
MEASLES (RUBEOLA)				
MUMPS				
CHICKEN POX				
RUBELLA (3-DAY OR GERMAN MEASLES)				
WHOOPING COUGH				
SEIZURES, FITS, OR SPELLS				
TONSILLECTOMY				
ANY HOSPITALIZATION				
EXPOSURE TO TUBERCULOSIS OR PERSON WITH CHRONIC COUGH				
FREQUENT BEDWETTING (AFTER AGE 4)				
ANY KNOWN CHRONIC DISEASE OR HANDICAPPING CONDITION				
OTHER SERIOUS ILLNESS				

DEVELOPMENTAL HISTORY

COMPARED WITH HIS BROTHERS AND SISTERS AND WITH OTHER CHILDREN HIS AGE, HAS THIS CHILD BEEN PARTICULARLY FAST OR SLOW IN:	DATE FAST AVE. SLOW	DATE FAST AVE. SLOW	DATE FAST AVE. SLOW	DATE FAST AVE. SLOW	DATE FAST AVE. SLOW
WALKING, RUNNING, CLIMBING					
TALKING					
PLAYING WITH TOYS, COLORING, DRAWING					
UNDERSTANDING WHAT IS SAID TO HIM					
GETTING ALONG WITH CHILDREN HIS OWN AGE					

IS THIS CHILD CONSIDERED BY HIS MOTHER OR BY OTHERS TO BE PARTICULARLY:	YES NO	YES NO	YES NO	YES NO	YES NO
"DIFFICULT" OR "DIFFERENT"					
HYPERACTIVE					
CLUMSY					

COMMENTS:

Figure 2-1, p. 2

Health Program For Children 13

PREADMISSION CHILD HEALTH RECORD

Name of Child   Address

Parents Name   Medical Insurance and No.

Physical Examination   Date of Birth

Height		Weight		Age	Blood pressure
In. or Cm.	Percentile	Lb. or Kg.	Percentile	Years	Months

Does the examination reveal any abnormality in:	ABNORMAL	NORMAL	NOT DETERMINED	Eye Color _____ Hair Color _____ Skin Color _____ Describe fully any abnormal findings
General appearance, posture, gait				
Speech				
Behavior during examination				
Skin				
Eyes: externals				
Optic fundi				
Ears: External and canals				
Tympanic membranes				
Nose, mouth, pharynx				
Teeth				
Heart				
Lungs				
Abdomen (include hernias)				
Genitalia				
Bones joints, muscles				
Neuroligical examination				
Other				
Screening tests				

Figure 2-1, p. 3

14 Preschool Health Program—An Overview

	Not Done	Normal	Abnormal	Not Testable	Remarks
Vision					
Hearing					
Tuberculin					
Anemia					
Urinalysis					
Other					

Summary of findings, treatments, and recommendations

Abnormal Findings	Advice and Treatment given	Recommendations or further evaluation, treatment or social or educational services.

Figure 2-1, p. 4

Health Program For Children 15

Immunization Record (Note date and any adverse reactions)						
Diphtheria, Pertussis, Tetanus, (DPT)	Original Series	#1		#2		#3
	Boosters	#1	#2	#3	#4	#5
Polio	For each immunization, indicate type of vaccine (OPV-T = Trivalent Oral; OPV-1 = Type 1 Oral; S = Salk)					
	#1	#2	#3	#4	#5	#6
Measles	Had natural infection	Live vaccine #1	Killed vaccine		#2	#3
Small Pox	1st Vaccination (Date)	Primary Take? Yes No	Revac- #1 vacination	#1 Take? Yes No	#2 (Date)	#2 Take? Yes No
Mumps							
Rubella							
Other Immunizations							

Special examinations, operations or injuries (give dates) _____
_____

Comments: _____
_____

Is there any apparent reason why the child should not enter day care? _____
_____

Signature of physician: _____ Date: _____

Print name: _____
Address: _____
Tel. No.:   _____

Source. *Modified by E.H. Reinisch and R.E. Minear from DHEW Publication No. (OCD) 72-4.*

Figure 2-1, p. 5

Preschool Health Program—An Overview

Application for Admission
Sunny City Preschool

Name of Child:_____
      (Last, First, Middle)   Sex   Birthplace   Birthdate

Address: _____
    (Street & Town, or City)   Zip Code   Home Phone No.

Identification Information: _____
      Eye Color   Hair Color   Skin Color   Height

Father _____ Occupation_____Hrs. of work_____

Business Address _____ Tel. No._____

Mother _____ Occupation_____Hrs. of work_____

Business Address _____ Tel. No._____

Guardian Is: Father_____Mother_____Other (Name & Address)____

Any other person who will care for child in emergency_____Tel. No.

_____
(Address)

Name of other members of household with whom child resides. If there are children, give ages. _____
_____
_____

Family Physician or Source of Medical Care_____
                  (Name and Address)
_____ Tel. No._____

When is the best time to contact you?_____

Please continue with Background Form (Figure 2-3) Interviewer_____

Source. *E.H. Reinisch and R.E. Minear.*
Figure 2-2

ADMISSION INFORMATION
BACKGROUND FORM
(Confidential)

Child's Name _____ Date of Birth _____

Male/Female _____

Nickname _____ Name called in school _____

Relatives living in home, including parents (Give ages of brothers and sisters, cousins, etc.)
_____
_____
_____

Does the child show a preference yet for either left or right hand? _____

Napping habits _____

Eating habits (any food allergies?) _____

Favorite kinds of play or special interests _____
_____

Particular likes or dislikes _____

Bathroom language (what you refer to at home): _____

Additional comments (language at home other than English; special circumstances)
_____
_____

Has the child had any other school experience? _____ Where? _____

Reason for enrollment _____

To Parents: Do you have any particular talent or interest you would like to share with the children—your job, play piano, instrument, songs, a pet, a movie, etc.
_____
_____
_____

Date   Parental Signature

       Interviewer: _____

Source: *E. H. Reinisch and R.E. Minear.*
Figure 2-3

habits, favorite kinds of play and special interests. Social, cultural, and family characteristics should also be noted. An application form (Figure 2-2), and a background form (Figure 2-3) may be used to record this information.

The interview is a good time to discuss and plan to carry out recommendations from the preadmission evaluation that the physician and dentist may have made for additional testing or treatment.

The parents should be shown the medical forms that will be kept as a part of the child's health record. The interview with the parent is also an excellent time to have the parent sign the numerous types of permission forms required in the care of their child while in preschool. The permission or consent form should be dated and signed and it may cover all types of activities, for example, tests, examinations, first aid, and medical care in case of emergency. The permission may be requested for each activity individually. Other permission forms are used to determine who may call for a child at the preschool. This type of consent is important for the safety of the child for various reasons. For example, when parents are separated or divorced, custody of the child may be an issue. In the event that parents reject immunizations and medical care of their child on the basis of their religious belief, they should sign a statement certifying that they refuse immunization and medical care and accept full responsibility for their child's health. Then the child can be exempted from the preschool's health requirements. Examples of consent or permission forms are found in Figure 2-4.

The preschool administrator and the parents should discuss and understand their dual responsibility for the child's health. Then the parents and the preschool administrator should sign an agreement concerning the cooperative arrangement for caring for the child's health. A sample agreement is found in Figure 2-5.

2.1.2. Continuous Health Supervision

Policy

The goal of a continuous health supervision plan for each child is to attain the best health for the child. The preadmission health evaluation information serves as a basis for the continuous supervision of the child's health.

Permission Forms

1. I give my permission for _____ to have all necessary medical examinations, immunizations, laboratory tests, and treatments from the physicians, dentists, and other health personnel of the preschool and school health programs.

   _____
   Date   Signature of parent or guardian

2. I give permission for _____ to have emergency first aid measures and emergency medical treatment administered if necessary.

   _____
   Date   Signature of parent or guardian

3. I give permission for an appointment to be made for dental checkup since I do not have a private dentist for _____.

   _____
   Date   Signature of parent or guardian

4. I give permission for the following persons to take _____ _____ home from day care:

   _____
   _____
   _____
   _____

   _____
   Date   Signature of parent or guardian

Source: *E.H. Reinisch and R.E. Minear.*
Figure 2-4

> **Parent's Agreement with Goals and Philosophy of Health Program**
>
> I _____ the parent/legal guardian of _____ have read and agree with the goals and philosophy of Sunny City Preschool's health program.
>
> I understand that I have responsibility for the health care of _____. I also understand that Sunny City Preschool is very interested in helping me carry out my responsibility. Therefore from time to time the day care center staff will want to meet with me and they will also make requests of me to obtain medical care of my child. If I am unable to meet any requests from the day care center I will clearly let the staff know why. I understand that my child may be dismissed from the day care center if I am unable to work out a way to meet the requests of the day care center's staff concerning my child's health.
>
> Signed_____
> Parent/Legal Guardian
>
> Witness: _____
> Title: _____
> Date: _____

Source: *E.H. Reinisch and R. E. Minear.*
Figure 2-5

Procedure

In order to achieve this goal the health supervision should consist of the following activities:

Daily Health Observations.

Daily health observations consist of two phases: (1) the morning or "on-arrival" inspection, and (2) observations throughout the time the child remains in the center. It should be decided who will perform health observations at the time of the child's arrival. This inspection may be done by a health professional or the child's teacher.

A routine procedure for observations should be established at the time of arrival. A checklist of items to look at or look for is a good starting point (Checklist for Daily Health Observations, Figure 2-6). An attendance record (Figure 2-7) can be completed at the same time. Subsequent absences due to illness should be marked on the attendance record. All personnel who perform the health observa-

Checklist for Daily Health Observations

Facial expression: carefree, smiling, sad, pale, tired, concerned.

General appearance: neat, clean, washed.

Posture: erect and apparently normal; limp, shuffling feet, other suggestion of abnormality.

Skin on face, neck, forearms and hands: flushed, warm, sweating; pale; rash; scratches, bruises, infection.

Eyes: clear, bright; red, crusty; appearance of eyelids.

Ears: discharge.

Hair and fingernails: cleanliness, evidence of lice.

Nose: discharge.

Mouth: rash, swelling of lips, bleeding or swollen gums, appearance of teeth.

Does the child cough, rub eyes or nose or he scratch himself?

Child's comments: does he indicate discomfort, pain, or any other abnormality?

Observations during the day: in addition to the above observations, is there a change in his usual behavior, eating, sleeping, or toilet habits?

Source: *E.H. Reinisch and R.E. Minear.*
Figure 2-6

tions at the time of the child's arrival should be given instructions in how to detect signs of illness. This is discussed in the chapter on health assessment (Chapter 5). For ease, the checklist used at the time of arrival may also be used during the day. A similar form, Day Care Staff Health Observations, (Figure 2-8) also may be helpful.

Care of the Child Who Becomes Ill

When health observations seem to indicate an illness or an abnormality then procedures discussed in Chapters 6 and 7 should be followed.

Care of Injuries and Other Emergencies

Accidents and other emergencies always disrupt the activities of a preschool but they must not find the staff unprepared and unable to cope with these events. A procedure to meet any of these problems is discussed in Chapter 8.

22 Preschool Health Program—An Overview

Attendance Record — Continuing Health Supervision

Name of Child _____

	1	2	3	4	5	6	7	8	9	10	11	12	13	14	15	16	17	18	19	20	21	22	23	24	25	26	27	28	29	30	31	TOTAL ABS.	PRES.
JAN.																																	
FEB.																																	
MAR.																																	
APR.																																	
MAY																																	
JUNE																																	
JULY																																	
AUG.																																	
SEPT.																																	
OCT.																																	
NOV.																																	
DEC.																																	

Absence due to sickness is marked S.
ABS. — absent
PRES. — present

Source. Modified by E.H. Reinisch and R.E. Minear from DHEW. Publication No. (OCD) 73–1054

Figure 2-7

Health Program For Children 23

DAY CARE STAFF HEALTH OBSERVATIONS	NAME OF CHILD (LAST, FIRST, MIDDLE)			
IDENTIFICATION OF PROGRAM OR AGENCY				
	NAME OF RECORDER		DATE FORM COMPLETED	

DOES THIS CHILD COMPLAIN OF OR DEMOSTRATE ANY OF THE FOLLOWING MORE SEVERELY OR MORE FREQUENTLY THAN MOST OF HIS PEERS?

	YES	NO		YES	NO
TEMPER TANTRUMS					
IMPULSIVE OR EXPLOSIVE BEHAVIOR			SKIN RASH		
HYPERACTIVITY OR RESTLESSNESS			FREQUENT SCRATCHING		
WITHDRAWN			SORES ON SKIN		
INACTIVE OR SLUGGISH			PALE OR SALLOW SKIN		
SLEEPY OR LETHARGIC					
TICS OR GRIMACING			CONTINUOUS RUNNY NOSE		
			FREQUENT NOSE PICKING OR RUBBING		
CLUMSY			COUGH		
LIMP OR ABNORMAL GAIT			WHEEZING		
POOR COORDINATION			SHORT OF BREATH WITH EXERCISE		
POOR WRITING OR DRAWING					
CONVULSIONS, FITS, OR SPELLS			OVERWEIGHT		
SPELLS OF INATTENTION OR STARING INTO SPACE			STOMACH ACHES		
			VOMITING		
HEADACHES			FREQUENT URINATION		
			WETS PANTS		
			SOILS SELF WITH BOWEL MOVEMENTS		
EYES CROSSED OR OUT					
POOR VISION					
RED, RUNNY OR ITCHING EYES					
POOR HEARING					
DISCHARGE OR RUNNING FROM EAR					
UNCLEAR SPEECH					

WHAT IS YOUR OPINION OF THIS CHILD'S HEALTH?
☐ PERFECTLY HEALTHY   ☐ SPECIFIC PROBLEM(S) AS NOTED BUT GENERALLY HEALTHY
☐ NOT IN GOOD HEALTH

FURTHER OBSERVATIONS AND EXPLANATION OF ITEMS MARKED "YES" ABOVE

Source: *DHEW Publication No. (OCD) 72-4*

Figure 2-8

Management of Cases of Suspected Child Neglect and Abuse

This problem may be found among people of all socio-economic groups, all racial and ethnic groups and all educational backgrounds. It is discussed in Chapter 6. It is best to develop a procedure with the advice of an appropriate social service agency such as the Children's Protective Services. A form similar to the one in Figure 2-9 may be used to file a report alleging neglect or abuse.

Specialized Care for Children

Frequently a child has to receive medicines while attending school. If the preschool agrees to accept children who may need to be given medicines or any other special health care, a procedure must be written. This procedure should specify who will perform the task and how the task may be done safely. The medicines must be kept in the labeled bottle obtained from the pharmacy and must be locked up and out of reach of all children in the preschool. In addition, the physician prescribing medicines must do so in writing (Figure 2-10) and the parents should give written permission to the preschool to administer what the physician prescribed (Figure 2-10). Both of these records must be on file with the preschool administrator.

Some preschools accept children with handicaps. They may include those with perceptual abnormalities, chronic lung or heart disease, mental retardation, and abnormalities of bones, joints, and the nervous system. Prior to admission these children should be evaluated by an appropriate agency or specialists in your community and a special program for each handicapped child should be recommended.

2.1.3 Periodic Health Evaluation: Care and Follow-up of Health Problems

Policy

There should be a periodic evaluation and review of the health of each child. The medical consultant should determine what methods will be used to evaluate health and how often they will be employed. The evaluation of a child's health may be done within the preschool setting or by the health professionals selected by the parents. The significance of health evaluation and the commonly used methods are found in Chapter 5.

Health Program For Children 25

MASSACHUSETTS DEPARTMENT OF PUBLIC WELFARE

REPORT OF CHILD ALLEGED TO BE SUFFERING FROM

SERIOUS PHYSICAL OR EMOTIONAL INJURY BY ABUSE OR NEGLECT

Please complete all sections of this form. If some data is unknown, please signify. If some data is uncertain, please place a question mark after the entry.

DATA ON CHILD REPORTED:

Name: _____ Last _____ First _____ Middle

Address: _____ Street & Number _____ City/Town _____ State

Sex: ☐ Male ☐ Female   Age: _____

DATA ON MALE GUARDIAN OR PARENT:

Name: _____ Last _____ First _____ Middle

Address: _____ Street & Number _____ City/Town _____ State

Telephone Number: _____   Age: _____

DATA ON FEMALE GUARDIAN OR PARENT:

Name: _____ Last _____ First _____ Middle

Address: _____ Street & Number _____ City/Town _____ State

Telephone Number: _____   Age: _____

_____ Date of Report   _____ Report received by telephone

_____ Mandatory report/Voluntary report   _____ Report received in writing

Name of Reporter: _____ Last _____ First _____ Middle

Address of Reporter: _____ Street & Number _____ City/Town _____ State

Telephone Number of Reporter: _____   Relationship of Reporter to Child: _____

Name and Location of Reporting Institution, School or Facility: _____

_____ Street & Number _____ City/Town _____ State

_____ Telephone Number

Figure 2-9, p. 1

26 Preschool Health Program—An Overview

Figure 2-9, p. 2

Health Program For Children 27

SPECIAL PROCEDURES, PHYSICIAN'S INSTRUCTIONS

Date_____

To whom it may concern:

I give medical care to _____ who needs to receive the following medicines. (child's name)

_____ in the dose of _____ for _____
                                              (length of time)

_____   _____   _____

_____   _____   _____

while in the preschool. If there are any reactions or problems that may be due to the medicine please call me at _____.

Sincerely yours,

_____ M.D.

SPECIAL PROCEDURES, PARENT'S PERMISSION

Date_____

To whom it may concern:

I give the Sunny City preschool permission to give the medicines prescribed by _____. Please see the physician's instructions for giving the medicines.
(physician's name)

Thank you,

_____
Parent/Guardian

Source: *E.H. Reinisch and R.E. Minear.*
Figure 2-10

The information obtained from the periodic evaluation and review must be used to help improve the child's health. Therefore, it is important to know if a child was referred to a medical service because of abnormalities. The outcome of the medical care of those children who were referred for medical service should be known and recorded.

Procedure

Periodic Health Evaluation

The child's health record should be one guide for such an evaluation. The results of these evaluations including dental examinations and immunization status should be recorded on forms similar to the dental health record (Figure 2-11) and periodic health evaluation record (Figure 2-12). All of these should become a part of the child's cumulative health record.

Periodic Review

Information within the child's cumulative health record should be the prime source for evaluation. The periodic review should consist of a health team conference either regularly scheduled or called for a special reason. The health team should include the child's teacher and any health professionals who work with the preschool either as consultants or as direct providers of health services. The parents should be made aware of the team's health evaluation of the child. Then with the parent's cooperation, a plan to meet the child's need is made.

Care and Follow-up

The preschool center and medical consultant should establish a system to record the abnormalities found in a review of the child's cumulative health record. The system should be able to demonstrate what action had been taken on the reported abnormalities and if the problem is solved or needs further examination. For one type of recording system see Figure 2-13.

2.1.4 A Cumulative Health Record

Policy

There should be a complete, comprehensive, up-to-date health record of each child because it will assist in understanding the child's on-going health care. This is particularly important because

Health Program For Children   29

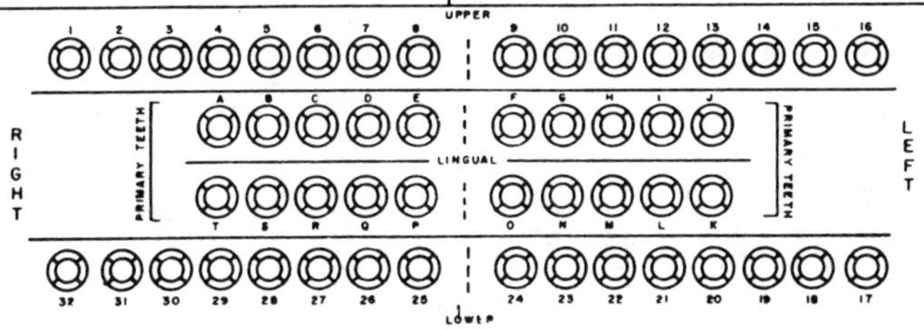

Source: *DHEW Publication No. (OCD) 72-4*

Figure 2-11

30 Preschool Health Program—An Overview

PERIODIC HEALTH EVALUATION RECORD (PRESCHOOL AND SCHOOL AGE CHILD)	NAME OF CHILD (LAST, FIRST, MIDDLE)
IDENTIFICATION OF PROGRAM OR AGENCY	DATE OF THIS EVALUATION
	LOCATION OF THIS EVALUATION
	☐ THIS IS FIRST EVALUATION (COMPLETE SEPARATE FORM CAP HS 30) ☐ A HISTORY AND EXAMINATION WAS PERFORMED (DATE) (PLACE)

ILLNESS, INJURIES, HOSPITALIZATIONS SINCE LAST EVALUATION

SCREENING TEST SINCE LAST EXAMINATION

	NOT DONE	NORMAL	ABNORMAL	NOT TESTABLE	REMARKS
VISION					
HEARING					
TUBERCULIN					
ANEMIA					
URINALYSIS					
OTHER					

PROGRESS ☐ PROGRESSING NORMALLY WITH AGE GROUP ☐ OTHER (EXPLAIN)

OBSERVATIONS ☐ NO APPARENT DIFFICULTY ☐ SLOW OR POOR READER
☐ HYPERACTIVE OR IMPULSIVE BEHAVIOR ☐ EPISODIC CHANGES IN STATE OF CONSCIOUSNESS, SEIZURES
☐ OTHER (EXPLAIN)

CHANGES IN HOME OR FAMILY SETTING SINCE LAST EXAMINATION (MOVES, NEW SIBLINGS, DIVORCE, UNEMPLOYMENT ETC.)
☐ NONE   ☐ OTHER (EXPLAIN)

HEALTH PROBLEMS NOTED BY PARENT OR CHILD

Figure 2-12, p. 1

Periodic Health Evaluation Record (Preschool and School Age) page 2

PHYSICAL EXAMINATION

HEIGHT		WEIGHT		AGE		BLOOD PRESSURE
IN. OR CM.	PERCENTILE	LB. OR KG.	PERCENTILE	YEARS	MONTHS	

DOES THE EXAMINATION REVEAL ANY ABNORMALITY IN:	ABNORMAL	NORMAL	NOT EXAMINED	DESCRIBE FULLY ANY ABNORMAL FINDINGS
GENERAL APPEARANCE, POSTURE, GAIT				
SPEECH				
BEHAVIOR DURING EXAMINATION				
SKIN				
EYES: EXTERNALS				
OPTIC FUNDI				
EARS: EXTERNAL AND CANALS				
TYMPANIC MEMBRANES				
NOSE, MOUTH, PHARYNX				
TEETH				
HEART				
LUNGS				
ABDOMEN (INCLUDE HERNIAS)				
GENITALIA				
BONES, JOINTS, MUSCLES				
NEUROLOGICAL EXAMINATION				
OTHER				

DEVELOPMENTAL SCREENING EXAMINATION

	NORMAL FOR AGE	OTHER (EXPLAIN)	REMARKS
GROSS MOTOR FUNCTION			
FINE MOTOR AND MANIPULATIVE FUNCTIONS			
ADAPTIVE FUNCTION			
LANGUAGE FUNCTION			
PERSONAL-SOCIAL FUNCTION			

SUMMARY OF FINDINGS, TREATMENTS, AND RECOMMENDATIONS

ABNORMAL FINDINGS	ADVICE AND TREATMENT GIVEN	RECOMMENDATIONS FOR FURTHER EVALUATION, TREATMENT OR SOCIAL OR EDUCATIONAL SERVICES.

SIGNATURE OF PHYSICIAN   DATE

Source: *DHEW Publication No. (OCD) 72-4*
Figure 2-12, p. 2

Care and Follow-up of Child's Health Problems

1. Prepare a 3-inch x 5-inch or 5-inch x 7-inch alphabetical card file divided into *active cases* and *inactive* (closed or completed).
2. Make a card for each child with an abnormality or an incomplete immunization record.
3. Record the abnormality and recommendations for remediation.
4. Record all actions pertaining to the problem.
5. Review the card file periodically and check to see if problems have been corrected.
6. The cumulative health record of the child should also contain the abnormalities and reports of actions taken and resolution of the problem, if it occurs.

Example:

Josea, Maria		
2/8/76	Failed vision test	
	To see Dr. Watts 3/1/76	
4/10/76	Wears glasses, to return every year to Dr. Watts	
5/6/76	Needs DPT, polio boosters	
	To see Dr. Black 5/20/76	

Source: *E.H. Reinisch and R.E. Minear.*
Figure 2-13

the information should be available for use by the child's parents or other individuals in case the child leaves the program or the preschool program closes.

Procedure

A child's cumulative health record should contain the following information:

1. Identifying information: child's name and address and date of birth, parents' name and address, and telephone number where the parents can be reached at all times in case of an emergency.
2. The child's physician or health agency where he has been examined or treated and code used to identify the child at a hospital or clinic where he has received medical care.
3. Arrangements for emergency medical care and all written permissions from parents authorizing emergency medical care.
4. Reports of accidents or illnesses which involved the child.
5. Written permissions from parents authorizing nonemergency health care, administration of medicines, or special health remedies.
6. Information about the child's financial arrangements for any type of medical care.
7. The preadmission health evaluation.
8. The continuous health supervision data including all tests, growth measurements and examinations, and their evaluation.
9. Reports of referrals that were made and follow-up of medical care received.
10. Notes of the communications with parents in the form of conferences, visits, and written reports.

2.1.5 A Nutrition and Food Service

Policy

A nutrition and food service should provide part of the child's daily nutritional needs and should incorporate nutrition education into the learning experiences of the child.

The food service may be provided by the preschool organization or it may be furnished by another agency through a contractual arrangement. The program should be planned in consultation with a nutritionist and a food service director should be in charge of the program. All policies regarding the food service and methods for implementing them should be in writing. Parents must be informed of the preschool's policies and procedures so that there is a coordination of meal planning between the home and the preschool.

Procedure

What type of meals and how many should be served will be determined by how long children remain in preschool on a particular day. When the children stay a half day or less, a snack should be served. But when the stay is longer than half a day, a meal should be served in addition to a snack. Recommendations from *Food Service in Child Care Centers* by the United States Department of Agriculture for appropriate type and amount of food to be served are shown in Figure 2-14. When parents are required to provide the meals, a suggested list of food items that could be included in the lunch bag should be given to them.

The person providing the food service should have adequate knowledge of child nutrition, food preparation and serving, sanitary handling of food, food purchasing, and menu planning. Preschool staff members who do not have nutrition education before employment should receive it in in-service education. This program may be offered to parents at the same time. Because this topic is so important it is presented in detail in Chapter 3.

The food service director should keep menus on file and maintain a record of the food budget, which includes records of food purchases. Menus must be planned in advance and posted a week ahead so that parents may see them. The food service director should review periodically each of the responsibilities. The food budget tends to be the one most subject to dramatic price changes, therefore plan for price increases. It is not advisable to skimp on the food budget. The parents should be included in decisions about changes in type and quality of food offered as a result of the changing market prices.

The children must not be in the kitchen unless they are under direct supervision of the staff.

Daily Food Plan and Serving Portions

PATTERN	CHILDREN 1 up to 3 years	CHILDREN 3 up to 6 years
BREAKFAST		
Milk, fluid whole	½ cup	¾ cup
Juice or Fruit	¼ cup	½ cup
Cereal and/or Bread,[1]		
enriched or whole grain		
Cereal	¼ cup	⅓ cup
Bread	½ slice	½ slice
MID-MORNING OR MID-AFTERNOON SUPPLEMENT		
Milk, fluid whole, or Juice or		
Fruit or Vegetable	½ cup	½ cup
Bread or Cereal,[1]		
enriched or whole grain		
Bread	½ slice	½ slice
Cereal	¼ cup	⅓ cup
LUNCH OR SUPPER		
Milk, fluid whole	½ cup	¾ cup
Meat and/or Alternate		
One of the following or combinations to give equivalent quantities:		
Meat, poultry, fish, cooked[2]	1 ounce	1½ ounces
Cheese	1 ounce	1½ ounces
Egg	1	1
Cooked dry beans and peas	⅛ cup	¼ cup
Peanut butter	1 tablespoon	2 tablespoons
Vegetable and/or Fruit[3]	¼ cup	½ cup
Bread,[1]		
enriched or whole grain	½ slice	½ slice
Butter or Fortified Margarine	½ teaspoon	½ teaspoon

[1] Or an equivalent serving of cornbread, biscuits, rolls, muffins, etc. made of enriched or whole grain meal or flour.
[2] Cooked lean meat without bone.
[3] Must include at least two kinds.

Source: *Food Service in Child Care Centers. Food and Nutrition Service. U.S. Department of Agriculture, Washington, D.C. FNS-64.*

Figure 2-14

Assessment of any child's nutritional status is part of both the preadmission evaluation and the continuing health supervision. The food service director should be notified about any special nutritional needs discovered by either of these assessments.

Some examples of learning experiences associated with food and nutrition that might be included in the educational program are the following: identification of different foods and food groups, choosing and eating foods never eaten before, participating in the preparation of food, learning that mealtime may be a good social experience, enjoying food, selecting and eating foods that are important to health, understanding the role of nutrition in health and disease, and establishing good eating habits.

2.1.6 A Safety and Accident Prevention Program

Policy

The goal of this program is to protect both children and staff by making the preschool facility and its activities as safe as possible. Any existing hazards should be recognized and controlled or removed. All preschool staff must be concerned, involved, and educated in making the facility and its programs safe. The methods to achieve such safety are presented in detail in Chapter 9.

2.1.7 Healthful Activities

Policy

The preschool program should offer a variety of activities that provide intellectual, social, creative, emotional, nutritional, and cultural experiences. Whenever possible the child should be taught about his health. Early childhood education textbooks will help with planning of activities and choosing learning experiences.

The proper balance and distribution of activities during the child's stay in preschool is as important as the activities offered.

Procedure

The schedule of activities should be planned ahead of time. It should be flexible but offer regularity so that the child will have the security of knowing what to expect. There should be indoor and outdoor play, vigorous physical activities, and free play as well as activities that exercise small muscle groups. The schedule should allow time each day for naps, time for eating, time for going to the toilet, and group and individual activities.

Interaction between children is very important but child/adult relationships should also be formed. Therefore, plan activities that will permit these types of relationships. However, do not neglect providing opportunities for the child who desires to play alone at times. Solitude is important also.

Intense and stimulating activities should not be scheduled before rest periods, snacks or meals and before going home.

A rest period of 10 to 20 minutes is desirable for children who stay half a day and an hour of rest for those staying longer.

2.2.0 A HEALTH PROGRAM FOR THE PRESCHOOL STAFF

Policy

A health program for the children of a preschool would fail or at least be inferior if the health of the staff were neglected or ignored. Therefore a health program for the preschool staff must exist. Its goal should be to make certain that the staff's mental, emotional, and physical well-being is conducive to good child care. This means that all staff, including volunteers and students, must be evaluated under such a health program.

Procedure

2.2.1 Preemployment Health Evaluation

Prior to employment in the preschool each individual should have their health evaluated by a physician. This evaluation should include a tuberculin test or a chest X ray. To obtain standardized information a form similar to Figure 2-15 can be used.

2.2.2 Continuous Health Supervision and Evaluation

Each staff member should have their personal health reevaluated once a year. If a staff member develops an illness he should be excluded from work until he is well. He should have a statement from a physician certifying that he is able to return to care for children.

EMPLOYEE PREEMPLOYMENT HEALTH EVALUATION

Mr./Mrs. _____ currently operate the Sunny City Preschool. Information on the health condition of all employees and prospective employees is an important part of the preschool program. General physical examination is required for employment at the Sunny City Preschool. We would appreciate your completing the following form.

Applicant

I hereby authorize Dr. _____ Address _____
to give medical information concerning my health to a representative of the Sunny City Preschool.

Signed _____

To Be Completed by Physician:

Date of examination _____
Name _____ Age _____ Height _____
Weight _____ BP _____ Do you consider this to be within normal limits: _____ Chest _____ Heart _____ Chest X ray _____
Tuberculin Test _____ Veneral Disease _____
Approximately how long has the individual named above been under your care? _____
What is your opinion concerning the general health of this person in relation to his/her suitability to work in a preschool?
Excellent _____ Good _____ Questionable _____
Comments or recommendations: _____
I have examined _____ and found her/him free from contagious and infectious disease.

_____ M.D.

Address _____

Please Mail Directly to Sunny City Preschool

Source: *E.H. Reinisch and R.E. Minear.*
Figure 2-15

2.2.3 Health Record for Personnel

Health record for personnel should include:

1. Preemployment physical examination and medical evaluation.
2. Reports of yearly X rays or tuberculin tests.
3. Reports concerning medically excused absences.
4. Reports of injuries or accidents in the preschool.
5. Physicians and individuals to be notified in case of emergency.
6. Type of health insurance coverage.
7. Any reports concerning emotional difficulties during employment in the preschool.

The staff's emotional health and attitudes toward the care of children should be reexamined periodically also. A guide to help with this task is given in Figure 2-16.

2.3.0 EDUCATION OF THE PRESCHOOL STAFF ABOUT CHILD HEALTH

Policy

The goal of educating staff about health matters, particularly child health, is to have them become active, informed participants on the health team and to prepare them to incorporate health principles in the learning experiences of the children. The total health program would not be very successful if the staff had minimal knowledge about child health.

Procedure

2.3.1 Preemployment Education

When child health knowledge is a preemployment requirement then topics in this book are a good source for acquiring it. A formal course in child health or integration of this book's content in a course in early childhood education are two ways of accomplishing the task. A course in early childhood growth and development should supplement the education in child health.

Teacher Evaluation

Teacher's Name_____ Date____
Director_____

WORKING WITH CHILDREN

1. _____ Creates a warm and accepting environment.
2. _____ Likes children, shows a real enjoyment of them.
3. _____ Recognizes when children are happy and relaxed.
4. _____ Enjoys humorous incidents with children. Seems to enjoy laughing with them.
5. _____ Understands children on their own level.
6. _____ Accepts each child as he or she is.
7. _____ Recognizes that each child is a sensitive, thinking individual and treats child accordingly.
8. _____ Shows awareness of progress or lack of it in a child's behavior.
9. _____ Relates easily to children.
10. _____ Impartial in dealing with children.
11. _____ Aware of differing moods of children, adjusts standards for them at time when they are fatigued, irritated, overstimulated, etc.
12. _____ Uses different, though consistent, methods in dealing with different children.
13. _____ Is imaginative and creative.
14. _____ Is resourceful in a practical way, has common sense.
15. _____ Uses positive approach.

Figure 2-16, p. 1

Education Of The Preschool Staff About Child Health   41

16. _____ Helps children accept limitations.
17. _____ Makes suggestions without antagonizing.
18. _____ Does not overstimulate or cause tension in children.
19. _____ Removes distracting influences.
20. _____ Alert to total group, even when dealing with a part of it.
21. _____ Remains controlled in startling or difficult situations.
22. _____ Encourages and guides the expression of feelings.
23. _____ Assists children in gaining confidence.
24. _____ Treats the child's possessions and projects with care.
25. _____ Gives children opportunity for manipulating various kinds of creative materials.
26. _____ Explains relations between a child's individual rights and group rights.
27. _____ Guidance of children in group relationships.
28. _____ Guidance of activities according to group needs and interests.
29. _____ Guidance of children in developing motor coordination.
30. _____ Guidance in music experiences.
31. _____ Guidance in story and language experiences.
32. _____ Guidance in science experiences.
33. _____ Guidance in use of creative materials.
34. _____ Guidance in toileting routine.
35. _____ Guidance in resting.
36. _____ Guidance in eating experiences.

Figure 2-16, p. 2

WORKING WITH ADULTS

37. _____ Is interested in people, thinks in terms of helping them rather than criticizing.

38. _____ Cooperates well with adults.

39. _____ Is considerate of activities of other adults.

40. _____ Welcomes new ideas, flexibility as shown by willingness to consider new ideas.

41. _____ Maintains high standards of professional ethics in regard to children and staff.

42. _____ Realizes that situations cannot always be handled in the home as they are at school.

43. _____ Attitude in working with parents is cooperative.

SPECIFIC STRENGTH OF TEACHER:

SPECIFIC LIMITATIONS OF TEACHER:

OTHER COMMENTS:

Indicate evaluation by using numbers 1 through 5; 5 meaning high, appropriate or very good; 3 average; and 1 low, inappropriate, or poor in that particular characteristic.

Source: *Modified by E.H. Reinisch and R.E. Minear from DHEW Publication No. (OCD) 72-20.*

Figure 2-16, p. 3

2.3.2 In-service Education

In-service education is very important. This supplements and/or updates the health knowledge of those who already have had preemployment education and educates those who have minimal health knowledge and understanding.

The in-service education program must be flexible and adjusted to the education level of each person. The education should start with each individual's previous knowledge and should be directed toward their tasks in the preschool. Often preeducation and posteducation tests are useful guides as to what to teach and how much success was achieved. To illustrate techniques, individuals in charge of daily health observations and periodic health observations should have educational programs directed at how to perform health observations and how to administer certain tests—for example, vision and hearing. All staff, no matter what their function, including volunteers, should receive orientation to the health program and safety and accident prevention education.

Education in first aid is necessary for those who do not have it. The standard course in First Aid and Personal Safety taught by an American Red Cross instructor and a course in cardiopulmonary resuscitation taught by either an American Red Cross or American Heart Association instructor should be successfully completed by all staff members and a certificate should be issued to them by the instructor. The advanced course in First Aid and Emergency Care

Credit: *Marshall R. Hathaway*

should be taken at least by persons who are in charge of first aid in the preschool although it would be advantageous to any staff members. Refresher courses should be conducted yearly. Sanitary food handling is another example of in-service education for all staff connected with any phase of the food service. Other child health topics may be selected as needed.

The in-service education program may take place within the preschool itself or it may be offered elsewhere. The program may be shared with staff from other preschools and it may be taught by any variety of experts. In many circumstances local experts rather than those from out of town offer such a program with greater success. Your knowledge and experience with the staff will indicate whom to choose.

2.4.0 ADMINISTRATION OF THE PRESCHOOL HEALTH PROGRAM

Policy

The health program must be administered efficiently in order to satisfy all the goals and objectives established. The administration must integrate the efforts of the preschool staff with those of health professionals and parents so that the health needs of the children and their families are met.

Procedures
2.4.1 Responsibility for Administration

The policies and procedures for all phases of the program that were established during the planning period should be very visible to everyone and should be clearly understood by your staff and all parents using the center.

Responsibility for the various components of the health program must be clearly defined and assigned to one or more members of the permanent staff (Figure 2-17). Not every health service will be offered within the preschool. Contracts for health services should be negotiated where it is appropriate. A sample contract for health services is found in Figure 2-18. An advisory committee to the health program should consist of (a) representatives of community agencies that may provide resources for the health program, (b) parents, and (c) staff of the preschool. Members of the preschool staff who should be represented on the advisory

Administration Of The Preschool Health Program 45

```
Responsibility for the Administration of the Health Program

                    Overall Health Program

         Name_____(Preschool Director)

         Nutrition        Inservice Health Education    Safety and Inspection
Name _____        Name _____          Name _____

         Sanitation       Medical Emergencies
Name _____        Name _____

Daily Health Observations

Name _____    Name _____
Names of children responsible for:       Names of children responsible for:
_____          _____
_____          _____
_____          _____
_____          _____
```

Source: *E.H. Reinisch and R.E. Minear.*
Figure 2-17

```
                    Contract for Health Services

                              Date_____

    The Sunny City Preschool enters into an agreement with _____
(agency) for the purpose of performing the following services _____
_____ . The Sunny City Preschool agrees to pay_____(amount)
for the services upon receipt of a voucher of completion. This contract is for
_____(length of time) from this date.

    Witnesses                            Signatures of appropriate persons
```

Source: *E.H. Reinisch and R.E. Minear.*
Figure 2-18

committee are the individual in charge of safety, a teacher, a custodian, a representative of the clerical staff, and the administrator. The director of the preschool should call all advisory committee meetings and serve as the chairman or moderator. The functions of the advisory committee should be supportive and advisory.

A letter of invitation (Figure 2-19) should be sent to persons who are asked to serve on this advisory committee. Information about the philosophy, organization, and policies of the preschool should be included with the letter of invitation. Also clearly outlined functions and organizational makeup of the advisory committee should be sent with the letter of invitation (Figure 2-20). When the invitation is accepted, a letter of acknowledgment and thanks should be returned along with the time, place, and agenda of the next meeting. At the conclusion of a committee member's term a letter of appreciation should be mailed.

2.4.2 Financial Management of the Health Program

Both the planning and the advisory committee should assist the administration in arriving at the appropriate financial arrangements. Budget experts and accountants would be very valuable members of such committees. The cost of every aspect of the health program must be known and there should be some identifiable source of payment for these costs. Grants, loans, or donations from community agencies or public organizations, fees from parents, and payments from a variety of insurers are some of the ways to meet the costs for the health program. A guide similar to Figure 2-21 may be used to prepare a budget.

2.4.3 Health Program Record Keeping

Records for the health program are extremely important because they contain all the information about what is being done. The records of certain activities are subject to inspection by licensing agencies. The purpose of the inspection is to ascertain if the preschool is performing activities required by rules and regulations before reissuing a license.

Health records of each child and each staff member must be regarded as confidential in nature and maintained in such a manner. Therefore, it should be established who will have access to the

Letter of Invitation to Serve on the Advisory Committee
to the Health Program

Date

Mr. or Ms._____
Speech and Hearing Center
100 Main St.
Sunny City, State

Dear_____:

    A Day Care Center for preschool children is being established at the Sunny City Community Center. The health program of the day care center will need the advice of health professionals in the community.

    We would like to invite you to serve a one-year term on the Advisory Committee to the Health Program. Because of your extensive experience in the field of speech therapy we can profit greatly from your guidance. The Advisory Committee will meet at least twice a year.

    Information about the Day Care Center's objectives and policies, and the committee's functions is enclosed. Do not hesitate to call me if you have any questions.

Very sincerely yours,

, Director

Enclosure

Source: *E.H. Reinisch and R.E. Minear.*

Figure 2-19

Preschool Health Program—An Overview

Functions and Organization of the Advisory Committee to the Health Program

Functions of the Committee.

The general responsibility of the Advisory Committee is to offer advice concerning the Health Program in the following areas:

1. Implementation of the health program.
2. Evaluation of the health program.
3. Liaison with the community at large and community resources.
4. Selection and procurement of health professionals and community resources.
5. Assessment of parent needs and liaison with parents.
6. In-service education. Planning of programs, selection of teachers, and procurement of teaching materials.

Organization of the Advisory Committee

The membership of the committee will consist of the director of the Day Care Center, the medical consultant, three health professionals, three members of the day care staff, and three parents. The day care director will act as chairperson. Members will be appointed to serve on the committee for terms from one to three years. The terms will be staggered so that there will always be some members continuing their term while new members start their terms. There will be at least two meetings per year.

Source. *E.H. Reinisch and R.E. Minear.*
Figure 2-20

individual records and where they will be kept. There must be a written statement for everyone to see that clearly defines under what circumstances health information may be released to anyone. Each time health information concerning either staff member or a child is to be released there must be a permission for release signed by that staff member or the child's parents. This permission for release of information must state what information is to be released and to whom. An illustration of such a release form is found in Figure 2-22.

Individual Records

All individual health records of staff and children must be kept up to date, complete, concise, and clear so that they may adequately fulfill the important role that they play in a person's health program. The content of these records has been discussed previously.

BUDGET GUIDE FOR HEALTH PROGRAM

Costs to the Preschool

1. *Supplies to carry out health program*
   (a) Items used from year to year
   (b) Repair and maintenance of nonconsumable supplies
   (c) Items consumed
2. *Equipment*
   (a) Purchases
   (b) Maintenance and repair
3. *Salaries to health program staff*
   (a) Preschool staff
   (b) Consultants
4. *Contracts to perform health program services*
5. *Health and safety insurance*
   (a) Accident insurance for each child
   (b) Health insurance for staff
   (c) Accident and fire insurance for preschool
6. *Transportation related to the health program*
7. *Food*
8. *Miscellaneous day-to-day operations*

Sources of Income

1. Volunteer time—professional and nonprofessional
2. Grants
3. Loans
4. Donations of supplies and cash
5. Fees and charges to users of day care
6. Health insurance payments

Source. *E.H. Reinisch and R.E. Minear.*
Figure 2-21

Authorization to Release Health Information

I hereby authorize Sunny City Preschool to release the following information

(specify what may be released)
about the heath and background of:

Name

Address

to a physician or agency for consultation, service or because of transfer or because of the following reason(s):

Date: _____ Signed: _____
                            Print Parent's Name: _____
Witness: _____ Address: _____
(Name)

(Title)

Fill in relationship of individual signing to the above name child

Source: *E.H. Reinisch and R.E. Minear.*
Figure 2-22

Administrative Records

1. Accident reports and medical emergencies (Chapter 8).
2. Reports listing what was found in the routine inspection of the preschool for fulfillment of safety requirements (Chapter 9).
3. Procedures in case of a disaster (Chapter 9).
4. Reports about the evaluation of health program and statistics about the health of the staff and children.
5. Nutrition records that include copies of special and general menus (Chapter 3).
6. Financial records.
7. Statistical reports.

Credit: *Marshall R. Hathaway*

2.4.4 Communication with Parents About Their Child's Health

Communication between preschool staff and parents is very desirable because it strengthens the dual responsibility for the child's health care. Quick personal conversations or written or telephone contacts centered around one or two issues of the moment rarely allow the parent or preschool staff a good view of the child's current health. Therefore, it is necessary for the center to set aside regular times for conferences between staff and parents. One good time is

52 Preschool Health Program—An Overview

```
Record of Health Conferences with Parents

Name of Child _____
Address _____
_____

Persons Present at Conference: _____
Date: _____   Purpose: _____
Result: _____

Persons Present at Conference: _____
Date: _____   Purpose: _____
Result: _____

Persons Present at Conference: _____
Date: _____   Purpose: _____
Result: _____

Persons Present at Conference: _____
Date: _____   Purpose: _____
Result: _____
```

Source: *E.H. Reinisch and R.E. Minear.*
Figure 2-23

following periodic health evaluations. During that time the parents could learn of the findings and should want to share in the decisions about any number of medical recommendations. In order to be assured that each child receives follow-through for each medical problem, keep a record of the health conferences with parents. Examples of such records are found in Figure 2-23.

2.4.5 Evaluation of the Health Program

All aspects of the health program should be examined continuously. The object of evaluation is to determine if what is being done satisfies or meets the goals that were established during the planning stages. How current health-related problems are solved also needs evaluation. Furthermore, the evaluation must determine if what is being done is accomplished in the best possible way (good quality) and for the lowest cost (good efficiency). The evaluation must be based on facts, exact data, statistics, objective judgments, as well as experience. Once the information is collected changes may be made in the health programs so that they really accomplish what is expected of them. It is important to have consultants or an advisor to assist in evaluations. The outsider who is an expert can offer a great deal in terms of evaluation. But there must be an agreement to act according to the recommendations of such an evaluation, otherwise it is a useless and costly process.

For each aspect of the health program that has been discussed there should be requests for specific information. For example, how many problems were discovered by periodic evaluation? Have preschool activities included learning experiences about health? How many children have no health problems? How many children failed to get care when it was needed and why? Remember that evaluation of a health program is the way that a preschool staff measures its progress in meeting the needs of the children.

2.5.0 LAWS, RULES, AND REGULATIONS

The high standards of the preschool health program just presented may not be required by existing rules and regulations. However, one purpose of the previous discussion is to stimulate you to aim for child health care beyond the legal requirements. This is particularly important because generally rules and regulations establish minimal standards and not optimal ones.

2.5.1 How Is Preschool Child Care Controlled?

It is regulated by laws enacted in every state. These laws respond to the particular needs of individuals within each state and therefore differ accordingly. There are no federal laws that regulate all preschool programs but there are federal requirements for preschools receiving federal funding. However, those programs not controlled nationally may obtain nonbinding advice from the Administration for Children, Youth and Families (HEW).

2.5.2 Why Were Laws Concerned with Child Care Enacted?

In recent years more and more preschool children require care away from home because family structure and activity has changed to include single-parent families and families in which both parents work. Therefore, children are not cared for by their parents primarily but rather by a group of individuals. In addition to that, some children are considered disadvantaged while at home and therefore some education and health authorities recommend an improved environment for these children for at least part of the day. Children cannot take care of themselves. Therefore, parents and other concerned groups felt a need to protect the children by extending their control into the preschool environment. Laws were developed in response to this need and demand.

2.5.3 Who Makes the Rules and Regulations for Preschools?

The law designates a public agency to be responsible for all preschool activities supported by private or public money. This agency develops some practical guidelines (rules and regulations) to insure that the intent or reason for the law is carried out. The public agency uses its staff, numerous experts, and public hearings to develop the rules and regulations. This process not only guarantees that many interests are represented in the final rules and regulations but also that they are a compromise of all the represented groups. Rules and regulations similar to laws are not permanent and may be changed in order to meet the changing needs of the children as interpreted by any persons in the community, parents, preschool staff, or staff of public agencies. Rules and regulations therefore should not be thought of as rigid, impossible hindrances to anyone working in preschools.

2.5.4 What Is the Purpose of the Rules and Regulations?

The purpose of rules and regulations is to establish a common baseline of quality for the care of children in preschools. Rules and regulations also act as a yardstick against which all preschools may compare. For some facilities the rules and regulations demand upgrading and improvement. In these cases only provisional or temporary licenses to operate a preschool are issued until the deficiences are corrected. Other facilities, however, may find that their standards for quality care exceed in numerous areas the standards demanded in the state's rules and regulations. Most preschools should be in this category because as noted earlier the rules and regulations establish only minimal standards. But it is here where a controversy always errupts. One group of advocates defines the minimal standards so that almost all preschools become

Laws, Rules And Regulations 55

licensed without much upgrading. The other group believes that minimal standards should be rather high so that almost all preschools must be improved before they are licensed. Whatever group you find yourself in, always try to remember that good effective preschools should be your goal. *Recommendations for Preschools for Infants and Children*[1] was developed to direct preschool personnel toward improved child care services and obviously beyond minimal services.

2.5.5 Licensing

Licensing is a formal permission (legal document) or authorization to operate a preschool. A license to operate is granted under the supervision of state, county or other controlling agency and is usually renewed on a yearly or two-year basis. The preschool is inspected and a plan for the complete preschool program is reviewed before a license to operate is issued. The license is used to enforce the rules and regulations and may be revoked when the facility no longer complies with the rules and regulations. Both private and public facilities must meet this test.

2.5.6 Examples of Rules and Regulations

Rules regulate all phases of the preschool: licensing, administration, personnel, and program that includes health of the child, nutrition and food service, and buildings and grounds.

In the state publications a preschool may be referred to as a day care center or nursery school. It may be defined as a preschool that takes care of unrelated children on a regular basis part or all of the day separate from their parents. The age of the child in this type of preschool is approximately three to five or up to seven years in some states. Different rules and regulations apply to younger children.

We only concern ourselves with rules and regulations relating to the health of the child in preschool. After examining the rules and regulations of several states we formulated some examples to demonstrate the range of subjects that are being regulated. The examples do not represent any particular state. A review of the examples compiled provides a summary of the main concepts presented in this chapter.

[1] American Academy of Pediatrics, P.O. Box 1034, Evanston, IL 60204.

Consultants

The total plan for the preschool's health program must be reviewed by a pediatrician or physician interested in child health while nurses or other health professionals may supervise the health aspects of the preschool program.

In addition, a dentist, nutritionist and, where appropriate, a social worker should be used as consultants.

Admission Procedures

A preadmission examination of the child by a physician and appropriate immunizations are required. A waiver of this requirement based on religious beliefs of the parents is allowed.

An interview with the parent is required. The purpose is to obtain a health history and other information about the child and give information about the preschool to the parent.

Telephone numbers of parents or responsible adults to call in the event of an emergency must be available and arrangements for a physician or health facility must be made and recorded.

Whenever it is found that the child is handicapped, the preschool should comply with the state's provision for this type of child.

Continuing Health Supervision

Staff members who are qualified by special instruction in the detection of signs of childhood illness should be responsible for initial and continued observation of the child throughout the day. Children who appear ill should not be permitted to attend. Any unusual signs of physical, mental, or emotional problems should be reported to the parent.

The staff may request that the parent provide a dental, vision, or hearing examination if the child's behavior or appearance indicates a need for it.

A suitable space, under supervision of the staff, should be provided for ill children, and parents should be notified.

A written plan for reporting suspected child abuse or neglect to an appropriate agency should be prepared.

Medication should not be administered to a child without a written order of a physician and written parental authorization. A record should be kept of the administration of prescribed medication.

Laws, Rules And Regulations

At least one person trained in first aid should be present at all times.

The preschool should train all staff in approved emergency first aid procedures.

First aid supplies should be available at all times.

Prompt arrangements should be made for notification of parents and for medical care in case of illness or injury.

Telephone numbers of persons or agencies needed in case of an emergency should be posted.

There should be a procedure to be followed for the protection and evacuation of children in case of fire or other disaster.

There should be at least two responsible adults on the premises at all times.

Child's Cumulative Health Record

The child's comprehensive record should contain the following: identifying information, health history, physician's preadmission examination and record of immunizations, notes of staff and/or nurse about the child's health and development, medical and dental examinations, information about special medication required, dates and summaries of parent conferences, plan for medical care in case of emergency, parent authorizations for emergency medical care, and any other necessary actions. The record should be kept up to date.

Nutrition and Food Service

A snack should be provided for children staying less than five hours. A nutritionally adequate meal should be provided for children staying five hours or more.

Menus should be prepared and posted at least one week in advance.

Parents required to provide meals should be given a list of items to put into the lunch bag.

One person should be responsible for the food service.

Food should be prepared under sanitary conditions.

The kitchen should be maintained in a sanitary condition. Proper storage, refrigeration, and sanitizing of dishes should be provided. Food requiring refrigeration should be stored at a temperature between 32° and 45°F. Food unfinished by a child must be discarded. Meals should be tasteful and served in an appetizing manner.

Children should not have access to the kitchen except under supervision.

Dining furniture and utensils should be appropriate to the ages and needs of the children.

Buildings and Grounds.

The preschool should have certificates of inspection from the appropriate safety and health agencies in compliance with the state's licensing law.

The preschool should obtain an inspection for lead detection. If lead is found to be present, steps should be taken to remove all material containing lead.

The building of the preschool should be in good repair and free from accident hazards.

There shall be at least 35 square feet per child of indoor usable space. This space should not include areas used for other than children's activities. There should be at least 75 square feet per child of outdoor play area. This area should be protected and made safe for children to prevent bodily injury from accident hazards.

The rooms used by children should receive an adequate amount of light and sunshine and should be adequately heated and ventilated.

There should be at least one toilet and one wash basin with hot and cold water for every 15 children. The temperature of the hot water should be between 100° and 130°F. Individual washcloths and towels should be provided.

A telephone for preschool use should be on the premises.

Equipment

Equipment should be sturdy, safely constructed, flame retardant, and easily cleaned. It should be free from hazards and maintained in good repair.

Healthful Activities

The preschool should have a well-balanced, planned program. It should include indoor and outdoor activities, quiet play and rest. The length of the rest period should depend on the daily length of stay of the child in the preschool.

Individual cots and blankets should be provided. There should be at least two feet between the cots on all sides.

Staff of the Preschool

Staff members should provide a preemployment physician's certificate of good physical and emotional health including a negative tuberculin test or normal chest X ray. During employment, an annual certificate will be required, and a tuberculin test or chest X ray every three years.

Staff members should receive special training in the detection of symptoms of childhood illness and be responsible for initial observation of each child on his arrival and continued observation throughout his stay at the preschool for signs of illness.

The preschool should provide orientation to the preschool program and continuous in-service training to staff members.

Staff members should have personal qualities needed to work with young children. They should have an interest in and liking for children, understanding of children, personal competence, and emotional stability and dependability.

Discipline should meet the needs of each child. There shoud be no harsh punishment. Witholding of food should not be used as punishment.

Parent Involvement

The director or staff member should meet with the child's parent at least three times per year.

CONTENTS

3.1.0 FACTORS INFLUENCING WHAT AND HOW MUCH A PERSON EATS
3.2.0 WHAT A NUTRITION PROGRAM SHOULD ACCOMPLISH
3.3.0 THE REQUIREMENTS OF NUTRITION
    3.3.1 Nutrients
    3.3.2 Digestion
    3.3.3 Metabolism
    3.3.4 Energy
3.4.0 WHICH NUTRIENTS ARE NEEDED?
    3.4.1 Water
    3.4.2 Carbohydrates
    3.4.3 Fats
    3.4.4 Proteins
    3.4.5 Vitamins
    3.4.6 Minerals
3.5.0 FOR WHAT ARE NUTRIENTS NEEDED?
    3.5.1 Water
    3.5.2 Carbohydrates
    3.5.3 Fats
    3.5.4 Proteins
    3.5.5 Vitamins
        Fat Soluble
        Water Soluble
    3.5.6 Minerals
3.6.0 SOURCES OF NUTRIENTS AND HOW TO INSURE THEIR ABSORPTION
    3.6.1 The "Basic Seven" Food Groups
        Group 1—Leafy, green and yellow vegetables
        Group 2—Citrus fruits, tomatoes, raw cabbage and salad greens
        Group 3—Potatoes and other vegetables and fruits
        Group 4—Milk and milk products
        Group 5—Meat, poultry, fish, dried beans, and peas and nuts
        Group 6—Bread, flour, and cereal
        Group 7—Butter and fortified margarine
    3.6.2 The "Basic Four" Food Groups
        Group 1—Milk and dairy products
        Group 2—Meat, poultry, fish, eggs, legumes and nuts
        Group 3—Fruits and vegetables
        Group 4—Cereals and Breads
3.7.0 SERVING FOOD TO YOUNG CHILDREN
3.8.0 ABNORMALITIES ASSOCIATED WITH POOR NUTRITION

CHAPTER 3

Nutrition

What a person eats is important. The food that is eaten is necessary for survival but the amount and type helps to determine if an individual will be healthy. For the young child the quantity and quality of food eaten is especially critical because he is growing and preparing for his future and that of his children.

3.1.0 FACTORS INFLUENCING WHAT AND HOW MUCH A PERSON EATS

Almost every thoughtful individual believes that the effect of food on the body must be important. The difficulty is how to eat or supervise eating so that the food ingested will be most advantageous to health. This chapter tries to minimize this dilemma. First, it introduces you to the essential food requirements. Second, it teaches you that numerous circumstances control what and how much a person eats, regardless of (your) knowledge about nutritional requirements. Some examples follow:

1. Cultural and ethnic customs include and exclude all types of foods for many reasons. For example, some Puerto Ricans may eat rice and not milk; some Negroes may eat corn bread, peas, beans and ham hocks almost exclusively; some Mexicans may eat corn and beans rather than milk and a wide variety of vegetables; vegetarians exlude meats and meat products; some Jewish persons exclude nonkosher food and some people who originally came to the United States from Northern Europe may eat large amounts of milk and dairy products.
2. How much money a family has to spend on food also determines what types of food are eaten. High-income families may buy more meats, dairy products, and fresh fruits and vegetables. Low-income families, on the other hand, may buy more starchy foods, fatty cuts of meat,

and "junk food" (tonic, soda pop, potato chips, candy, and various snacks.) However, money to supplement the low-income family's food budget may influence what types of food are purchased.

3. Social, technical, and economic changes in the society have motivated the creation of new foods; fast food or takeout foods, precooked, and previously prepared foods of every possible type are readily available now. Clever, persuasive advertising gimmicks encourage their use. All these factors strongly influence what an individual eats today. Furthermore, current practices often keep one from knowing what is eaten because packaged foods rarely include an accurate list of the ingredients contained.

4. The environment in which a child resides strongly influences eating habits and how well food is utilized. If the surroundings are unsanitary the child may develop vomiting and diarrhea and will not benefit from food eaten (Chapter 4). A child may develop very irregular eating habits, a poor appetite for appropriate and nutritious food, anemia, dental cavities, or overweight if allowed to eat anything at any time.

5. The state of health of the child affects nutrition. In Chapter 6 many types of illnesses are discussed that may change the quantity of food eaten and how well food will be used. The conditions may be temporary or continue for a long time.

The teacher should be familiar with these conditions and plan ways to keep them from being a hindrance to the child's program of nutrition.

3.2.0 WHAT A NUTRITION PROGRAM SHOULD ACCOMPLISH

The objectives of a nutrition program in a preschool should be the following:

1. Make certain every staff member knows the necessary food requirements for the children in the center.
2. Reduce barriers to good food utilization.

3. Attempt to meet that part of a child's daily nutritional requirements not provided at home.
4. Encourage the development of good eating habits.
5. Introduce appropriate foods with the expectation that these will benefit him in later life.

3.3.0 THE REQUIREMENTS OF NUTRITION

3.3.1 Nutrients

Nutrients are the important parts of food. They are necessary because they permit an individual to function or work; they are used to get energy from what is eaten and they allow a young person to grow. These nutrients are water, carbohydrates, fats, proteins, vitamins, and minerals.

3.3.2 Digestion

Digestion is the process of changing foods that have been eaten into substances that may be absorbed and incorporated into the makeup of the body. The process begins immediately when food enters the mouth. Chewing and the saliva are the factors that begin digestion there. Digestion continues in the stomach where gastric juice is provided. From the stomach the processed food continues to the small intestine and then the large intestine where additional juices are used for digestion. By means of very complicated processes the nutrients are taken into the body through the blood vessels and lymphatics in the intestines. Those parts of the food that may not be used by the body are eliminated through the rectum. The liver and pancreas are additional organs playing an important role in digestion. At each successive area between the mouth and the rectum the food is changed. The extent of the change is different for each type of nutrient.

3.3.3 Metabolism

Metabolism is the process of utilizing the nutrients that have been absorbed. The chemical reactions involved occur in every cell of the body and need complex substances, *enzymes*, which make the chemical reactions occur. These chemical reactions enable the digested nutrients to be used for the growth of an individual and they release energy so that a person may carry on normal daily activities.

3.3.4 Energy

Energy keeps bodily functions operating. It is needed also for growth. Energy is produced when fats, carbohydrates, and proteins react chemically with oxygen. The amount of energy that is produced by this reaction is measured in units called calories. When metabolized by the body, fats give almost twice the amount of calories compared to carbohydrates and proteins. That is, one gram of fat yields nine calories, one gram of carbohydrates four calories and one gram of protein also four calories. The total amount of calories or energy needed from nutrients depends on the following:

1. Size: a larger person needs more energy than a small one.
2. Temperature: more food is needed in colder climates than hot ones.
3. Growth: more energy is needed during those times when physical growth is the greatest, for example, childhood, adolescence, pregnancy.
4. Amount and type of work or exercise done: the more physical activity, the greater the calorie need.

To guide an individual in what to eat three sources of information are available. First, the number of calories which are required in various times of life have been determined. For example, for a child between one and three years of age it is recomended that 45 calories per pound per day be supplied for normal activities. Second, a variety of foods have been analyzed for the number of calories contained in a specific quantity. For example, 200 calories per cup or 400 calories per six ounces of a given food. This enables a person to measure food and know how many calories will be available. Third, the best mixture of fats, carbohydrates, and proteins to be eaten daily has been determined. That is, 15 percent of the calories should come from protein, 35 percent from fat and 50 from carbohydrates.

3.4.0 WHICH NUTRIENTS ARE NEEDED?

The following nutrients are required by every individual.

3.4.1 Water

Water is the most important nutrient needed. Without water a person could survive approximately one week. Water comprises about 70 percent of a young child's weight. The blood, digestive fluids, fluids within each cell of the body, the liquid environment surrounding the cells, urine, and sweat all contain water. Most of the water requirements come from fluids that a person drinks but some is obtained through metabolism of foods. As the child gets older the amount of water needed per pound of body weight decreases. That is, the needs for an average one-year old are 120 to 135 milliliters of water per kilogram (2.2 pounds) of body weight per 24 hours; at two years of age it is 115 to 125 milliliters of water and at four years of age it is 100 to 110 milliliters of water. For simplification, these water needs may be estimated as follows:

1. Two ounces per pound for children between one and three years.
2. One and one half ounces per pound for children between four and six years of age.

3.4.2 Carbohydrates

Carbohydrates are the sugars and starches. They supply the greatest amount of energy in the diet. The starches and sugars are complex compounds that are broken down by the digestive process into simple compounds. These simple substances are absorbed and then metabolized. The most important simple carbohydrate is glucose. The glucose that is absorbed is used to supply energy for every cell of the body while some is stored in the liver and muscles. The glucose that is stored is changed chemically and represents only one percent of the body weight. If the carbohydrate is not consumed in meeting energy needs and is not stored it is converted into fat.

3.4.3 Fats

Fats are the nutrients that are most likely to produce a feeling of fullness or appetite satisfaction. Food tastes better if it contains fat. Fats are substances that are added to food, such as butter, shortening, and cooking oils or they are substances already in foods such as eggs, cheese, nuts and milk. Fats are either solid or liquid at room temperature. The compounds known as fats are very complex but one part is known as a fatty acid. The characteristic of the fat depends on its chemical structure, more specifically the fatty acid part. Certain fats contain complete or saturated fatty acids. Other fats contain fatty acids that have either a small or relatively large part of a chemical structure that is incomplete. Unsaturated fatty acids are partially incomplete and polyunsaturated fatty acids have a large part of the chemical structure that is incomplete. The saturated fatty acids cause cholesterol (a hard waxy substance that gets deposited in arteries) to be increased in the bloodstream. Unsaturated fatty acids in the diet have no effect on cholesterol. The cholesterol in the blood may be dangerous because it can clog the arteries and cause stroke and heart attack when a person gets old.

3.4.4 Proteins

Proteins make up about 20 percent of the total body weight. Most of the solid structure of the body is composed of protein. Therefore, much of the growth, restoration, and maintenance of a person's body depends on protein. Proteins may come from animal or vegetable sources and number in the thousands. However, all proteins are made from the same 20 chemical structures—amino acids. Some amino acids are made in the human body (nonessential ones) while others (essential ones) have to be supplied by proteins in animal or plant nutrients. Any one animal protein contains an adequate amount of all essential amino acids whereas individual vegetable proteins do not. The digestion of proteins breaks them down into amino acids which are metabolized in the body. It is recommended that a child between one and three years of age be given 2 to 2.5 grams of protein per kilogram (2.2 pounds) of body weight a day while a child between four and six years of age should be given 3 grams.

3.4.5 Vitamins

Vitamins are complex substances that are needed in minute amounts by the body so that metabolism may occur. A specific amount is required each day because vitamins are part of many of the enzymes used by the body. Most of the vitamins are labeled by the letters of the alphabet. There are water soluble vitamins—B_1, B_2, niacin, pyridoxine, B_{12} folic acid, and C. These vitamins are not stored within the body but are used quickly or excreted. The fat soluble vitamins may be stored and they include A, D, E, and K.

3.4.6 Minerals

Minerals not only give support and structure to the body but they are essential to metabolism and maintenance of the human body. Also the delicate balance between the acidity and alkalinity of body fluids depends on the concentration of certain minerals in the body. Large amounts of calcium, magnesium, and phosphorus are needed daily while small amounts of iron and iodine are needed daily. The amounts needed do not determine the importance of the substances because all are essential to normal human functions.

3.5.0 FOR WHAT ARE NUTRIENTS NEEDED?

The essential nutrients supply the following needs or perform the following functions:

3.5.1 Water

1. Is within and surrounds body cells.
2. Transports nutrients and waste products.
3. Regulates the body's temperature.

3.5.2 Carbohydrates

1. Supply quick, easy source of energy.
2. Supply energy to the brain.
3. Spare protein use and prevent acidity in the body.
4. Help to utilize fat.
5. Are a source of stored energy.

3.5.3 Fats

1. Permit the absorption of Vitamins A, D, E, and K.
2. Are a concentrated source of energy.
3. Are essential for growth and normal skin.
4. May be stored and used for energy.
5. Spare protein use.

68 Nutrition

    6. Cushion vital organs and serve as **insulation** against cold environmental temperature.

3.5.4 Proteins

1. Regulate the balance of fluids within the body's cells.
2. Supply amino acids.
3. Are essential for growth and maintenance of the body.
4. Are used in the formation of hormones, enzymes, and antibodies.
5. Are important in regulating the balance between alkalinity and acidity in the tissues of the body.
6. Serve as a source of energy.

3.5.5 Vitamins

Fat Soluble

Vitamin A

1. Contributes to skin and covering of internal organs.
2. Prevents night blindness (poor vision in a dim light).
3. Is used in the development of bones.

Vitamin D

1. Is necessary for the utilization of calcium to form bone.
2. Promotes absorption of calcium.
3. Contributes to the use of certain enzymes and phosphorus in the production of bone.

Vitamin E

1. Stops the breakdown of red blood cells.
2. Protects certain vitamins and fats so that normal metabolism may occur.

Vitamin K

1. Is important in blood clotting mechanism.

Water Soluble

Thiamine (B_1)
1. Is important to the enzymes that metabolize nutrients and release energy.
2. Helps in the metabolism of carbohydrates.

Riboflavin (B_2)
1. Is necessary for growth.
2. Is an important factor in assisting the metabolism of nutrients.

Niacin
1. Is essential in proper metabolism of proteins.

Vitamin B_6
1. Plays a key role in metabolizing nutrients.
2. Allows the body to make nonessential amino acids.
3. Is vital to the functioning of the brain and spinal cord.
4. Is important in blood cells.

Pantothenic Acid
1. Is a key part of the chemical reaction that releases energy.

Biotin
1. Is essential in getting energy from carbohydrates.
2. Is important in the metabolic process of fats and proteins.
3. Contributes to the utilization of vitamin B_{12} and folic acid.

Folic Acid
1. Prevents a form of anemia.
2. Is important in the metabolism of amino acids.

Vitamin B_{12}
1. Is important to the brain and spinal cord, digestive system, and bone marrow.
2. Prevents anemia.
3. Aids in metabolism of fats, carbohydrates, and proteins.

Vitamin C (Ascorbic Acid)
1. Prevents bleeding.
2. Is an essential part of supporting tissues in the body.
3. Helps in the metabolism of certain amino acids.

3.5.6 Minerals

Calcium
1. Is part of bones and teeth.
2. Is used for blood clotting.
3. Is needed for heart muscle activity.

Phosphorus
1. Is part of bones and teeth.
2. Regulates the balance between acidity and alkalinity in the body.
3. Is part of every cell in the body.
4. Is important in the transmission of nerve impulses.
5. Metabolizes fats, carbohydrates, and proteins.

Magnesium
1. Is part of bones and teeth.
2. Regulates muscle and nerve action.
3. Is used in carbohydrate metabolism.

Sodium
1. Regulates muscle and nerve action.
2. Maintains balance of water inside and outside body cells.
3. Is important to the balance between alkalinity and acidity of the body tissues.

Chloride
1. Regulates the balance of acidity and alkalinity of body tissues.
2. Is part of acid in stomach juices.
3. Maintains balance of water inside and outside of body cells.

Sulphur
1. Is contained in some proteins of cells.
2. Is important part of fluid within bone joints.

Iron
1. Is an essential part of the pigment of red blood cells.

Iodine
1. Is part of the hormone secreted by the thyroid gland.

Other Minerals
There are several minerals in addition to those discussed above that are important to normal body function. Some examples are potassium, cobalt, manganese, selenium, and zinc.

3.6.0 SOURCES OF NUTRIENTS AND HOW TO INSURE THEIR ABSORPTION

Natural food containing various nutrients offered to a child may be in a fresh (raw or cooked), canned, or frozen condition. Each food substance does not contain all of the nutrients necessary for a person's growth and survival. Therefore, a variety of food substances must be eaten. In order to be certain that all of the nutrients that are needed are eaten on a regular basis, we recommend a system using a number of basic food groups.

3.6.1 The "Basic Seven" Food Groups

About 30 years ago the U.S. Department of Agriculture introduced the "basic seven" food groups. For good nutrition, a serving of food from each group should be eaten every day. Another system, the "basic four," was recommended in 1955. This system is used commonly today. Several servings of a variety of foods from within each of the four groups should be eaten daily. Some nutritionists consider the "basic four" as a practical guide to meal planning. Others prefer the "basic seven" because the "basic four" food groups do not include all dietary needs. There are indications that still another classification of foods will be introduced in the future.

Because opinion about the food group system is divided, both systems are described here.

72 Nutrition

The "basic seven" classification is as follows: *Group 1*—leafy, green and yellow vegetables; *Group 2*—citrus fruits, tomatoes, raw cabbage, and salad greens; *Group 3*—potatoes and other vegetables not in Group 1 and Group 2, and fruits not in Group 1 and Group 2; *Group 4*—milk and milk products; *Group 5*—meat, poultry, fish, dried beans, peas and nuts; *Group 6*—bread, flour and cereals and *Group 7*— butter and fortified margarine.

Manufactured or synthetic or artificial foods are not included in this scheme. Their nutrient content as well as nutritional value may be found on the containers. Unfortunately, the contents of such foods may not be known and the nutritional value therefore is also unknown. "Junk foods" or foods that are high in carbohydrate content are not included in this scheme because they may offer only calories of energy without nutrients, also called empty calories. The foods in each of the groups should always be prepared so that the greatest amount of nutrients are preserved. This may be done by not pouring out the juices in which the food was cooked, cooking with a cover on the pan containing the food, not frying foods, and not destroying the vitamins or other nutrients with heat or prolonged exposure to sunlight.

Group 1—Leafy, Green, and Yellow Vegetables

This group provides vitamin A, iron, calcium, thiamine, riboflavin, niacin, and vitamin C. The following food substances are in this group: stringbeans, spinach, green peas, broccoli, kale, asparagus, carrots, squash, pumpkin, sweet potatoes, wax beans, rutabagas, and brussel sprouts.

Group 2—Citrus Fruits, Tomatoes, Raw Cabbage, and Salad Greens

This group offers vitamin C, vitamin A, iron, and calcium. The following food substances are in this group: *berries* (blackberries, loganberries, boysenberries, red and black raspberries, youngberries, blueberries, cranberries, huckleberries, and strawberries); *citrus fruits and their juices* (lemon, line, orange, tangerine, grapefruit, kumquat, and citron); *tomatoes* (all types); *cabbage* (green to red in color and all types); *salad greens* (endive—curly, escarole, lettuce—leaf, crisphead, Romaine, butterhead such as Boston and Bibb, stem).

Group 3—Potatoes and Other Vegetables and Fruits

This group offers vitamin C, other vitamins and minerals, starch, and carbohydrates. The following substances are in this group: *potatoes* (all types from high to low solid content); *vegetables* (beets, onions, garlic, celery, egg plant, corn, parsnip, cucumbers, radishes, turnips, okra, peppers, and cauliflower); *fruits* (apricots, cherries, peaches, plums, prunes, grapes—American and European types—watermelon, cantaloupe, honeydew, Persian, casaba, honeyball, and crenshaw melons, apples, pears, quince, avocado, banana, dates, figs, raisins, pineapple, papaya, and pomegranate).

Group 4—Milk and Milk Products

This group offers calcium, vitamin A, riboflavin, and a good quality of proteins.

The milk may be fresh whole, skim, dried, condensed, or cultured (buttermilk or yogurt). The chief milk product is cheese, which may be natural or processed. The milk and cheese may come from the cow, goat, or sheep.

Group 5—Meat, Poultry, Fish, Dried Beans, and Peas and Nuts

This group is the chief source of protein and it also produces iron, phosphorus, thiamine, and niacin. The types of food in this group are: *meat*—beef, pork, lamb, and veal. These meats may be cured, smoked, precooked, fresh (some aging up to one and one half months), or freeze dried when purchased. It is better to boil, roast, braise, or stew meat than to fry it. In the process of frying added fat is necessary. *Poultry*—chickens, turkeys, ducks, geese, and eggs of the chicken. *Fish*—fresh water and salt water types, nonshell fish and shellfish, fish with varying amounts of oil (less than 2 percent up to 20 percent). *Dried beans and peas*—lima beans, kidney beans, pinto beans, peas, navy beans, black-eyed peas, and crowder peas. *Nuts*—peanuts, cashews, pecans, walnuts, and chestnuts.

Group 6—Bread, Flour, and Cereal

This group offers vitamins and minerals as well as carbohydrates. Because of the deleterious effect of processing and milling, these substances should be fortified if unprocessed types are not used. The food substances in this group are: rice, barley, corn meal, wheat, bread, biscuits, crackers, oats, millet, rye, and sorghum.

Group 7—Butter and Fortified Margarine
These offer vitamin A and energy in the form of fat.

3.6.2 The "Basic Four" Food Groups

The "basic four" classification follows: *Group 1*—milk and dairy products; *Group 2*—meat, poultry, fish, eggs, legumes, and nuts; *Group 3*—fruits and vegetables; *Group 4*—cereals and breads.

The young child should consume daily some foods from each group as follows: *Group 1*—three or more 4 to 6 ounces glasses a day; *Group 2*—one or more child-size servings a day; *Group 3*—four or more child-size servings a day; orange or dark-green leafy vegetables should be included at least every other day; *Group 4*—a serving from this group at every meal. Butter should be used on bread and vegetables. For a daily food plan refer to Figure 2-14, page 35.

3.7.0 SERVING FOOD TO YOUNG CHILDREN

Standards for sanitary and safe conditions to be observed when food is prepared and served are discussed in Chapter 4.

Rules and regulations that govern the operation of preschools are specific as to what meals are to be offered (Chapter 2). The condition of any child, the time, and the atmosphere at the meal affect a child's eating habits. For example, children should have a regular mealtime; the intervals between meals should not be too long so that irritability or snacking becomes a problem; the mealtime should be a congenial time; children should be in small groups and mixed with adults during eating times; children should not be asked to carry their plates containing food to the table; it is better to have small containers partially filled with liquid rather than adult-sized drinking cups or glasses; offer foods that may be eaten easily either with fingers or with utensils; do not expect a child to cut up large pieces of food with a knife and fork.

Good attitudes toward eating and mealtime should be encouraged. This means that there should be no conflict over how much to eat or about a refusal to eat certain food types. The staff should not become excited or agitated if a child will only eat one type of food for awhile, for example, peanut butter sandwiches. The child should have one helping of food at a time; usually one tablespoon or one slice. All foods prepared should be offered but forcing a child to eat

Credit: *Marshall R. Hathaway*

every food type is neither necessary nor advisable. Food should never be used as a bribe to the child for any good or bad behavior. "Junk food" should not be in the preschool center and thus it will not be a temptation to a child. Allow the children to help in planning the menus, setting the table, preparing some types of food, serving the food, and cleaning up after eating. For a suggested daily food plan and size of serving portions see Figure 2.14, page 35.

3.8.0 ABNORMALITIES ASSOCIATED WITH POOR NUTRITION

Abnormalities due to a child's poor nutrition are difficult to recognize by the teacher in a preschool unless they are extreme. Most individuals would recognize, then, that the child has some serious problem that needs medical attention. Some observable characteristics in a child that may be the result of poor nutrition are:

1. Irritability, bleeding of the gums, and bleeding under the skin.
2. A loss of weight or lack of growth.
3. Sluggishness, tiredness, puffiness of the face, arms and legs.
4. Complaints of a sore, burning tongue, cracks in the skin at the corners of the mouth.
5. Severely decayed teeth.

6. Bowed legs, large lumps at the end of ribs, or a square shape to the head.

Obesity or overweight is usually equated with poor dietary habits. However, a young child who is obese or overweight is not always so because of faulty food intake. Scientific studies have demonstrated that genetics are also a factor in overweight. That is, if a child has both parents or even one parent who is overweight, there is a much greater chance that he will also be overweight. Severe emotional stress or physical damage to specific parts of the brain may produce abnormalities that could lead to overweight. Other scientific investigations have shown that the young child who is overweight seems to remain in such a way throughout life in spite of strenuous attempts to control what is eaten.

The amount of food eaten more than the type appears to be important in producing obesity. For example, if overweight is to be avoided there must be a balance between the energy obtained from food and the energy spent for growth, development, and exercise. Thus, the presence of obesity is not always simply a lack of nutritional information.

The child who eats poorly, goes on food binges, or appears ill may have a nutritional problem. Such a problem will probably be found if the teacher, parents, and medical consultant get together and review the child's growth information, eating patterns, and medical findings after a comprehensive medical and dental examination.

CONTENTS

4.1.0 INFECTION AND INFECTIOUS DISEASE
4.2.0 THE INFECTIOUS PROCESS
    4.2.1 Infectious Agent
    4.2.2 Reservoir
    4.2.3 Transmission
    4.2.4 Susceptible Host
        Stages Of Infectious Disease
        Period of Communicability
4.3.0 SUSCEPTIBILITY AND RESISTANCE
4.4.0 IMMUNITY
    4.4.1 Types of Immunity
4.5.0 IMMUNIZATION
4.6.0 CONTROL OF INFECTIOUS DISEASES
    4.6.1 Control of Reservoir
    4.6.2 Control of Transmission
        Children's Diseases
        Food-borne Diseases
    4.6.3 Control of the Infectious Agent within the Body
    4.6.4 Control of Infectious Diseases by Legal Means

CHAPTER 4

The Infectious Process

Infectious diseases are an important part in the young child's life. In spite of tremendous progress in medical knowledge, infectious diseases are still among the most frequent causes of absence from school. Every infectious disease is the result of a successful chain of events—the infectious process. This process and ways to control or prevent it is explained in this chapter. A teacher who understands the basic principles of this infectious process and its control will be more alert to symptoms that might indicate an oncoming infectious disease; might be able to alleviate or avert infectious disease by proper action; will be better able to communicate with the parents, the nurse, or the doctor; will understand why children with certain infectious diseases should be separated from others, why they should stay home a certain length of time, and, finally, will understand the importance of immunization.

In the beginning of this century the average life expectancy was about 49 years, whereas today it is about 70 years. Much of this difference is due to prevention and treatment of infectious diseases. The leading cause of death in the year 1900 was due to such infectious diseases as tuberculosis, influenza, pneumonia, and others, while today they only comprise about 5 percent of all the causes of death. Up to about 100 years ago it was believed that the agents that caused infectious disease could arise from filth, dirt and vapors, decaying animals, and plants. This was called spontaneous generation. Then it was discovered that each infectious disease is caused by a specific agent or microorganism. For example, measles is caused by a special virus, whooping cough by a special bacterium, and ringworm by a particular fungus. And it was also discovered that these microorganisms do not arise spontaneously from dead matter but only by multiplication from already existing microorganisms. Later, much was learned about immunity to disease and today we are able to prevent or alleviate diseases by immunization against them. With the discovery of antibiotics such as penicillin, for instance, we are able to treat many of the infectious diseases and effect a recovery.

Immunization, giving almost complete protection, is available against diseases such as poliomyelitis, diphtheria, tetanus (lockjaw), whooping cough (pertussis), mumps, measles, and rubella (German measles). These diseases are preventable. However, because of public apathy toward immunization, some of these onetime childhood threats are on the rise again in some communities. One of the reasons for lack of immunization of young children today is that parents do not remember how dreadful these diseases can be and they neglect to have their children immunized. Older children receive immunization in public schools as required by law in most states. Many men have been immunized in the military service but adult women and some of the younger children are the two population groups that frequently are not immunized.

4.1.0 INFECTION AND INFECTIOUS DISEASE

What is infection? Is it the same as infectious disease? When a living organism that can cause disease enters the body and multiplies in it, we call it an infection. The body will react to this in some way, but there may be no outward sign of this reaction. But when the body reacts with signs and symptoms such as fever, running nose, watery eyes, aches and pains, and sore throat, then we call it infectious disease. The body is visibly reacting to the invading organism. It is a struggle between the two. Infection does not necessarily imply disease. The distinction between infection and disease is not clearcut but gradual. If we think of infection on one end of a line and severe disease on the other, we could devise the following scale:

Infection, no disease	Very mild disease, "subclinical" cases	Mild disease	Moderate disease	Severe disease
Disease not visible			Disease visible	

Some people exposed to a person with an infectious disease, will become infected but will have no symptoms or very mild symptoms. The "subclinical case" with slight symptoms is not ill enough to go to a physician. Even the physician would not be able to diagnose the disease because of lack of symptoms. These "missed" or "subclinical" cases, however, do transmit the disease to others. Because some persons become only slightly ill while others may be quite seriously ill with an infectious disease, their symptoms vary. Even though we identify signs and symptoms for a disease, such as fever, cough, sore throat, nasal drip, fatigue, and rash for measles, not every case of measles will have all these symptoms. In a slight case, there may not even be the typical rash or it may be so light or of such short duration that it might be overlooked.

4.2.0 THE INFECTIOUS PROCESS

In discussing the infectious process, immunity, and control of infectious diseases, we limit the subject to childhood diseases and food-born illnesses as much as possible.

In order for an infectious disease to develop, the following factors have to exist:

1. Infectious agent.
2. Reservoir.
3. Transmission.
4. Susceptible host.

The infectious agent causing the disease has to exist. It has to be present in a reservoir or a place from which it can be transmitted to a susceptible host. When this chain of events is broken, then infection will not take place. The control of infectious disease is based on this principle.

4.2.1 Infectious Agent

The infectious agent, also called causative or etiological agent, that gives rise to an infectious disease is a very small living organism called microorganism (micro = small). There are different types of microorganisms. Most of the infectious diseases in children are caused either by viruses or by bacteria. Viruses are even smaller than bacteria and they differ in several other ways from bacteria.

Some of the diseases caused by viruses are measles, German

measles, mumps, poliomyelitis, the common cold, smallpox, and infectious hepatitis. Bacteria, on the other hand, cause whooping cough, tetanus, scarlet fever, conjunctivitis ("pinkeye"), and others. The infectious agent is specific for each disease. Measles is caused by a specific measles virus and not by a virus that causes German measles or by one that causes a cold. However, pneumonia, which is not a specific infectious disease but is an inflammation of the lungs, can be caused by various microorganisms and even by nonliving substances. Similarly, bronchitis and meningitis can be caused by different microorganisms. We must distinguish between a specific infectious disease such as measles or whooping cough and a disease of an organ of the body, such as disease of the lung, bronchi, or coverings of the brain. Some disease-producing organisms do not cause one specific infectious disease but the disease depends on how and under what circumstances they enter the body of the susceptible person, and where they establish themselves. The staphylococcus, commonly called "staph," may cause a local infection in the skin, or may invade the lungs and cause pneumonia, or cause conjunctivitis or other infections. Infectious diseases vary in degree of infectiousness. Measles and chickenpox are highly infectious while mumps are less infectious.

4.2.2 Reservoir

The place where the causative agent resides and from where it can escape and be transmitted to the susceptible person or host is called reservoir. The reservoir for most of the infectious agents we are concerned with is a human being. The causative agent lives and multiples in the reservoir. Most infectious agents cannot survive for any appreciable length of time outside of a living body. The reservoir can be a person ill with the infectious disease but it can also be the person with a very slight case of the disease or one not ill at all, as we discussed above. Usually the person who is obviously ill stays at home and is less likely to transmit the disease than the one who is only slightly indisposed or who is infected but not ill at all. Thus we are unable to protect people from contact with the infectious agents. There are other reservoirs besides the human. The bacterium that causes tetanus (lockjaw) can survive in the soil for a long time. In this case the soil is the reservoir. This is one of the few exceptions where a reservoir is not a living organism. The fungus that causes ringworm of the skin may come from another human or from a dog or cat. The bacterium causing salmonellosis, a food infection, frequently comes from poultry, other animals, or another person. Thus animals also serve as reservoirs for some human infections.

4.2.3 Transmission

How does the infectious agent leave the reservoir and get to a susceptible person? There are several ways depending on the infectious disease itself. The most common route of escape of the infectious agent from an infected person is through the nose and mouth, by breathing, coughing, and sneezing. But of course only infectious agents that are present in the respiratory tract (lung, bronchi, windpipe, voicebox, throat, or nose) can be discharged in this manner. We breathe out moisture or droplets and microorganisms in the droplets will be directly breathed in by other persons nearby. Sometimes they can be carried for quite a distance before reaching another person, especially when forced out in a cough or sneeze. Some of the diseases of concern to us that are transmitted in this way are chickenpox, diphtheria, influenza, measles, mumps, poliomyelitis, the common cold, German measles, smallpox, scarlet fever, and whooping cough. Another route of escape for some of the infectious agents is the intestinal tract. While feces contain many harmless microorganisms, they can also contain disease-producing ones. These can be transmitted by fingers directly to other persons or to food that can transmit the agent to other people. In places where waste disposal is not satisfactory, flies can carry the microorganisms and contaminate food. The wastes can also leak into drinking water and contaminate the water supply. The importance of personal hygiene such as washing hands, proper waste disposal, food and water protection, and milk pasteurization is readily apparent. Poliomyelitis can be transmitted by the fecal route as well as by the respiratory route. Dysentery, typhoid, other intestinal diseases, and hepatitis are also transmitted from the intestinal tract. The respiratory and intestinal tract are the most common routes of escape of the infectious agent from a human reservoir. The discharges and scales from infected skin or mucous membrane lesions are also infectious. The liquid from the vesicles (small blisters) in the skin in chickenpox and the skin scales from ringworm lesions are infectious to the susceptible host. The mode of transmission to the new host is by direct or indirect contact. Direct contact includes not only physical contact but also breathing in organisms exhaled by another person. With indirect contact there is an intermediate carrier involved. It could be a handkerchief or towel, freshly soiled with nasal discharge from a child with measles used by another susceptible child. "Pinkeye," a bacterial infection of the mucous membrane covering the eyeball and lining the lids, can also be transmitted in this manner. The intermediate carrier can be an animal such as the fly mentioned above. It could be water, milk, other foods, or other objects. Books, toys, and similar objects do not play a significant role in transmission of infectious diseases, while freshly soiled towels with discharges from infected persons immediately used by susceptible persons do transmit diseases such as colds and measles. Milk has been the cause of severe outbreaks of scarlet fever and throat infections especially among children. Pasteurization is a process during which milk or other beverages are heated to a certain temperature, which destroys disease-producing microorganisms. Before pasteurization was used, milk-borne outbreaks of infectous diseases were much more frequent. Milk is a medium in which bacteria multiply easily, especially when milk is not refrigerated. Today the milk we consume is pasteurized. However, it is important not to contaminate milk, once a container of it has been opened, and it is also important to keep it refrigerated. The same principle applies to foods in general.

Entry of the infectious agent into the new host occurs through the respiratory tract by inhalation or by ingestion of contaminated food, through the skin or mucous membrane or by less common means. Most of the causative agents of common children's diseases enter through the respiratory tract. They also leave through the respiratory tract to be transmitted to other children. Some infectious agents must use a certain mode of entry in order to produce an infection. For example, the tetanus bacterium must enter through a deep wound to produce lockjaw. If ingested, no infection will result.

4.2.4 Susceptible Host

In order to know when and for how long an infected child can transmit the infection to others, we should first know something about the course of the infectious diseases. Once the infectious agent has entered the susceptible child, most infectious diseases follow a similar pattern of development. The disease is either acute or chronic. In acute diseases symptoms appear, rise to a certain level and then subside abruptly. The acute disease follows a rapid and severe course, usually of a few days duration. The chronic disease runs a slow course over a period of weeks, months, or even years. Most children's infectious diseases are acute.

Stages of Infectious Disease

The course of acute diseases can be divided into four stages or periods: incubation, prodromal, acute, and convalescent. The duration of the various periods are usually characteristic for a particular infectious disease.

1. *The Incubation Period.* The time between exposure to an infectious agent and the appearance of the first signs and symptoms of the disease is the incubation period. The infectious agent is "incubating," establishing itself and multiplying, while the host is not yet visibly reacting. The incubation period for each infectious disease is specific and can be expressed as a range of days or the most common number of days. The incubation period for chickenpox is two to three weeks, most commonly 13 to 17 days; measles 8 to 13 days, most commonly 10 days till first symptoms, and 14 days till rash appears; German measles 14 to 21 days; whooping cough usually within 10 days, most often 7 days and not more than 21 days; infectious hepatitis 15 to 50 days, commonly 28 to 30 days; tetanus 4 days to three weeks, commonly 10 days; influenza 24 to 72 hours[1].

2. *The Prodromal Period.* This stage usually lasts only one or two days and it is the time when the very first symptoms appear before the acute stage. Prodromal means "running before" or preceding. It may show itself by a feeling of uneasiness, a slight sore throat, or headache. At times there may not be a prodromal stage; the disease may have a definite, sudden onset.

3. *The Acute Period.* During this stage the child is obviously ill. Each infectious disease has characteristic symptoms, although most have many symptoms in common, such as fever. Rashes are one of the signs of certain children's diseases and their appearance and body distribution are

---

[1]Obtained from *Control of Communicable Diseases in Man*, published by the American Public Health Association, 1975.

typical for each disease such as chickenpox, measles, and scarlet fever. The appearance of the throat will be different in such diseases as "strep" sore throat and diphtheria. The distinctive cough is a particular symptom of whooping cough. It is well to remember that the course of disease and symptoms vary with each child and not all symptoms are present in each case.

4. *The Convalescent Period.* Unless the disease is so severe that the child does not recover, but dies, or the disease is followed by complications, the acute stage is succeeded by a recovery or convalescent stage. The symptoms subside and the patient gradually feels better. One of the dangers of the children's infectious diseases are complications that may follow. Some of the complications of measles are ear infection, bronchitis, pneumonia, and encephalitis. Mumps may be followed by involvement of the testicles. This rarely happens in the male before puberty. The complications of German measles will be discussed later in this chapter.

Period of Communicability[2]

The infected child becomes a reservoir for the infectious agent and a source of infection to others during the time when the infectious agent can leave the child and can be transmitted to another person. The time during which transmission is possible is the period of communicability. This time varies with each disease. In diseases where the infectious agent is in the respiratory tract, the person is communicable as long as the infectious agent can be discharged by breathing, coughing, and sneezing. When the infectious agent is in the intestinal tract, the host is communicable whenever the agent is present in feces. In diseases with skin involvement, such as chickenpox, the organism is present in the skin lesions, the tiny blisters filled with fluid. As long as the infectious organism is there, it can be transmitted. When the scab forms, the period of communicability ends. However, in chickenpox the infectious agent is also present in the respiratory tract. Some examples[3] of period of communicability follow:

[2]The term *infectious disease* means a disease resulting from an infection. Not all infectious diseases are communicable. A *communicable disease* also results from an infection and it can be transmitted from humans (or animals) to humans by direct or indirect means.

[3]*Control of Communicable Diseases in Man*, a publication of the A.P.H.A. (American Public Health Association), 1975.

The Infectious Process

Chickenpox	As long as five days before the eruption of chickenpox; not more than six days after the first crop of vesicles.
Measles	From the beginning of the prodromal period to four days after appearance of the rash.
Infectious mononucleosis	Unknown but presumably from before symptoms appear to end of fever and clearing of oral-pharyngeal lesions.
Mumps	The virus has been isolated from saliva from 6 days before salivary gland involvement to as long as 9 days thereafter, but the height of infectiousness occurs about 48 hours before swelling commences. Urine positive as long as 14 days after onset of illness. Persons with unapparent infection can be infectious.
Poliomyelitis	Polio virus is demonstrable in throat secretions as early as 36 hours and in the feces 72 hours after infection in both clinical and unapparent cases. Virus persists in the throat for approximately one week and in the feces for three to six weeks or longer. Cases are most infectious from 7 to 10 days before and after the onset of symptoms.
Common cold	Nasal washings taken 24 hours before onset and for 5 days after onset have produced symptoms in experimentally infected volunteers.
German measles (Rubella)	For about one week before and at least 4 days after onset of rash. Highly communicable. Infants with congenital rubella syndrome may shed virus for months after birth; the period of shedding is extremely variable.
Tetanus (Lockjaw)	Not directly transmitted from one person to another.
Whooping cough (Pertussis)	Highly communicable in the early catarrhal stage, before paroxysmal cough. Thereafter, communicability gradually decreases and becomes negligible for ordinary nonfamilial contacts in about three weeks despite persisting

spasmodic cough with whoop. For control purposes, the communicable stage extends from 7 days after exposure to three weeks after onset of typical paroxysms.

The infected child, as seen from the above examples of children's diseases, is communicable to others not only when obviously ill and the disease has been diagnosed, but often before anyone knows that he or she might become ill. It is not possible to protect children from exposure to most common children's diseases.

4.3.0 SUSCEPTIBILITY AND RESISTANCE

If a group of children comes in contact with a child who has measles, some of the children will get the disease. These children are susceptible to measles. The majority of those who will not come down with the disease have protective substances called antibodies. These children are immune to measles. The rest of the children are susceptible but will resist the disease at this time. However, at a later time, after contact with a measles case, they might contract the disease.

While we may not understand all the reasons why at times a disease develops after exposure yet at other times it does not, we know some of the factors involved. The amount of infectious agent received by the child on exposure is one of the factors. If he receives a massive dose by being directly coughed at he is more apt to come down with the disease than if he is at some distance away from the infected child. How long he is exposed to the infectious agent is another factor. Does he spend all day or night with the sick child or is he just a short-time visitor? Infants and the very young child are usually more susceptible to infections than older children, thus age is a factor. Malnutrition, exposure to cold, tiredness, and the presence of a chronic disease all play a role in making a child more prone to the development of infectious disease. These factors will also influence the severity of the disease. Resistance to disease is a very broad term. The type of resistance associated with the factors above, such as age, good nourishment, rest, and absence of chronic disease, is considered nonspecific resistance. It is effective against all kinds of infectious agents, not against a particular one. Specific resistance, on the other hand, refers to immunity.

4.4.0 IMMUNITY

A person who is immune to an infectious disease has antibodies in his or her body or can quickly develop them when exposed to the infectious agent causing the disease. These antibodies will usually prevent the development of the disease. The immunity is specific, which means that there are specific antibodies for each infectious agent. Immunity against measles will not protect the child against German measles. There are four types of immunity, two are called active and two passive immunity, according to how the antibodies were acquired.

4.4.1 Types of Immunity

1. Active immunity that follows the actual disease.
2. Active immunity that is the result of vaccination.
3. Passive immunity that newborn infants have to some disease because their mother's antibodies entered their blood through the placenta during pregnancy.
4. Passive immunity due to injection of antibodies.

The term active immunity means that the child has actively produced his own antibodies, either in response to illness or after having received an artificially prepared vaccine.

Active Immunity Following Disease

While the susceptible child is developing the infectious disease after invasion by the infectious agent, he will also be stimulated to develop antibodies (protective substances) against the infectious agent; when enough antibodies are produced, they will inactivate the infectious agent, symptoms of the disease will subside, and the child will be on the road to recovery. The antibodies will persist in the body for a time, and then their level will gradually diminish. When the child is exposed to the same infectious agent again, he may not have enough antibodies but his body will know how to produce the antibodies to it. This time it will do it quickly before the disease can develop. The child has active immunity as a result of the disease. Some children will be immune to a disease even though they never had the disease. They most probably had a very slight or so-called subclinical form of the disease. The symptoms were so mild as not to be recognized. It is also possible that repeated exposure to the infectious agent in very small doses produced immunity gradually.

Active Immunity Following Immunization

The terms vaccination and immunization are used interchangeably. Vaccination will also stimulate the active production of antibodies in the child but without the presence of the disease. The term vaccine is derived from the Latin word *vacca*, which means cow (*vaccinia* means cowpox, a disease of cattle). Almost 200 years ago Edward Jenner, the English physician, observed that many persons milking cows became infected with cowpox, a very mild infection. Later, when exposed to smallpox, they would not get the dreaded and very often fatal disease of smallpox. In spite of severe opposition and criticism from his contemporaries, Jenner demonstrated that he could protect people from an attack of smallpox by rubbing the cowpox vaccine, material from actual cowpox, into their skin. This procedure, refined, is still in use today when smallpox vaccination is necessary. The cowpox virus is similar to the smallpox virus and, although antibodies are specific, in this case antibodies to cowpox will also protect against smallpox. The principle of Jenner's discovery underlies modern vaccination methods. A vaccine is the material used to immunize persons. It is prepared from dead or attenuated (weakened) live bacteria or viruses, or from toxoids that are weakened toxins (poisonous products) of some bacteria. Immunization of children is of great importance to us and it will be discussed later.

The term passive immunity means that the child becomes immune because antibodies are given to the child.

Passive Immunity of the Newborn

The newborn baby may be immune to a number of infectious diseases because some antibodies from the mother pass into the blood of the fetus during pregnancy. The newborn can be immune to a disease only if the mother has antibodies to that disease. She may have acquired these antibodies by having been immunized or by having had the disease. This passive immunity of the newborn gradually diminishes as the infant grows older. The duration of immunity in the newborn child varies for each disease but usually does not exceed the first few months of life. See Figure 4-1 for some of the diseases in which immunity may be transmitted from the mother and for the duration of the immunity.

Disease	Duration of Immunity in Infant
Diptheria	Six to nine months
German measles	Three to six months
Measles	Six weeks to six to nine months
Mumps	Two to six months
Poliomyelitis	Several months
Scarlet fever	Up to six months
Smallpox	Variable, not reliable
Tetanus	Some immunity, but not enough to be reliable for protection

NOTE: Immunity is transmitted only if the mother has active immunity due to previous disease or active immunization. The immunity in the infant is temporary and gradually diminshes. Unnecessary exposure of infants to any infectious disease is unwise.

Figure 4-1 Transmission of immunity from mother to newborn.

Passive Immunity Due To Injection of Antibodies

When a child is vaccinated against a disease, it takes some time, weeks or months, for the immunity to develop, but it is usually of long duration. It is a procedure to protect him from the disease in the future. However, there are instances when one cannot wait until the child develops his own immunity. When he has already been exposed to an infection and indications are that the disease or its complications would be very serious and would endanger him, then he must be protected immediately to prevent the disease or to make it at least milder. This is done by injecting him with antibodies produced by another person or by an animal. Antibodies against diphtheria and tetanus are produced by injecting animals with a vaccine. The antibodies will appear in the animal's blood and can be prepared from the blood for injection to protect exposed children against the disease. However, animals are not susceptible to some of man's diseases such as measles or infectious hepatitis. In these instances antibodies from humans have to be used for protection by passive immunity. Convalescent serum, hyperimmune serum, and gamma globulin are all preparations from blood of persons who have had the disease in question and whose blood is high in antibodies to it. Convalescent serum or gamma globulin is used when it is considered advisable to prevent measles in an exposed child. When given, a mild case of measles might still develop but prevent the dangerous complications that often follow. This has the additional advantage of allowing active immunity with its lasting protection to develop. Gamma globulin is also used to protect those exposed to infectious hepatitis. In case of exposure to whooping cough, immune serum—together with antibiotics—has been found effective. Compared with active immunity, which develops slowly but has lasting effect, passive immunity is only of short duration.

4.5.0 IMMUNIZATION

To demonstrate how vaccination produces immunity, let us use diphtheria as an example. This is one of the infectious diseases that can be successfuly eradicated by immunization of children. Systematic immunization was begun in the 1920s and since then diphtheria has been extremely rare in the United States. Only recently, because of neglect of immunization, especially by certain population groups, cases of diphtheria are appearing again. The usual procedure is to give three injections of the diphtheria vaccine between the age of two to six months. Following the first injection, antibodies usually start to appear in the body approximately after a week. The amount gradually increases and with the help of the two subsequent injections, the level of antibodies becomes high enough to protect against a diphtheria infection. However, the amount of antibodies does not stay at a certain level but decreases after a time and therefore, after a year an additional injection of vaccine is given. This is called a booster dose. It is repeated every few years according to a set immunization schedule. A booster injection is a dose of vaccine given to a previously immunized child. In some diseases, it is given when a child is exposed to a case of the disease, to make sure that his antibody level will be high enough to protect him. A previously immunized child can develop antibodies much faster in response to a booster dose than to a first vaccination. The immunity following vaccination varies in different diseases. In diphtheria, the immunity is very protective while in whooping cough (pertussis) it is less efficient but still very worthwhile. Chances are that if a child comes down with whooping cough in spite of vaccination, the disease will be milder. Immunization against tetanus is very reliable. The vaccines for these three diseases are often injected together ("DPT"=diphtheria, pertussis, tetanus). The recommended immunization schedules for common childhood diseases are summarized in Figure 4-2.

Immunization 93

Age of Child	Vaccine	
2 months	DTP[a]	TOPV[b]
4 months	DTP	TOPV
6 months	DTP	TOPV (optional)
1 year		Tuberculin test[d]
15 months	Measles	
	Rubella	
	Mumps	
1½ years	DTP	TOPV
4 to 6 years	DTP	TOPV
14 to 16 years	Td[c] and every 10 years thereafter	

Adapted from Report of The Committee on Infectious Diseases, 1977. American Academy of Pediatrics.
[a] DTP—diphtheria, tetanus and pertussis (whooping cough) vaccine.
[b] TOPV—poliomyelitis vaccine (trivalent oral polio virus vaccine).
[c] Td—combined diphtheria and tetanus vaccine.
[d] Frequency of repeated tuberculin tests depends on local circumstances.

Figure 4-2 Recommended schedule for active immunization and tuberculin testing of normal infants and children.

Vaccination is not a totally harmless procedure and there are instances, although rare, when complications follow vaccination. However, generally, the advantages of vaccination far outweigh the rare disadvantages. Because of increasing medical knowledge and because of other developments, changes do take place in recommended immunization procedures. A disease may become so rare in some countries that the necessity for immunization is being reconsidered. In other diseases, vaccines are only now becoming available. Yet in another instance, it has been discovered that a communicable disease in a pregnant woman can cause birth defects in the child, making it imperative to take special precautions. Different populations also react differently to some communicable diseases and, therefore, recommended immunization procedures may vary with geographical location.

Smallpox is one of the diseases that has been virtually eradicated in this country. While vaccination against smallpox used to be compulsory, some states now do not require routine vaccination to this disease any more. The reason is that it is unlikely for children to come into contact with a case of it and although adverse reactions to this vaccination are very rare, they can be quite serious in nature.

The development of some vaccines, such as against poliomyelitis, measles, and German measles, has been quite recent. The drop in incidence of these diseases has been dramatic due to vaccination. Measles is a very serious and highly fatal disease among children of less developed countries and of isolated populations such as on islands. Vaccination in such places is very important. German measles (rubella) is of special significance because of the danger it poses to an embryo and a fetus carried by a pregnant woman who has German measles. The product of conception is called an embryo up to about eight weeks of pregnancy. After eight weeks it is called a fetus until it is born. In children German measles is mild. However, after careful studies of health records of mothers who had spontaneous miscarriages or whose infants were stillborn or born with abnormalities such as heart defects, liver and spleen damage, cataracts and brain damage, it was frequently found that these mothers have had German measles very early in pregnancy. Infants of mothers who had rubella early in pregnancy are infected with the virus and can spread it to others, especially adults, caring for them. According to recent studies as many as 80 percent of the infants are affected when the expectant mother has the disease during the first four weeks of pregnancy. She may not even be aware of the pregnancy at the time of the disease. The danger to the infant decreases when the disease is acquired by the mother later in pregnancy. A vaccine made from live, weakened virus has been developed recently. It protects 90 to 95 percent of susceptible persons from getting the disease when exposed to the German measles virus. The reason for immunizing all children is to build up immunity in the population to a point where transmission would cease because of the drop in incidence of the disease. Immunization of pregnant women should not take place, because the vaccine is a live virus. However, susceptible women of childbearing age who through their work might be exposed to infected infants should be vaccinated at least two months before a pregnancy might occur. The success of passive immunization of exposed pregnant women by gamma globulin is not established yet. When this disease occurs among children in preschools it is very important for the teacher, the health team, and the parents to follow a previously established school health policy for this particular situation.

We do not have vaccines for all infectious diseases; for instance, there is none against infectious hepatitis. Immunity does not follow all infectious diseases. A person can contract the common cold repeatedly without becoming immune to it. Immunity to tuberculosis, a usually chronic infectious disease, differs from immunity to common children's diseases. It is complex and not completely understood. Tuberculosis is not as highly infectious as measles. It usually takes prolonged contact with a case of tuberculosis to get the disease. There is a vaccine available but it is advisable to use it only in high-risk areas such as countries where there are still many cases of tuberculosis. In this country instead of vaccination, a skin test, the tuberculin test, is used. This test is discussed in Chapter 5.

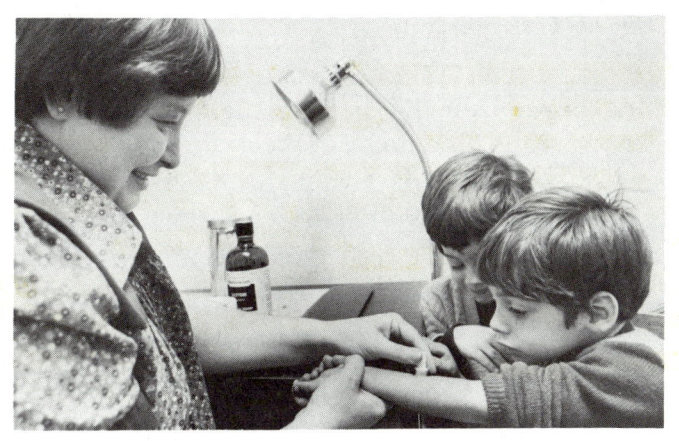

Credit: *Marshall R. Hathaway*

4.6.0 CONTROL OF INFECTIOUS DISEASES

Control procedures vary with the type of disease, circumstances, and local conditions. Only some of the procedures apply to children's diseases. The control measures can be divided into four general areas although some overlap exists.

1. Control of reservoir.
2. Control of transmission (preventing spread).
3. Control of the infectious agent within the body.
4. Control of infectious diseases by legal means.

4.6.1 Control of Reservoir

It was previously mentioned that before infection of a susceptible person occurs, a series of events takes place. An infectious agent has to exist in a place or reservoir and there has to be some way in which the agent is transmitted to the new host and enters the body. One way to stop the infectious process is to eradicate the reservoir. This can be done only where the reservoir is not man. Eradication has actually been used with cattle that were infected with tuberculosis which through their milk could infect people, especially chidren. All cattle were tested and those with a positive test were eliminated. Since the reservoir for most children's diseases is human beings, the reservoir cannot be eliminated.

4.6.2 Control of Transmission

Transmission from the reservoir to the host can be interrupted by controlling the exit from the reservoir, the direct or indirect contact, or the entry into the host. Some of the methods for controlling the exit are proper handling of feces and urine, covering of open sores, proper handling of wound dressings, bed linen, towels, and other objects. Methods for controlling direct or indirect transmission are avoiding close contact, pasteurizing milk, sanitizing food, providing proper sewage treatment, disinfecting objects, controlling animals or animal products. Methods of control of entry into the host would include wearing of a mask over mouth and nose, personal hygiene such as washing hands, avoiding intake of contaminated food or water, and protecting open wounds.

Children's Diseases

Control of transmission of most children's diseases is generally not possible because the diseases are usually communicable before detected. Once the disease has been identified, it is important to isolate the child to protect those who are especially vulnerable, such as very young children or, in case of German measles, pregnant women and those who might become pregnant within a few weeks.

Food-borne Diseases

The purpose of food sanitation, and rules and regulations (Chapter 2) pertaining to food service is prevention of food-borne diseases. To understand food sanitation it appears appropriate to apply the principles of the infectious process to disease transmitted by food. The term food includes milk and other liquids as well as solids. The two food-borne diseases that are most common and could occur in preschools are salmonellosis and staphylococcus food poisoning.

The infectious agent causing salmonellosis is a bacterium called salmonella. When salmonellae enter the digestive tract, they settle there and multiply and cause gastroenteritis, an inflammation of the lining of the stomach and intestines.

The salmonellae live in humans and in animals, in turkeys, chickens, turtles, and others. Thus the reservoir is humans, and domestic and wild animals.

The bacteria spread from animal to human, from one person to another and from human to animal. Transmission occurs usually by ingestion of food, which is contaminated by feces of infected animals or humans. Salmonellosis outbreaks are frequently traced to food such as poultry and meat, and their products, meat pies, chicken salad, gravies, eggs, (fresh frozen or dried), potato salad, custard-filled pastries, unpasteurized milk, and fish. There is no way to determine by its appearance, taste, or odor, that food is contaminated. Animals get the infection from contaminated feed and fertilizer. Contamination of food by animals occurs before it reaches the consumer but contamination by man occurs by food handlers who have the infection and do not wash their hands thoroughly. The bacteria are also transmitted directly by touch from contaminated hands to the hand or mouth of another person.

The incubation period of salmonellosis is 8 to 72 hours and the onset of symptoms is sudden, with nausea, vomiting, diarrhea, abdominal pain, and usually fever. The period of communicability is anywhere from three days to three weeks or even longer, and the severity and duration of the disease is quite variable. When an outbreak occurs, for example, and a number of children in a preschool become ill with the symptoms described, it must be reported to the local health authority. All food-borne diseases are reportable.

Now that we know the chain of events leading to salmonellosis infection, how do we break this chain and prevent the disease? To eliminate either the infectious agent or the host is impossible. It is the transmission from the reservoir to the host that has to to prevented. What are the conditions that make it possible for bacteria to multiply in food and what will destroy or prevent bacterial growth?

An investigation of a typical outbreak revealed that a turkey was thawed out and prepared on a wooden cutting board. After the turkey was cooked, the giblets were diced on the same cutting board, which was only rinsed off slightly. Bacteria on the board from the uncooked turkey contaminated the giblets, which were then added to gravy. During the following two to three hours the gravy was kept warm on top of the stove until served. The temperature and time were ideal for sufficient growth of the bacteria to make everyone who consumed the gravy ill. This is only one example. Slow refrigeration of food, especially when it is in large bulk so that the cold cannot penetrate it quickly, is another frequent cause of bacterial multiplication. Prevention steps for salmonellosis apply to other foodborne diseases also. Therefore, let us discuss staphylococcus food poisoning first before explaining preventive measures.

A large number of persons became ill with nausea, vomiting, diarrhea, and abdominal cramps two to four hours after consuming a luncheon at a social gathering. An investigation revealed that cream-filled pastries contained staphylococci. These bacteria were traced to the baker who prepared the pastries. He had an infected cut on his hand. The pastries were immediately refrigerated after preparation and also after reaching the place of the luncheon on the day before it took place. However, the delivery truck with the pastries inside broke down on the way and was kept in a repair shop for several hours on a hot summer day. This gave the bacteria the right time and temperature to grow and produce a poison in the food. A similar outbreak occurred among school children after eating lunch. The poisoning was traced to chicken salad that was improperly handled by persons with staphylococci in their throat and was insufficiently refrigerated.

The causative agent of the food poisoning is the staphylococcus, a bacterium present in some persons' throat, nose, in pimples, boils, or infected wounds. It is also present in animals—in cows with an infected udder, for example. Thus the reservoir is human and animal. The foods most frequently contaminated are meat, poultry, egg products, salads, custard-filled pastries, and unpasteurized milk.

The staphylococcus does not infect the intestinal tract of persons who consume contaminated food. The bacteria produce a poison called toxin as they multiply in the food. When consumed, it acts fast; within two to four hours, it produces the signs and symptoms described in the outbreak. The disease is acute and severe but recovery occurs usually within 24 to 48 hours.

The presence of the toxin will not alter the appearance, taste, or odor of the food. The bacteria will be destroyed by proper heating of

Control of Infectious Diseases

the food, but once the toxin is produced, heat will not destroy it. Refrigeration and freezing does not destroy bacteria or toxins but it inhibits bacterial multiplication.

Prevention of food-borne diseases can be achieved by observing the following rules:

1. Work with clean hands. Wash hands with soap and warm water thoroughly after going to the toilet and after handling raw food or any other possibly contaminated object.
2. Do not touch hands to face, mouth, or hair while preparing food. Keep hair in place. Protect food and hands from coughing and sneezing. Do not use cooking utensils to taste food and do not eat or smoke while preparing food.
3. Do not work in any area of food service when you have an infected wound, boil, acute respiratory infection, or other communicable disease.
4. Clean all kitchen equipment thoroughly with soap and hot water and prevent contact between raw and cooked food.
5. When refrigerating or freezing food, place it in small containers so that the temperature in the center will drop as quickly as possible. Refrigeration temperature must be 45°F or lower. When thawing out food, use it immediately or cook it as quickly as possible.
6. Bacterial growth occurs at temperatures between 50°F and 110°F, therefore, avoid keeping food at those temperatures.
7. When cooking food, make sure that heat penetrates all the food.
8. To keep food hot while serving, store it above 140°F.

4.6.3 Control of the Infectious Agent within the Body

Treatment and prevention by immunization as previously discussed is used to control the infectious agent in the body. Treatment of infectious diseases by antibiotics such as penicillin and other drugs usually shortens the period of communicability and contributes to reducing transmission. Treatment must be under the supervision of a physician because drugs can produce considerable reactions.

4.6.4 Control of Infectious Disease by Legal Means

There are several public health laws and regulations that exist specifically for the control of infectious diseases. The laws and regulations are intended to protect not only the individual, but the population at large. The purpose is to prevent the occurrence of infectious diseases and prevent their spread to others when they do occur.

Reporting of Communicable Diseases

In all states reporting of communicable diseases is required by law. Which diseases are reportable and the procedure of reporting varies in different communities. It is of great importance to identify a communicable disease and report it as soon as possible to the proper health authority. Even if the disease is not identified but the child is ill with apparently a communicable condition, a report is still required. Whose responsibility is it to report an infectious disease to the health authority? If a child with the infectious disease has been examined by a physician, it is the physician's responsibility. However, if a physician is not consulted, then the nurse, teacher, householder, or other persons having knowledge of the disease have the responsibility to report the disease. The physician identifies the disease in his or her report, the other persons simply report that a child appears to be suffering from a communicable disease. Some states require that school authorities exclude all children who are ill or suffer from what may be a communicable disease and notify the board of health of such exclusion. Data on communicable diseases are collected locally, on the state level, nationally, and worldwide. The collective reports serve as an indication and measure of community health problems and permit planning of control programs.

Immunization

There are variations among states regarding immunization requirements. These regulations have been discussed in Chapter 2.

Regulations for Schools

Initial and periodic health evaluation of teachers and children in preschools are required to detect infectious diseases (in addition to other health problems). There are also requirements pertaining to exclusion of ill teachers and children from school and to readmission after illness. Other requirements concerned with control of infectious diseases pertain to food handling. A discussion of the rules and regulations is found in Chapter 2.

CONTENTS

5.1.0 WHAT IS HEATH ASSESSMENT?
5.2.0 WHO ASSESSES HEALTH?
5.3.0 WHY ASSESS HEALTH?
5.4.0 HOW IS HEALTH ASSESSED?
    5.4.1 Health Histories
    5.4.2 Health Observations
    5.4.3 Screening
    5.4.4 Medical Examination
5.5.0 WHAT TO DO WITH THE RESULTS OF HEALTH ASSESSMENT

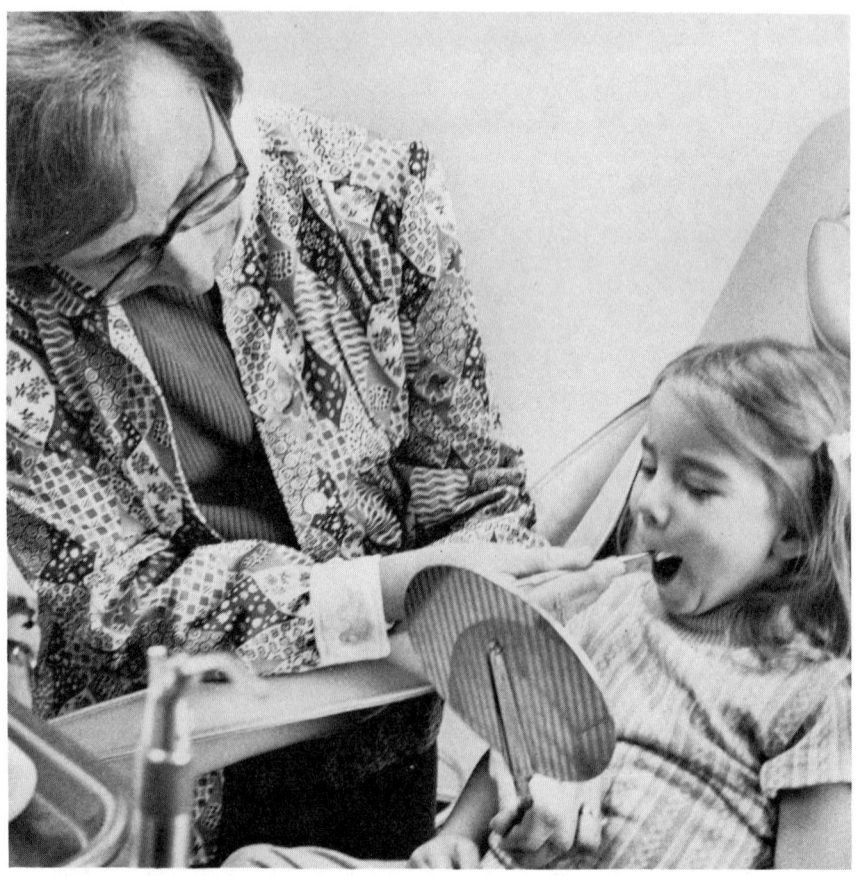

Credit: *Marshall R. Hathaway*

CHAPTER 5

Health Assessment; Health Observations and Sharing Information With Parents

Health assessment, as it pertains to the young child in a preschool, may seem to be a medical function that is the complete responsibility of health professionals. However, the preschool teacher plays a vital role in this process. This is done through day-by-day observations that make up an important portion of an assessment of the child's health status. Thus health assessment is a responsibility shared by health professionals and all other individuals who take care of the young child, particularly the teacher.

It will be helpful to understand where and how preschool personnel fit into the overall process of health assessment. This chapter surveys along broad general lines the whole concept of health assessment of preschool children, such as:

1. What is health assessment and why is it done?
2. What are the methods used and what can they tell us?
3. How are important measurements of assessment performed?
4. What follow-up action should be taken if a disorder or problem is revealed?

5.1.0 WHAT IS HEALTH ASSESSMENT?

Assessment of health is an evaluation or a measurement of health.

104 Health Assessment; Health Observations and Sharing Information With Parents

The concept of health itself is difficult to define and the assessment or appraisal of an individual's health certainly is not a simple procedure.

When a person goes to a physician for a "checkup," he is asked many questions and undergoes a series of tests, observations, and examinations. The individual may then receive a "clean bill of health" or, if a disorder is found, further tests may follow. In this case, eventually there will be some form of treatment. The checkup is a type of health assessment. It permits the physician to form a valid opinion about the individual's health at a certain point.

A mother makes an evaluation of health when she notices that her child sits very close to watch the television, does not respond when she talks in an ordinary voice or walks "pigeon toed." In each case the mother observes something that she believes to be abnormal. The mother's observations combined with an evaluation and examination by a physician is a health assessment. Either the child will be found to have a problem or will be found to be in "good health."

The teacher greets each child at the door and looks at her appearance. She notices if the child appears similar to the day before or if she acts very differently today. Every few months the teacher may measure each child's height and weight. Both these activities are measurements or evaluations of the child's health.

5.2.0 WHO ASSESSES HEALTH?

A health assessment is performed by any number of individuals who are under the leadership of a physician. They may be called the health team. Each member of the team should have a skill that is either acquired through experience or learned by study. The health team may be composed of parents, teachers, nurses, and a wide group of other health professionals such as the child psychologist, and speech and hearing specialist. Each member evaluates the child using expertise and the information gained is shared with the leader, who is usually a pediatrician.

5.3.0 WHY ASSESS HEALTH?

What is the purpose of checking the condition or status of an

Why Assess Health? 105

individual's health, in our case a young child? One reason is to detect any disorder that may not be easily recognized but needs medical attention, for example, anemia, a heart murmur, or exposure to tuberculosis. In some instances early detection and early treatment may be more successful than discovery and treatment at a later stage when the condition may have caused much damage. For example, a mild limp that is not recognized and treated early may have serious consequences because one leg is shorter than the other and was allowed to go uncorrected. The child who has crossed eyes needs early treatment to avoid the loss of vision in one eye. A child with speech problems or emotional conflicts does better if there is early recognition and intervention.

Another reason for health appraisal is to identify children who are at high risk of developing certain diseases so that the health team can be alerted to watch for evidence of their appearance. This may be so with specific inherited disorders. In other situations some children may be more susceptible to certain diseases because of poor habits or the environment in which they live. Examples of these high-risk conditions are described later in this chapter under Health Histories.

Still another reason for assessing health is to identify and make note of some signs that in themselves do not indicate illness but if they persist may indicate an abnormality. A one-time health assessment yields useful data but it would miss these persistent traits that identify slowly developing abnormalities. The best evaluation of an individual's health may be obtained by repeated or periodic health assessment. For example, failure to grow properly could be missed without periodic measures of height and weight. Perceptual abnormalities or developmental slowness are conditions that produce subtle changes in a child's behavior that might be missed without health assessment of a periodic nature.

Finally, health assessment is performed to determine the effectiveness of any treatments a child may be receiving or may have received in the recent past. Health assessment could give answers to questions similar to those which follow: Is the child's behavior changed now that the family is receiving professional counseling? Did the ear infection respond to treatment and clear up? Have the prescribed glasses improved the child's performance?

In some cases, early treatment of a disorder may be very simple, that is, a change in eating habits may correct a nutritional deficiency or wearing glasses may prevent the delay in developing important skills. However, there are other diseases for which treatment may not exist or for which treatment does very little. To know the child has a disease, regardless of the results of treatment, is important to the relationship between the teacher and child because it will help the teacher understand the child's behavior if it is affected by the disease.

5.4.0 HOW IS HEALTH ASSESSED?

What are the methods or tools available to the health team to appraise the health of young children? The state of an individual's health is always changing and ideally one should have available an up-to-date status of health. Continual assessment of health is not possible, therefore specific methods and tools are required in order to capture the best approximation of an individual's health status.

A single comprehensive health appraisal gives information about an individual's health only at that particular time as noted earlier. This has limitations. Periodic health appraisals (those done at specified time intervals) permit a more complete picture of an individual's health because results from each measurement may be compared with previous ones.

Not all disorders can be detected with the same test or method; neither is there a test for every disorder. Because an abnormality, disease or disorder may be manifest in different ways, a variety of techniques or tests may be required.

It may seem to you that the best way to assess a child's health is to have a physician perform a medical examination yearly. This is recommended and should be done. But the physician who examines the child sees the child only for a fraction of an hour. The doctor cannot follow the child's behavior during the course of a day. The doctor does not observe signs of a disease that may not be sufficiently obvious to be detected at the particular time of the examination. The doctor cannot see how the child's health was affected during the course of the previous year by episodes of illness, injury, or some other adverse conditions that have not been called to her attention. Although the medical examination is the central core of health assessment, it is not sufficient in itself.

Health information from all sources is brought together by the physician, usually a pediatrician, at the time of the examination. He interprets and evaluates all of the supplementary health information before coming to a conclusion that the child is in good health, needs medical treatment, or requires additional examinations.

Regardless of who performs the health assessment of the young child it is based on the combined information obtained from:

1. Health histories.
2. Health observations.
3. Screening tests.
4. Medical examinations.

5.4.1 Health Histories

A health history is an up-to-date written account of all events known to affect a person's health in the distant as well as the very recent past. It is used as a starting point in health assessment because it reveals an individual's susceptibility, risks, and prior health experiences. The child's health history should contain information about the health of the family as well as her own.

The family health history can give clues to illnesses that may be inherited by the child or that may develop because of family circumstances. Allergies, diabetes, skin disorders, mental retardation, cystic fibrosis, hemophilia, sickle cell anemia, and color blindness are just a few conditions that may be inherited. Poor health of the mother or bad health conditions during pregnancy may have damaging effects on the child. Some illustrations are the use of drugs, tobacco, and alcohol; the presence of syphilis; prolonged anemia; relatively advanced age at the time of the pregnancy; and the absence of general medical care. If a family lives where overcrowding, poor housing, and poor sanitation exist, then the child has an increased risk of developing tuberculosis, scabies, food-borne diseases, lead poisoning, and a failure to grow appropriately. Behavioral and emotional difficulties are likely to be found in a child when family relationships are disturbed.

The child's health history should include facts about his birth. Difficulties at birth or shortly thereafter may have damaged the child, for example, stoppage of breathing, jaundice, prematurity, and the birth of more than one child at the time. A record of illnesses, injuries, operations, hospitalizations, treatments of all types, and immunizations received give an overall view of the child's health. A child who is inadequately immunized is likely to develop the disease an immunization would prevent. If a child had meningitis (inflammation of the covering of the brain and spinal cord), when younger, it might explain some developmental learning difficulties that a child has at the present time. If a child has been hospitalized for asthma in the past, it is likely that she may now require special care to prevent additional hospitalizations.

The health history should also contain information about the child's development. For example, at what age did the child start to walk, speak, and play with toys?

Usually, the health history is obtained by a nurse or a physician when interviewing parents as part of the preadmission examination. The health history becomes part of the cumulative health record.

The teacher should be familiar with the content of the child's health history. It may often give the teacher clues to understanding a child's behavior and may help the teacher explain some health abnormality.

5.4.2 Health Observations

Observations consist of everything noticed through the senses of smell, taste, hearing, seeing, and feeling. These sensory perceptions become health observations when they are used consciously to evaluate the status of a child's health. They are most useful when they are precise, when they are based on a comparison with a previous observation on the same child or with those of other children, and when they are shared with all members of the health team.

Health professionals organize their observations into *signs* and *symptoms*. Signs are characteristics that any person may see or observe. They are objective evidence of something happening, for example, convulsions, vomiting, redness, or cough. Symptoms are what the affected person feels and must be described to others. This means that there is a change in condition that is subjective in nature, for example, dizziness, pain, or nausea. Symptoms may be accompanied by objective signs as well, such as staggering and falling because of dizziness, crying, or doubling over from stomach pain, or gagging and vomiting as a result of nausea.

We often do not have access to the subjective symptoms of young children because they do not express themselves or describe how they feel. Thus, the objective manifestations or signs are the clues upon which the health team relies.

Everyone engages in observation but not everyone is a good observer without some training and practice. It is important that an observation be precisely descriptive; for example, it is more valuable to say that Sarah has a runny nose, sore throat, red cheeks, and a cough, than to say Sarah looks sick. It is more useful to say "Jackie favors her right leg when walking" instead of "Jackie has an abnormal kind of walk." It is the specificity of these observations that permits meaningful communication between persons of widely different experience and knowledge. It avoids misinterpretation of what may be wrong with the child. In the case of Sarah when the signs are specifically described, everyone is able to visualize her appearance. Precise description lets Sarah's mother indicate that the child is sick with something she never had before. Sarah's teacher recognizes that the same condition was apparent in three other children in the preschool in the last week. The physician is alerted to look for symptoms of streptococcal throat; several cases have been seen recently and what is described in Sarah could be consistent with that diagnosis. The parent, teacher, and physician all contribute information that enables them to make plans quickly to treat not only Sarah but any other children with similar signs and symptoms.

Being precise in observations also includes being systematic and complete. This means observing with all of one's appropriate senses. For example, much is learned by looking at the color, shape, and size of a child's face as well as the condition of the hair, eyes, and skin. Odors also can give information important for health assessment. Does the child smell fresh and clean, or of urine or body odor? Is his breath offensive? Observers who listen carefully can hear many significant indicators of a child's condition. Does the child have a hoarse or squeaky voice? Does the child constantly sniff or cough?

The sense of touch can be developed to reveal differences in texture and temperature. Is the child's skin smooth? Does she have a rash that feels similar to sandpaper? Does the child's hair feel sticky or dry?

Another technique for getting useful information is observing general behavior. For example, watch a child walk, observe how the child eats, uses his hands, and tilts his head. Often the small unobtrusive signs provide important clues to factors affecting children's health.

The most troublesome problem for any individual who engages in health observation is how to know which observations are noteworthy. With experience this becomes less difficult. Train yourself to observe a number of individual characteristics. Note any differences in these manifestations. For example, observe how two year olds wash their hands. Look especially at those who need help. Why is this necessary? You might find that roughly half of the two-year-old children cannot wash their hands by themselves. This indicates that most two year olds need help to wash their hands. Said another way, it is not a significant observation for a two year old to fail to wash her hands without help from an adult. As another example, observe how all three year olds hold a pencil, turn the pages in a book, and sit in a chair. Any unusual characteristics should be noted along with how often they occur. If a small number of children are observed to be significantly different, that may be noteworthy and should be correlated with other developmental data.

Each observer uses a different perspective in obtaining health information. The parent compares the child from day to day with himself or with brothers and sisters when they were the same age. The teacher may have the perspective of a parent but in addition compares many similar children. The physician compares each child with what his knowledge and experience have led him to expect a child to be like under different circumstances. Each view alone is not sufficient to get a good assessment of the child's health. As discussed earlier, it is necessary that information collected from all perspectives be brought together. Only then is the health team under the physician's leadership capable of using the information to the child's benefit.

Much of this book is concerned with health observations that are considered to be important to preschool operation. This task of assessing health status through day-by-day observation is perhaps the teacher's most important health function. Consequently, every preschool teacher should learn well the art of making and recording health observations. Health professionals can guide the teacher in this responsible task. It is important to remember, however, that it is the health professionals who make the diagnoses; they determine what disease or dysfunction a child may have and subsequently what should be done about it. The teacher is the monitoring member of the health team and the one who provides the most intimate surveillance.

5.4.3 Screening

The preschool teacher must understand the objectives of screening. Often the teacher is the one who obtains parental permission for the testing; the teacher should be able to explain what disorder the test will identify and what the results of the test will mean. For this reason the concept of screening and some of the commonly used screening tests are discussed here. Source materials dealing with screening are available and should be consulted for details.[1,2,3]

The purpose of screening is to aid in the early detection of disease. Screening tests separate from a large group of apparently healthy persons those who are likely to have a specific disorder. Health observations on the other hand are primarily used to identify signs of disorders that a person may have.

The decision to screen a group of preschool children for a certain disorder, such as a vision or hearing defect, should be made by the medical consultant and advisory committee. Some screening tests may be administered in the preschool facility itself. They are usually performed by specially trained personnel. If teachers are to help with the screening, they must receive proper instructions.

Let us assume that a screening test for hearing impairment is administered to a group of preschool children. Most children will pass the test. This means that their hearing ability is normal. However, there may be some who have impaired hearing that the test did not detect. They are referred to as false negative cases. Other children will fail the test. Some of those will really have impaired hearing, while others will have normal hearing. This latter group, may have been distracted at the time of testing, uncooperative, or

[1] *A Guide to Screening—EPSDT—Medicaid*, U.S. Dept. HEW, Social & Rehabilitation Service in cooperation with The American Academy of Pediatrics, under contract SRS 74-24516. SRS Publications Office, Room G115, 330C Street, S.W. Washington, DC 20201.

[2] *Standards of Child Health Care*, 2nd edition, American Academy of Pediatrics, 1972. American Academy of Pediatrics, P.O. Box 1034, Evanston, IL 60204.

[3] *The Pediatric Clinics of North America*, Symposium on Ambulatory Pediatrics, Vol. 21, No. 1, February 1974, Evan Charney, M.D., Guest Editor, W.B. Saunders Co., Philadelphia, PA 13105.

failed for some other reason. These children have false positive results. The test showed "falsely" that they had impaired hearing. A more complete examination is necessary to confirm or disprove the hearing loss.

A screening test by itself is not diagnostic, that is, it alone does not definitely identify the presence of a certain disease. The same may be said of health observations. They only give a clue suggesting that a disorder may exist. Further examination and the expertise of a health professional is necessary for a final diagnosis of a disorder. Both of these methods of health assessment are equally important. Health observations should not be underestimated or ignored just because screening for a certain condition is also being performed.

A discussion of screening for specific disorders follows.

1. *Vision.* Poor vision and signs of visual defects are discussed in Chapter 6. Screening is performed to detect those children who are in need of a complete professional eye examination. The most common vision defects in children are farsightedness, decreased vision in one eye (amblyopia), and crossed eye (strabismus or squint). Early detection is important because it increases the success of treatment. A vision test or test for visual acuity screens out those individuals who are nearsighted and farsighted when using both of their eyes. Nearsightedness is not common in young children. A visual acuity test also screens for decreased vision in one eye or a difference in visual acuity between the two eyes. The test is suitable for all children beginning at the age of three years or in some cases slightly younger. From the very young to the older age groups test charts used for screening change from familiar easily recognizable pictures (Allen picture cards and Strycar minature toy test) to simple symbols (illiterate E or Snellen E) and finally to the alphabet (Snellen chart).

    It is important to remember that screening tests for vision only test visual acuity. They do not detect reading difficulties or any other visual problems due to developmental disabilities or brain abnormality.

    There are several screening tests for crossed eyes (strabismus) suitable for preschool children; the Hirschberg test and the cover test are examples. These, however, are used by the eye specialist during an eye examination. The

Credit: *National Society for the Prevention of Blindness, Inc.*

purpose of these tests is to determine if both eyes focus equally on an object. You may suspect strabismus if you observe that a child does not always focus on an object equally with both eyes.

In the general population, color blindness occurs in about 8 percent of the males and 0.4 percent of females. Young children, however, are not tested for defects in color vision because these defects do not delay learning and there are few reliable tests for preschool children.

There are many useful instructional guides for training in visual screening. Three excellent ones are *Preschool Vision Screening, A Guide for Eye Inspection and Testing Visual Acuity of Preschool Age Children,* and a film entitled *Before We are Six.*[4] Health professionals must train and supervise the teachers or volunteers who perform the vision screening tests.

2. *Hearing.* The early detection of hearing loss in the range of sound for normal speech is important because a very small loss in some sounds changes what the young child hears and consequently absorbs from the environment.

[4]National Society for the Prevention of Blindness, Inc. 79 Madison Ave., New York, N.Y. 10016.

The lack of proper hearing may seriously affect a child's development. Indeed, a child with poor hearing has sometimes been mistaken for one who has mental delay or mental retardation. In other situations children with hearing loss have been punished severely because they were thought to be unruly or undisciplined.

The principle of most hearing tests is simple. Sounds that match those produced by the pitch range of speech and music are reproduced by a machine. The instrument is called an audiometer (audio is sound, meter is measure). The sounds are produced as pure tones with a precise frequency. These sounds are then decreased in volume until the child indicates that she cannot hear them The lowest volume still perceived is recorded and compared to a standard. The standard is what other children known to have no hearing loss would hear under similar circumstances. The test is done for each ear separately and for both ears together. The tests are usually reliable when performed by well-trained personnel in a suitable environment.

Helpful information about hearing testing may be obtained from several sources. [5,6]

3. *Physical Growth.* The growth pattern is unique for each child but follows a well-established progression for all children. The growth process may be significantly inhibited by inherited traits, glandular abnormalities, environmental factors, or illnesses. Therefore, it is important to measure growth at regular intervals to determine if it is progressing normally.

An accepted composite indicator of physical growth is measurement of height and weight. These measurements should be made every six months or at least once a year.

To detect growth disturbances the measurements of a particular child are compared with his previous ones and also with the average for children of like age. Growth tables and charts are available for this purpose. An example of a growth chart is presented in Figure

---

[5] The American Speech and Hearing Association, 9030 Georgetown Road, Bethesda, Md.
[6] The National Association of Speech and Hearing Agencies (formerly American Hearing Society), 919 18th St. N.W., Washington, D.C.

How is Health Assessed? 115

5-1. The measurements of each child should be plotted on the chart and kept in the cumulative health record. The National Center for Health Statistics has recently issued growth charts based on new measurements of more than 20,000 children. They can be obtained from the center for Disease Control, Atlanta, Georgia.

4. *Lead Poisoning.* Recent testing of large numbers of children in cities and towns in the eastern half of the United States, detected that 5 to 10 percent of the children had some degree of lead poisoning. Among children living in older sections of cities and towns the cases of lead poisoning were as high as 20 to 30 percent. While most of the poisoning is caused by the eating of lead paint by children between one to five years old, lead is also found in plaster and putty in older houses, in drinking water drawn from lead pipes, in engine exhaust, contaminated dust, and in waste products of some industrial processes.

It is very important to detect lead poisoning early, before the children become ill. Immediate treatment is essential. Once a child becomes ill with lead poisoning the chances are that one in three will have permanent brain damage and some may die of the poisoning. Besides treatment, the source of the lead poisoning must be identified and removed so that the child is protected from further exposure. Because the dangers of lead poisoning are so serious every preschool child should be screened for this disease. This is best done at three-to six-month intervals particularly in areas where lead poisoning is known to be a community problem.

The screening test consists of obtaining a blood sample from the fingertip of the child after the hands are cleaned thoroughly. Because lead exists in the environment in various concentrations, it is important to collect the blood sample carefully. A positive test should indicate the level of lead in the child's blood and not in the environment. The blood is sent to a laboratory for examination. Some states now have laws that control the amount of lead allowed in paint. There are also public health programs to detect and treat lead poisoning. State

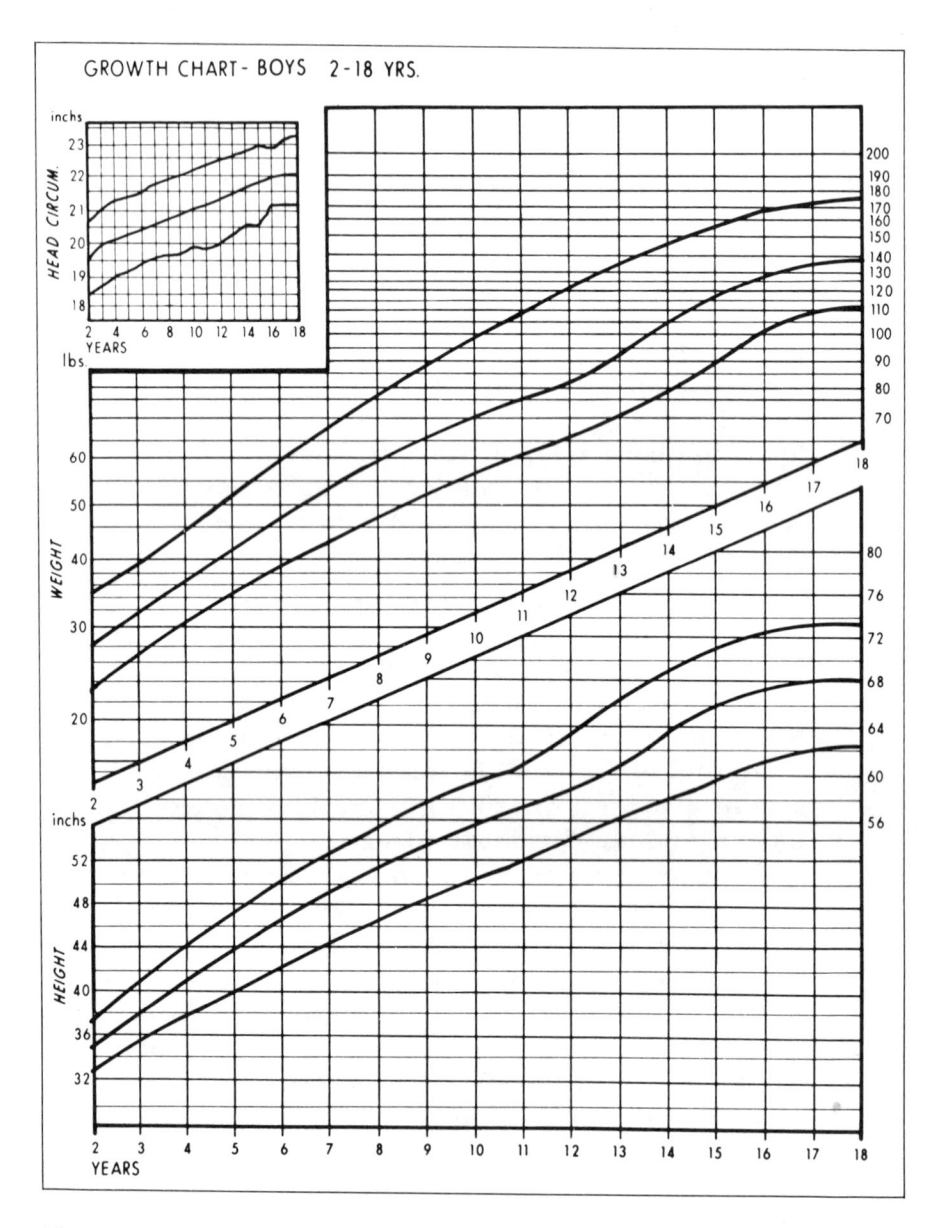

116 Health Assessment; Health Observations and Sharing Information With Parents

Figure 5-1, p. 1

How is Health Assessed? 117

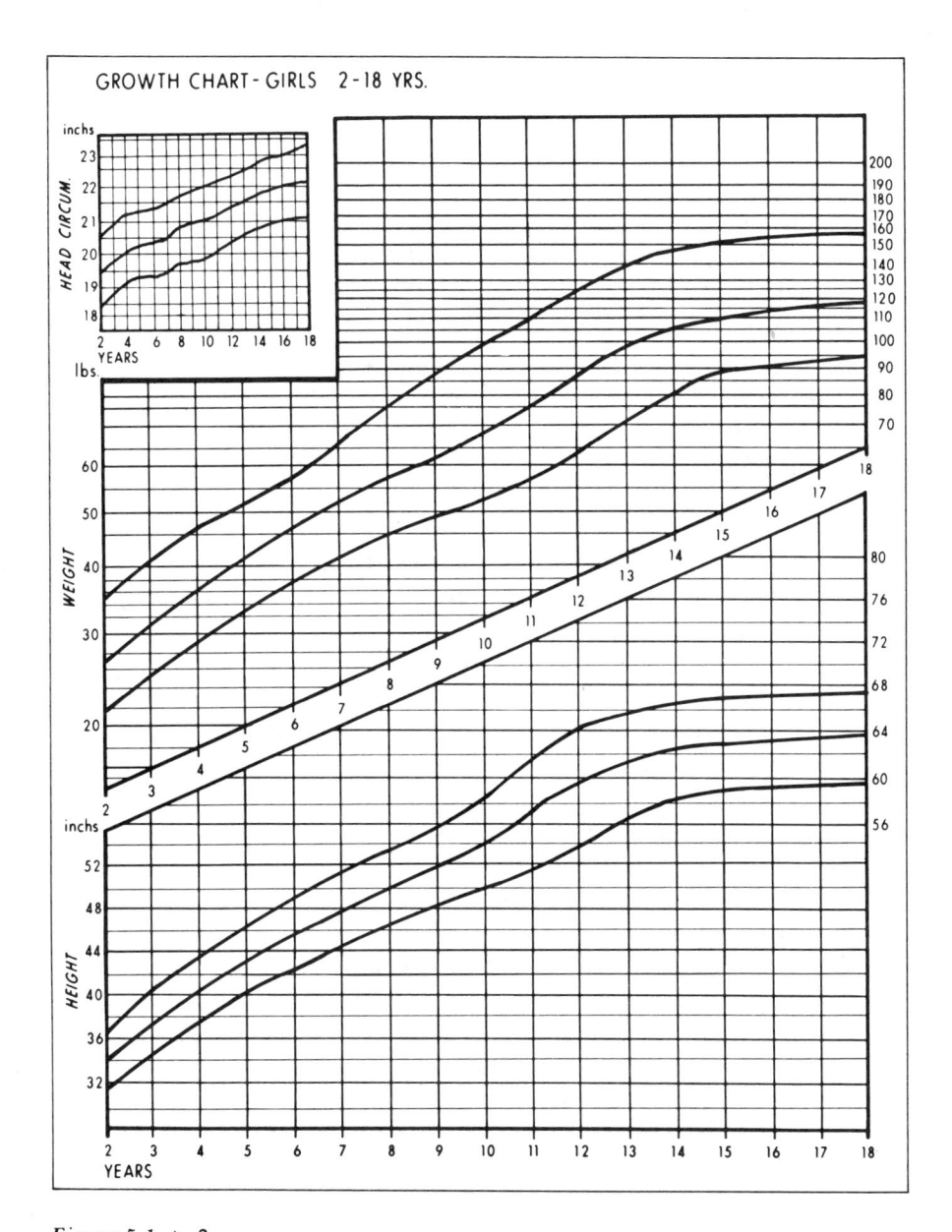

Figure 5-1, p. 2
Source: *DHEW Publication No. (OCD) 72-4.*

and local governmental health and housing agencies in some states will help to organize the screening program and perform the laboratory test. These agencies also have programs to detect the amount of lead in dwellings and to remove the lead containing substances.

If your community has an existing lead screening program, coordinate your intentions to screen with that program. For example, your facility might test children not tested previously or it might perform the repeat tests when the test has been positive sometime in the past.

5. *Infection with Tubercle Bacilli.* The infectious disease, tuberculosis, is discussed in Chapter 4. The tubercle bacilli that cause tuberculosis can infect a person without necessarily producing the disease. The purpose of tuberculin skin testing is to detect anyone, in our case, a child, who has become infected with tubercle bacilli by exposure to a person who has tuberculosis. As mentioned in Chapter 4, spread of the infection from person to person occurs only after prolonged contact such as living or visiting regularly with a person who has the disease. When a child is found to be tuberculin positive, then all the persons with whom the child maintains close contact should be tested in an attempt to find the one who has the disease.

A positive skin test in a young child indicates that it is likely that the child was in contact with a person who is spreading tubercle bacilli (has active tuberculosis). It is unlikely that this child has the disease even though he is classified as a positive reactor. This is important for the teacher and parent to know so as not to be unnecessarily alarmed. Approximately 3 percent of the individuals with a positive skin test (positive reactors) will develop active disease within a year after they become positive reactors. One percent of the positive reactors will develop active tuberculosis each year after that. Drug treatment of positive reactors is a preventive measure aimed at reducing the number of active cases of tuberculosis. Thus prompt attention to newly discovered positive reactors is very important. In the general population the tuberculin skin test has a low yield of positive reactors because tuberculosis has been declining in the United States. But persons living in poor socioeconomic conditions have a greater chance than average of contracting tuberculosis. Tuberculin testing of persons in this group should yield a higher number of positive reactors.

The skin test consists of placing an extract of killed tubercle bacilli just under the surface of the skin by injection with prongs (tine test) or a needle (Mantoux test). The disadvantages of the test are that there may be a few false positives, some false negatives, and a delay of 72 hours before the test may be read. In spite of these disadvantages the tuberculin testing is considered very reliable by health professionals. A positive reaction is swelling and redness of a specific size and appearance at 72 hours after administration of the tuberculin, not before.

Tuberculin skin testing should be done on a child once a year before the child is six years old. An adult working in the preschool is usually required to have a skin test at regular intervals. The test should be done by health professionals in their office or in the preschool. Should any individual be known to have a positive skin test, a chest X ray is done instead of another skin test. Of course any individual who is in close contact with a recently identified positive reactor should have a tuberculin skin test and be examined by a physician regardless of the time the last skin test was administered. All children who are identified as having a positive tuberculin skin test should be referred to a physician or a local public health tuberculosis clinic for further evaluation.

6. *Development Disorders.* It is estimated that 3 percent of the general population is retarded. The majority suffer from mild to moderate retardation and are capable of being educated. It is important to seek out children who might be in this educable group. Early detection is urgently indicated because some improvement may result from the provision of stimulating activities by teachers and parents. These are designed to encourage development of the child's senses and motor skills.

There are several screening tests that might be used

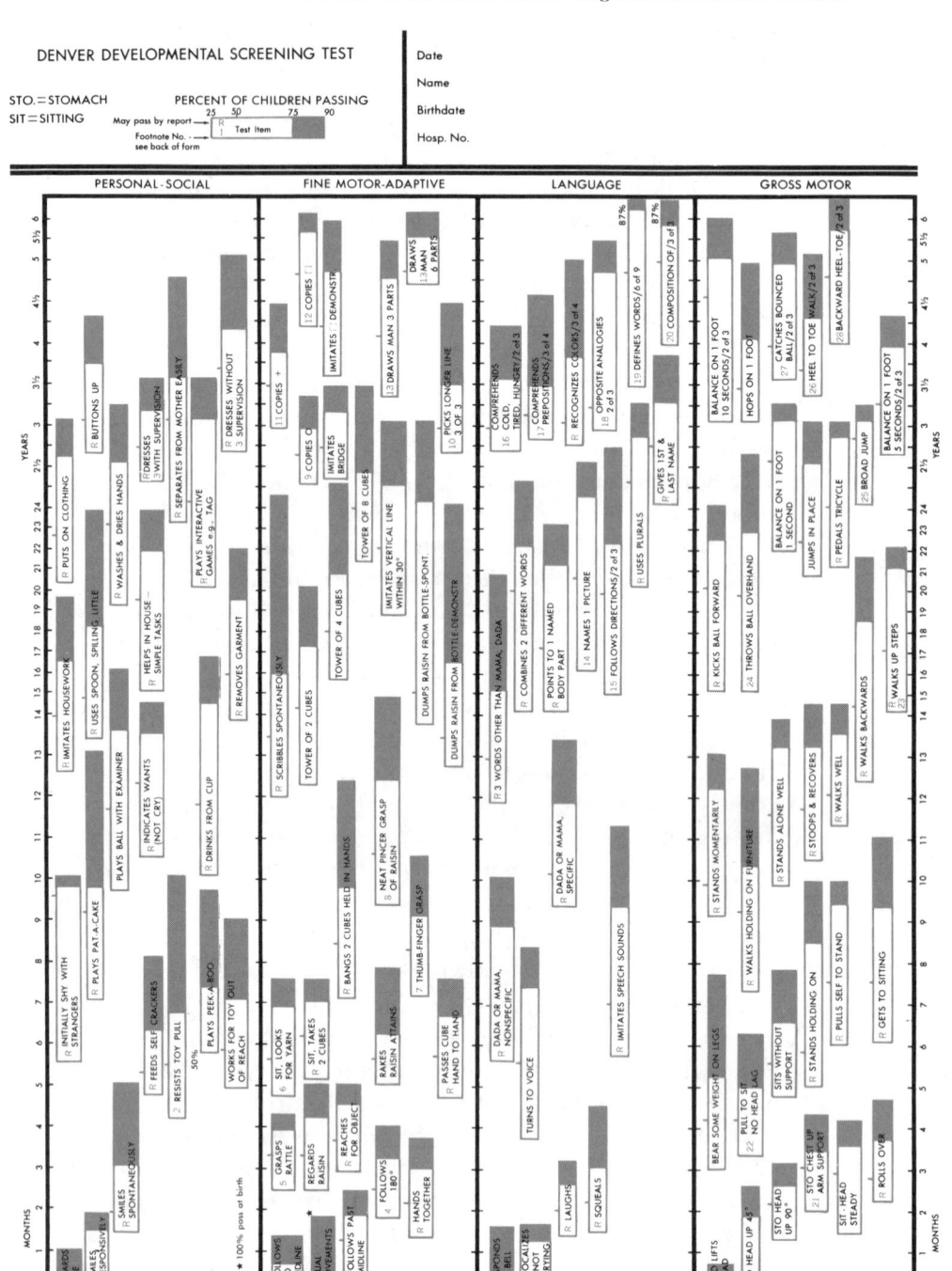

Figure 5-2, p. 1

How is Health Assessed? 121

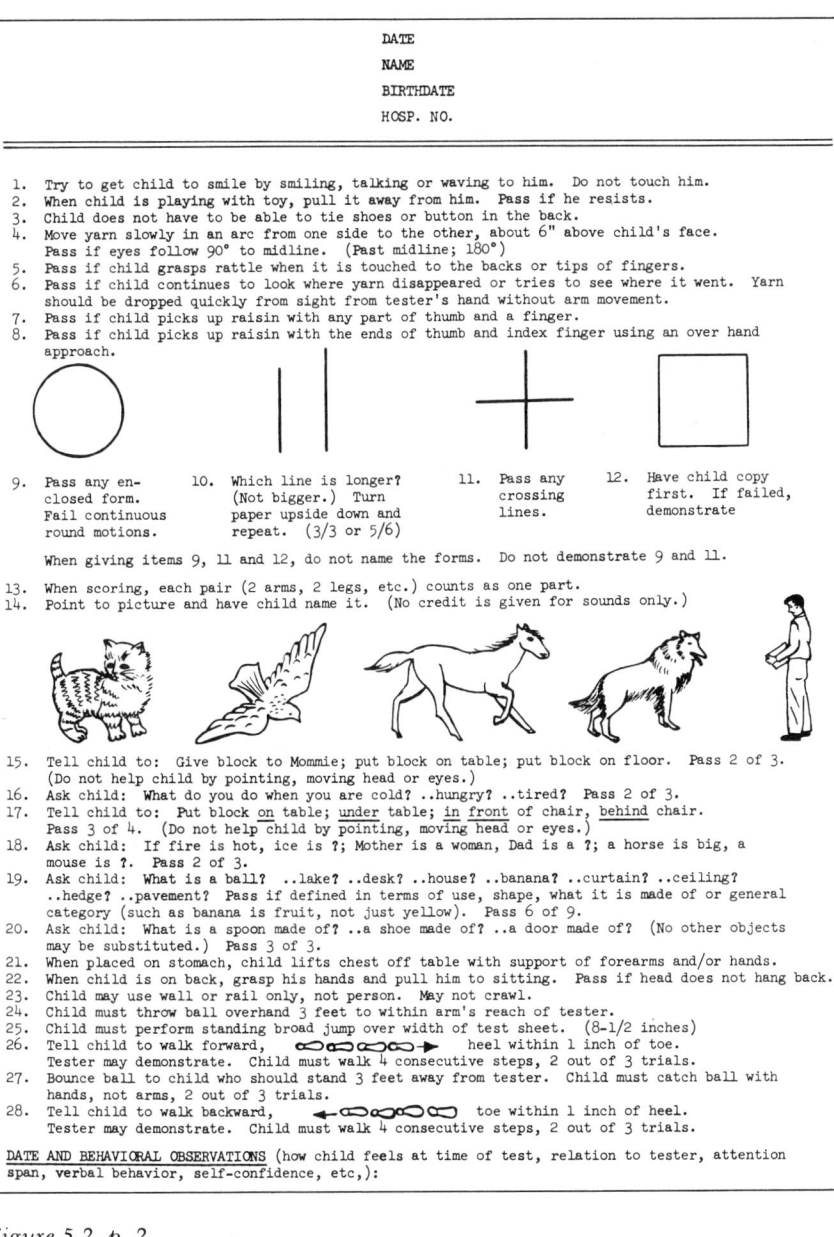

```
                        DATE
                        NAME
                        BIRTHDATE
                        HOSP. NO.
```

1. Try to get child to smile by smiling, talking or waving to him. Do not touch him.
2. When child is playing with toy, pull it away from him. Pass if he resists.
3. Child does not have to be able to tie shoes or button in the back.
4. Move yarn slowly in an arc from one side to the other, about 6" above child's face. Pass if eyes follow 90° to midline. (Past midline; 180°)
5. Pass if child grasps rattle when it is touched to the backs or tips of fingers.
6. Pass if child continues to look where yarn disappeared or tries to see where it went. Yarn should be dropped quickly from sight from tester's hand without arm movement.
7. Pass if child picks up raisin with any part of thumb and a finger.
8. Pass if child picks up raisin with the ends of thumb and index finger using an over hand approach.

9. Pass any enclosed form. Fail continuous round motions.
10. Which line is longer? (Not bigger.) Turn paper upside down and repeat. (3/3 or 5/6)
11. Pass any crossing lines.
12. Have child copy first. If failed, demonstrate

When giving items 9, 11 and 12, do not name the forms. Do not demonstrate 9 and 11.

13. When scoring, each pair (2 arms, 2 legs, etc.) counts as one part.
14. Point to picture and have child name it. (No credit is given for sounds only.)

15. Tell child to: Give block to Mommie; put block on table; put block on floor. Pass 2 of 3. (Do not help child by pointing, moving head or eyes.)
16. Ask child: What do you do when you are cold? ..hungry? ..tired? Pass 2 of 3.
17. Tell child to: Put block on table; under table; in front of chair, behind chair. Pass 3 of 4. (Do not help child by pointing, moving head or eyes.)
18. Ask child: If fire is hot, ice is ?; Mother is a woman, Dad is a ?; a horse is big, a mouse is ?. Pass 2 of 3.
19. Ask child: What is a ball? ..lake? ..desk? ..house? ..banana? ..curtain? ..ceiling? ..hedge? ..pavement? Pass if defined in terms of use, shape, what it is made of or general category (such as banana is fruit, not just yellow). Pass 6 of 9.
20. Ask child: What is a spoon made of? ..a shoe made of? ..a door made of? (No other objects may be substituted.) Pass 3 of 3.
21. When placed on stomach, child lifts chest off table with support of forearms and/or hands.
22. When child is on back, grasp his hands and pull him to sitting. Pass if head does not hang back.
23. Child may use wall or rail only, not person. May not crawl.
24. Child must throw ball overhand 3 feet to within arm's reach of tester.
25. Child must perform standing broad jump over width of test sheet. (8-1/2 inches)
26. Tell child to walk forward, ⟶ heel within 1 inch of toe. Tester may demonstrate. Child must walk 4 consecutive steps, 2 out of 3 trials.
27. Bounce ball to child who should stand 3 feet away from tester. Child must catch ball with hands, not arms, 2 out of 3 trials.
28. Tell child to walk backward, ⟵ toe within 1 inch of heel. Tester may demonstrate. Child must walk 4 consecutive steps, 2 out of 3 trials.

DATE AND BEHAVIORAL OBSERVATIONS (how child feels at time of test, relation to tester, attention span, verbal behavior, self-confidence, etc,):

Figure 5-2, p. 2

Source: William K. Frankenberg, M.D. and Josiah B. Dodds, Ph.D., University of Colorado Medical Center, 1969.

to detect a child who is developing slowly. One such test is the Denver Developmental Screening Test (DDST) (Figure 5-2). It is designed to detect developmental lag by testing social and personal capabilities; skills that require the use of hands, arms, feet, and body and language ability. These are important areas of general competence which are affected adversely by developmental retardation. The test may be done by trained teachers in about 20 minutes. The preschool child may be identified as developmentally slow by another test, the Goodenough Draw-A-Person test. This screening test may be administered easily by trained teachers.[7,8]

It must be emphasized very strongly that it is not always possible to identify correctly a child who has a developmental lag on the basis of a screening test. Some normal children may be classified erroneously as having developmental lag if the screening test results are not combined with many other health assessment tools. Normal children might be "labeled" retarded on the basis of one screening test; that could cause great harm to them. Therefore, regardless of the test used all children who are identified as having some delay in their development need a more complete evaluation by several specialists.

It is recommended that the Denver Developmental Screening Test be performed on all children between the first and second year of life and again when they are three and five years old.

There are many other conditions for which children may be screened but they are the function of health professionals. Some examples of these screening tests include determining blood pressure, testing for anemia, checking for the presence of sickle cell anemia, detecting speech disorders, and examining urine and stool specimens.

5.4.4 Medical Examination

A medical examination means the same thing as a physical

[7]F. Goodenough, *Measurement of Intelligence by Drawings*. Yonkers: World Book Company, 1926.

[8]D.B. Harris, *Children's Drawings as Measures of Intellectual Maturity*. New York: Harcourt, Brace and World, 1963.

examination to most people. That is true but it is more than that. It is a review of all available information about a person's health. Such personal health information comes from the previously discussed tools of health assessment, that is, health histories, health observations, and screening tests.

The purpose of the medical examination is to use the skills and knowledge unique to health professionals to determine the condition of a child's health. The experience of health professionals permits them to find previously undetected health defects. They have the ability and obligation to initiate correction of any abnormalities discovered.

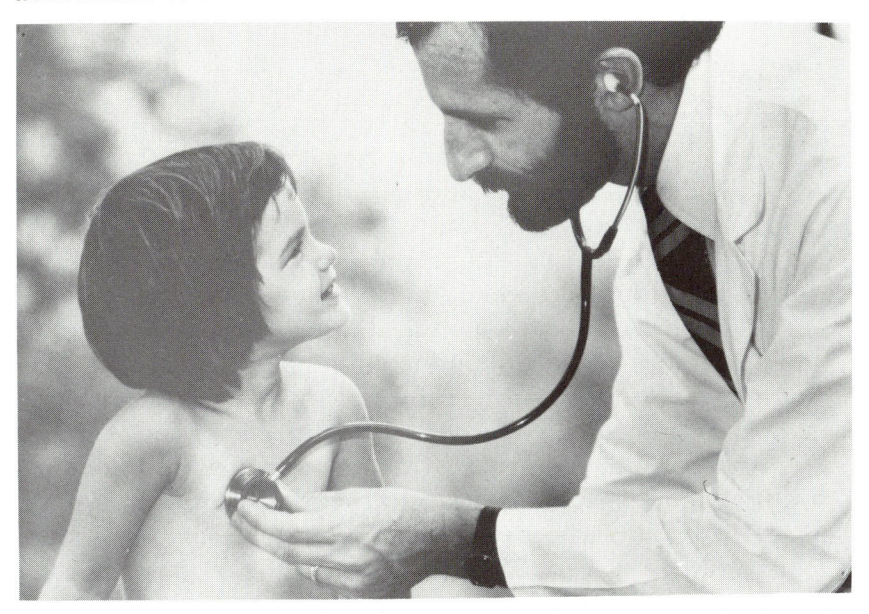

What does a child's medical examination consist of? First, the health professional interviews the child's parents to get new health information or to review all available health information; this includes a review of immunization requirements. Then the child is physically examined to determine body functions. This examination covers all parts of the body. It may be done by one person all at once, for example, by a pediatrician, or it may be done in parts, for example, dental examination by a dentist, eye examination by an eye specialist, ear examination by an ear specialist, and so forth. Developmental, behavioral, and emotional characteristics will be evaluated also. Next, the health professional will request a variety of laboratory procedures. This is done in order to assist in identifying health defects. In order that a medical examination performed now may be useful in the future, everything done and everything found must be recorded.

How often should a medical examination be done? Obviously it needs to be performed as often as there are specific health problems which need attention. Beyond that the preschool child requires a comprehensive examination of the kind just described, once a year after the age of two years. Some states require preschool programs to provide this. The details of medical examinations within preschool programs are discussed in Chapter 2.

5.5.0 WHAT TO DO WITH THE RESULTS OF HEALTH ASSESSMENT

All the data that have been obtained are brought together to serve as a basis for maintaining a child's health. This frequently changing information must then be used by everyone who has some responsibility for the child. In the preschool setting as discussed earlier, this includes health professionals, parents, and the teacher.

The physician must have all health information regarding a child, so that in consultation with other health professionals she may develop a treatment plan to correct deficiencies and prevent as many abnormalities as possible. Implementation of this plan requires the physician to provide interpretative information and counseling to both parents and teachers.

The parents who have primary responsibility to maintain the child's health must understand the condition of the child's health and should follow through with the recommendations made. Besides the health professional, the teacher can help in this important respect.

Because the teacher has observed the child's health behavior as much or more than a parent he has an obligation to share with the parent what is known. Acceptance of what the teacher says and action upon his recommendations are apt to occur more frequently if you adhere to the following principles:

1. *Do not confront the parents in an accusatory way.* For example, do not say, "Why did you allow Marianne to come to school with a fever?" Instead, say, "Marianne has a fever now. Did she appear ill or seem to have a

fever this morning?" Neither should you say, "Didn't you know that Kevin was ill?" Simply state, "We found Kevin to be ill and we think he should be taken home."

2. *Be tactful in your conversation.* As an illustration, you should state, "We noticed that Carey had puffy eyes and was sneezing quite a bit today. Is that usual at this time of the year? Have you noticed the same thing? You know, if Carey doesn't feel better by tomorrow you should keep her home or take her to see the doctor."

3. *Do not be discriminatory in your attitude or advice.* For example, do not tell the parent, "We expect the children who come here to be very clean and I am certain your child's illness is due to uncleanliness." Neither should the parent be told, for example, "Mary is pale and seems anemic. She probably does not eat properly when she is not in the center with us." In these cases, the assistance of a nurse or other health professional should be engaged.

4. *Be reasonable.* For example, allow a child to return while recovering from an illness if the child's doctor agrees. Permit parents time to rearrange work schedules and to make financial adjustments before nonthreatening health problems are corrected.

The teacher can take the initiative and arrange a meeting between the health professionals and parents. The purpose of such a meeting can be to make certain that every problem discovered by health assessment will be under treatment and that everyone will support this objective.

Unless abnormalities discovered by the process of health assessment are corrected the procedure has neither meaning nor purpose.

CONTENTS

6.1.0 GENERAL PLAN
6.2.0 CARE OF THE CHILD WITH SPECIFIC SIGNS, SYMPTOMS, OR ILLNESS
    Abdominal Pain
    Vomiting
    Diarrhea
    Fever
    Sore Throat
    Cough
    Asthma
    Earache
    Hearing Loss
    Pinkeye
    Toothache, Dental Cavities
    Skin Rashes
    Problems with Urination
    Unusual Walking Patterns
    Child Neglect and Abuse
    Poor Vision
    Speech Defects

CHAPTER 6

Care of the Child Who is III and the Child Who Needs Specialized Attention

Priscilla came to the teacher and complained, "My stomach hurts." She began to cry as she bent over, holding her abdomen. How would you handle this situation?

When Silvester took off his coat you hear Jackie exclaim, "Look at Silvester's arms! They are blue and bumpy!" Quickly Silvester put his coat on again and rushed off to be alone. Had Silvester been beaten? What would you do?

Tyrone did not want to be on the swings any more during playtime. He was breathing fast and coughing long after he sat down beside you to rest. Was he having another asthma attack? What would be your response?

6.1.0 GENERAL PLAN

Every preschool should have a plan for taking care of children who become ill. The plan should determine:

1. *Who should take care of the child who becomes ill or needs specialized attention?* Either the child's teacher, a designated staff member, or a nurse, if the center has one on duty, should attend to the ill child.

(2). *What should the preschool facility provide?* The preschool should have a quiet, isolated area containing a cot with linens and a blanket, a basin, a portable urinal, disposable drinking cups, clean wash cloths and towels, and first aid supplies.

(3). *What information should be available?*
   (a). Information about permission for and source of medical care for an emergency or illness (Chapter 2).
   (b). The child's cumulative health record should be available for a quick review. Look for the following information. First, are there illnesses that occurred in the past that might be similar to the present one? For example, stomach ache, toothache, ear infection. Second, has the child been absent due to an illness recently and could current problems be associated with that illness? Third, is there a plan or procedure to be followed to meet any special health need of the ill child? For example, is there:
   (1) a restriction on activities.
   (2) instructions about when to wear braces or how much rest is required.
   (3) instructions about giving special medicines.

(4). *What should you do?*
   (a). Isolate the child.
   (b). Determine what the child's problem is by gently questioning her. Ask her where she hurts and how she feels. Carefully look for signs of illness.
   (c). Plan your action. If there appears to be an emergency, notify the parent and follow the procedure outlined in Chapter 8. If you consider the illness to be serious enough for the child to be taken home, call the parents. If the problem appears to be temporary keep the child at rest.
   (d). Attend to the child's problem. Follow guidelines written by your medical consultant and directions in this chapter to take care of the most common illnesses occurring in the preschool. Your attitude is very important in dealing with an ill child. Be calm and reassuring and comfort the child; do not act hastily. His illness may interfere with your activities in the preschool. Arrange for another

staff member to take over your duties while you take care of the ill child.
5. *What records do you need to keep?*
   (a). Record of the child's illnesses (Figure 6-1).
   (b). A certificate from the child's physician stating the child may return to school after being absent for a prolonged period of time (Figure 6-2).
   (c). Authorization from parents and physicians for the preschool staff to administer medication (Figure 2-10).

A brief discussion of common health problems encountered in the preschool follows. The intent of the presentation is twofold: to prepare you to recognize and wisely cope with the health problems described, and to serve as a guide for your inservice education about detecting and managing childhood medical conditions.

6.2.0 CARE OF THE CHILD WITH SPECIFIC SIGNS, SYMPTOMS, OR ILLNESSES

Abdominal Pain

Priscilla, the girl who held her stomach and was crying half an hour ago was in no distress now. What had the teacher done? The teacher learned that Priscilla had a stomach ache that came on after arriving at school. She was not nauseated nor did she have an urge to vomit. The pain did not prevent her from walking to the isolation room nor did it seriously affect her. Because constipation (irregular or hard bowel movements) is a simple common cause of stomach ache, the teacher asked Priscilla to try to have a bowel movement and after she did the pain was gone. Constipation had been a recurring problem for Priscilla according to her health record. When her parents were made aware of the problem again, they corrected it as before by changing her diet at home.

Hard, firm bowel movements that are painful occur in children who do not drink enough liquids, refuse fruits, and leafy vegetables or rarely take bran and whole wheat substances. The exciting social stimulation of the child while in a group setting is often stronger than the urge for elimination. Bowel movements are postponed and constipation results. Constipation may occur for other reasons; for example, the child does not have privacy while at the toilet, has no scheduled time for use of the toilet, or finds toilets are not adequately

Diagnosis or Type of Illness	Date When Illness Was First Recognized or Treatment first Began	Date of Release by Physician for Return to Preschool	Comments or Recommended Action for the Future

Record of Acute Illnesses

Source. *Modified by E.H. Reinisch and R.E. Minear from DHEW Publication no. 72-20.*

Figure 6-1

Care of the Child With Specific Signs, Symptoms, or Illnesses 131

Physician's Certification That a Child May Return to Preschool
After An Absence Due to a Medical Reason
Date _____

To whom it may concern:
This is to certify that I have cared for _____
                                              (child's name)
_____ between _____ and
                                     (date)
_____ due to _____
        (date)   (type of illness)
The child may return to preschool on _____ and

may participate in all activities of the preschool program. OR The child
may return to preschool on _____ with the
following advice about: (date)
    Activity _____
    Medicines _____
    Special Instructions _____
I do/do not expect to examine the child again _____
                                                      (when)

                    Sincerely yours,

                              _____ , M.D.

Source. *E.H. Reinisch and R.E. Minear.*

Figure 6-2

cleaned. Make every effort to eliminate these conditions. A stomach ache seems to be the most common complaint of childhood. It may begin quickly in an apparently well child and disappear just as rapidly without any after effects. Or a child may develop abdominal pain that progresses either slowly or speedily into a very severe pain. The cause of the pain may be from an abnormality within the abdomen or from an unusual condition elsewhere in the body.

Keep the child quiet, lying down, while you determine how long she has had the pain and if there are complaints affecting other parts of her body. For example, if you find the child is hungry, food should be given. Should tension about an activity be the cause, then a short rest may offer relief. The child who has other complaints besides a stomach ache should be excluded from school until he or she becomes well again.

The most serious condition causing abdominal pain is one that may require surgery. Therefore, any child with prolonged, severe pain should be examined by a physician. Until the child gets health care he should rest quietly. Do not apply heat, cold, or any medication to the abdomen during the period of rest. If the child must take anything by mouth then only sips of water and ice chips are recommended.

It may require some practice to remain calm during numerous episodes of stomach aches. Respond to each incident and give appropriate care regardless of what you think the cause may be. A good relationship with a child ensures sensitive support and sympathy without revealing undue anxiety. Open communication with parents and your medical advisor will ensure that you neither ignore nor overreact to the many occurrences of aches.

Vomiting

This finding is almost as frequent as the stomach ache. Just about every illness in the young child triggers some degree of nausea if not vomiting. The swallowing of poisonous materials or a fall with a head injury are frequent causes for vomiting in the normally active child. Treatment for these problems are discussed in Chapter 8. If other children have vomited or appear nauseated also, it could indicate that poisoning from foods eaten in the preschool might be the cause. There might be an epidemic of illness causing vomiting in your community. If vomiting is severe, the child may be exhausted or have pains in the stomach areas. She should rest

Care of the Child With Specific Signs, Symptoms, or Illnesses 133

and be kept as quiet as possible during the period when not vomiting. Do not put anything cold or warm on the abdomen, such as an ice pack, heating pad, or hot water bottle. If you give anything by mouth it should be only sips of water or ice chips. Do not give milk or other foods because this may stimualte the stomach and intestines to cause more vomiting. If the child appears well after a rest it is best to offer only clear liquids and light foods at the next meal.

Try to reassure and comfort the child because vomiting may frighten him. Ask or look to see if the child has pain anywhere before vomiting and after he is quiet. Also determine if the child has a runny nose, cough, diarrhea, or a sore throat. All of these complaints may accompany vomiting due to a bacterial or viral infection. It is important to look at the material vomited. Look for foreign substances (those not normally expected in the stomach such as aspirin, other medicines, paper, small parts of toys), fresh blood (red material), as well as old blood (dark material resembling coffee grounds). Nosebleeds often contribute to material found in the vomitus. In this case the partially digested blood resembles coffee grounds as mentioned. The amount of vomiting, volume, and number of times should also be noted and written down. A single bout of vomiting should be reported when a parent comes for the child at the end of the day. But persistent vomiting, pains long after vomiting has stopped, severe exhaustion, and evidence of overall sickness that does not improve with rest and quiet are symptoms that clearly suggest that both the child's parents and your medical advisor should be contacted. Arrangements for excluding the child from the preschool and providing care should also be made.

Diarrhea

Diarrhea is defined as one or several watery bowel movements. The child may have cramps and stomach pains with diarrhea, or may soil her underpants or make frequent trips to the toilet. It is important that good personal hygiene be taught and practiced especially when this symptom occurs. Other children and adults may get diarrhea if the affected child's hands and the assisting teacher's hands are not washed properly after using the toilet. Many of the infectious causes for diarrhea are spread from bowel movements to the mouth (see Chapter 4).

An irritation of the intestines or a general infectious process may cause a child to have diarrhea. For example, kidney infections, infectious hepatitis, infectious diarrhea (dysentery, salmonellosis), or intestinal viruses all may cause diarrhea.

Antiobiotics taken for an infection anywhere in the body change the organisms normally found in the intestines. This process often leads to loose bowel movements temporarily. Spoiled foods may cause diarrhea and vomiting as well. As with vomiting, the frequency and volume of diarrhea is important. The appearance of the bowel movements should be noted. Are they greenish, bloody, containing mucus, or undigested foods? You might routinely count the number of times a child goes to the bathroom for an elimination. Once diarrhea occurs give only clear liquids, water, Coke, or ginger ale without the carbonation, juices, diluted Jell-O, and strained soups. Throughout the day you should record the number of liquids given and the volume (if possible). Try to obtain the number of times the child urinates. If the number of bowel movements is more than one or two the parents should be told when the child leaves for the day. It is more serious if the child also appears weak, sleepy, has frequent pain, looks pale or flushed, or has a fast pulse. Should the child take in less fluid than appears in the bowel movements, then medical help is needed. You will want to have the parents notified should the child also appear to have a dry mouth or not pass much urine during the time of diarrhea. All of these findings indicate a shortage of fluid in the body or some degree of *dehydration*.

A child with diarrhea may require only exclusion from the preschool for a few days while clear liquids, bed rest, and a gradual return to a regular diet are prescribed. But certification by a doctor that the child is able to return to preschool is certainly recommended.

Fever

Hal took off his sweater and said, "I'm hot." His teacher noticed his face was red and covered with drops of perspiration. When she touched his head she realized he was very hot.

Fever in a child is a temperature of 101°F or greater. A fever causes an increase in demand on the child's energy. Therefore, you are likely to observe that breathing is fast, the heart is pounding and the pulse is rapid. In addition, the child may be thirsty, have parched lips, or even complain that the mouth is dry. This occurs because moisture is lost by the body during the increased use of energy. The febrile child may be droopy because she does not feel well or shiver because of increased muscle contractions.

Fever is one of the most frequent signs of illness in the preschool child. The common cause of fever is infection. Therefore, it is often accompanied by cough, vomiting, diarrhea, sore throat, or pain elsewhere in the body. A child with fever should get rest and sips of water until he is excluded from the preschool.

One significant accompaniment of sudden, high fever in this age group is a convulsion. Convulsions associated with fever may have occurred in other family members when they were children. Once a child has a convulsion with fever, she is likely to have more convulsions. For this reason anticonvulsant medicine may be prescribed by the child's physician.

How to handle a child with a convulsion is discussed in Chapter 8. Of course, it is best to know beforehand if a child has a history of convulsions and it is of particular importance to know if the child has taken or is presently taking medicine to control convulsions. Unfortunately many parents are ashamed to admit such a condition exists. Their apprehension and shame are understandable, especially if people isolate or brand the child as being one of "those epileptics." Compassion and patience are needed to keep a child integrated into a group after his playmates have seen him have one or more convulsions.

Sore Throat

Tommie Sue failed to eat her snack in the morning and coughed frequently. At lunch time she grimaced when she swallowed some of her food and then cried and refused to eat more. Her teacher took her to the sickroom because she was breathing through her mouth and had flushed cheeks. The teacher noticed that Tommie Sue's neck looked swollen and when touched, hurt. Tommie Sue was sent home and her physician determined that she had a streptcoccal infection of the throat (Chapter 4).

A child with a sore throat frequently also has fever, cough, runny nose, and foul breath. Ulcers or sores on the tongue or gums, drooling, or a thick coating on the tongue may also accompany throat pain.

The most serious cause for a sore throat is a streptococcal infection. Under all circumstances a child thought to have a sore throat should be excluded from the preschool.

Cough

Ricky's teacher noted no change in his cough since yesterday even though Ricky said his father gave him cough medicine last evening. Today, Ricky was wiping his nose more and he seemed to be inattentive and sluggish in his actions. By lunch time he felt as though he had a fever and he held his side and cried when he had to cough. Ricky's father came for him. The following day the teacher learned that Ricky must stay at home and take an antibiotic because he had pneumonia.

A cough does not always indicate a child has pneumonia but it is suggestive if it occurs as it did in Ricky's case. A cough is simply a mechanism to expel irritants or foreign substances from the respiratory tract. However, if the child persists in coughing the parents should know about it and take the child home. In the meantime, for relief, try sips of water or honey with lemon juice. This should be given only after you have excluded choking from a foreign body (Chapter 8) as a cause for the cough.

A child who has a barking cough and raspy sound when taking a breath most likely has croup. This illness may come about slowly over several days or quickly in a few hours. Croup is serious because swelling occurs in the larynx (voice box) due to an infection there. The swelling may increase and block the child's breathing; therefore, call the parents and get medical care as soon as possible.

Asthma

In the preadmission interview with Tyrone's parents the teacher learned that he had asthma. Tyrone's mother told the teacher to call her whenever he began to cough frequently or breathe rapidly because she was eager to get medical care for Tyrone during the early stages of his asthma attack.

Asthma is an allergic disorder affecting the lungs. An attack might occur under the following circumstances:

1. When specific foods are eaten.
2. When certain substances in the air near the child are inhaled.
3. When emotional upsets occur.
4. When the child has a respiratory infection.

An asthma attack will cause the child to cough very frequently, struggle to breathe and produce a rattling, rasping, wheezing sound when breathing. If the child does not get care early in the attack she will develop dry, cracked lips and tongue, a fever, become nauseated and vomit, get sleepy and tired, or have stomach and chest pains. Most asthmatics are not "cured" but their condition may be controlled over a period of time. This permits the child to lead a nearly normal life.

Early attention to a child who has asthma is extremely important even if it means the child must stay at home for a few days while getting treatment.

If it is your preschool's policy, you may give antiasthmatic medication to a child under specific circumstances. Should an asthmatic child have an attack, bring the child to the isolation room and allow him to be quiet. Give the child water of fruit juice to drink until you are able to contact the parents. Liquid intake is important to offset the loss of fluids through rapid breathing.

Obtain from the parents a list of what the child with asthma should avoid. Then make every effort to remove these items either completely or as much as possible from the child's environment.

Earache

An earache may be very stressful to the child because of the intensity of the pain that develops when there is an abnormality in or around the ear. The ear as an organ of hearing has a unique structure but it also has a unique capacity for disease. The space behind the ear drum is connected to the upper throat by a small tube (eustachian tube). Therefore, any blockage or abnormal function of this tube may cause pressure changes behind the ear drum and result in an earache. A natural pressure change without earache may be observed in yourself when you blow your nose, swallow, or travel up or down in an elevator.

The connection of the ear to the throat means that the frequent colds and sore throats of the young child may involve the ear as well. Two illustrations follow. Roberto complained of a sore throat and soreness in his nose. He had been taking cold medicine bought by his mother. The teacher asked Roberto's mother to come for him when he did not eat because of pain in his ears. When Roberto saw the doctor he was diagnosed as having an infection of both his throat and ears. Cindy had an ear infection according to the physician who examined her today. But three days ago her mother noticed she was sneezing, had watery eyes and a runny nose, and yesterday her teacher observed Cindy to be breathing through her mouth and rubbing both ears.

Ear wax (cerumen) collects naturally in everyone's ear canal. If the wax does not come out it may form a plug that compresses the eardrum and causes pain. However, no one but a physician should attempt to remove wax by digging into the child's ear canal.

A child with allergies may have frequent earaches because the eustachian tube becomes blocked for long periods of time.

Ear pain may be due to mumps. This should be considered where the child has swelling around the ear, mostly in front and just below the lobe. With mumps the lower tips of the earlobes stick out when you look at the child's head from behind. Also the joint of the jaw cannot be felt easily when the child opens and closes her mouth.

A preschooler may have decayed teeth and in this situation the earache may be related to dental pain.

The eardrum may rupture if pus or fluid collected behind it is not released. Some decrease in ear pain often comes about after the eardrum breaks. You should look at a child's ear canal to determine if a liquid of any type is spilling out. Be aware that the fluid you see could be tears which trickled down into the canal. In general, when an ear infection is the underlying cause for a rupture of the eardrum, foul smelling, thick, cloudy, yellow-green material is released into the ear canal.

The child with an earache may hold his head, rub his ears, bang his head with his hands, hold his painful ear and cry, state he has an earache or simply be very irritable. The ways the child indicates pain is closely associated with age, temperament, the severity of pain, and past experience with an earache.

If a child has no relief from an earache within half an hour the parents should be notified so that the child may be taken for medical examination. Until the child's parents arrive keep her quiet in the sick room. Under no circumstances should material of any sort be placed into the ear canal before medical care is given. It hampers an adequate determination of the cause for the earache.

Hearing Loss

Jacqueline never understood directions given to her unless she was able to intensely look at the person speaking. Sydney asked, "What?" or "What did you say?" frequently after recovering from his last cold. Dick seemed to be confused and did not participate in the activities as usual; he kept putting a finger into his right ear and tilting his head to the right. What did all of these children have in common? They had a hearing loss.

Rarely do young children tell you that they cannot hear. Hearing loss should be suspected when you observe certain characteristics or know that specific conditions occurred which have a tendency to cause a hearing loss.

The child with an earache may also have hearing loss because both of these problems may share a common cause, for example, cerumen (ear wax) in the ear canal, an ear infection, or a sticky fluid behind the eardrum due to allergies. Because of the muffled sounds that the child with hearing loss experiences, it is not unusual to find that the child has stuffed paper, sticks, erasers, toothpicks, paper clips or other objects into the ear canal in order to alleviate the blocked sound. On the other hand, foreign materials pushed into the ear canal may be the cause of hearing loss and/or earache. When you suspect hearing loss look into the ear canal to determine if any foreign objects can be seen.

A hearing loss may affect a child's behavior in the following ways:

1. She may breathe through her mouth most of the time.
2. She may turn her head to one side when addressed.
3. She must be shown how to do something because she apparently is unable to follow spoken directions.
4. She mumbles (speaks too softly), yells (speaks too loudly), talks in a monotone or has an unusual sound to her voice.
5. She appears quiet, withdrawn, and rarely speaks to others in the preschool.
6. She gestures rather than speaks in any social situation.
7. She does well when alone or when engaged in activities not dependent on hearing someone else.
8. She tends to have periods of unexplained frustration in which there are temper tantrums, extreme irritability, hitting, biting, or other aggressive actions.
9. She imitates or closely follows the way others play.

Other characteristics of the child's appearance should also make you suspicious of hearing loss:

1. Any malformation of the face that involves the ear.
2. A cleft palate or cleft lip even after being corrected by surgery.
3. A malformation of the ear that causes a very small or no apparent opening into the ear canal.
4. Any malformation that involves the lower jawbone and neck.

The consequences of most of these unusual malformations will be known to parents by the time such a child comes to preschool. But the teacher has the responsibility to review what is known about the child during the initial interview with the parents. This will help the preschool plan and offer appropriate experiences for the child. Do not hesitate to consult with your medical advisor if the medical condition is complicated.

Certain conditions have a tendency to cause hearing loss in children, and they are the cause of approximately 70 percent of the cases. Suspect that a child might have a hearing loss if any of the following conditions exist:

1. Relatives of the child have had hearing loss other than that which occurs with old age.
2. The child's mother had rubella (German measles) or any other viral infection during the first three months of pregnancy.
3. The child was very jaundiced (yellow) at birth.
4. The child weighed less than 3½ pounds at birth.
This information should be obtained in the initial medical history.

If you suspect a child has a hearing loss from any cause, ask the parents if they have a similar suspicion. Together you may find an explanation for unusual behavior frequently associated with hearing loss. The child should be examined by a physician if you continue to be suspicious of hearing loss.

Pinkeye

Any type of irritation to one or both eyes makes the white part of the eye look red or pink. Any foreign substance may initiate the irritation. If the child responds by rubbing the eyes it will aggravate the condition. Therefore, all substances accidently introduced onto the surface of the eye should be treated quickly according to the first aid procedures in Chapter 8.

Care of the Child With Specific Signs, Symptoms, or Illnesses **141**

An infection on the surface of the eye (more commonly called pinkeye) needs your prompt and careful attention as well. Speed in care is essential because the infection is contagious and may spread to other children and adults in the preschool center through handling objects that are contaminated. In the beginning the child with pinkeye may have some discharge from the eye with crusting on the eyelashes or the eyelids may remain stuck together after sleep. Later the surface of the eye becomes pink or red, the eyelids puffy and cloudy material (pus) drains from the eye. Any child with these signs should be excluded from the center as soon as possible. All personal items (towels, washcloths, and toys, for example) of the affected child should be cleaned thoroughly and persons in contact with the child should wash their hands. Good personal hygiene for everyone is always extremely important but it is especially so when an infectious illness such as pinkeye occurs.

Toothache, Dental Cavities

Gregory was holding his mouth and complaining of pain. When you asked him to open his mouth you saw a cavity in one of his teeth. He pointed to a "gum boil" at the base of the tooth with the cavity. Apparently that sore was causing pain. Quiet and rest did not help the pain go away so Gregory was sent home. The parents told you later that the tooth was infected and after the infection was treated with an antibiotic the dentist pulled the tooth.

Loss of the white coating (enamel) on the tooth is the beginning of tooth decay. This usually is the result of faulty eating habits, poor hygiene, and/or an inherited tendency. The major cause of tooth decay is eating too much sweet, sticky food and failure to cleanse the mouth when a child has finished eating. An older child who goes to sleep with a bottle or with candy, cookies, or other sweet food is endangering his teeth and can expect dental cavities. Toothaches and abscesses (Gregory's situation, for example) are the ultimate result of untreated cavities and they frequently destroy teeth. Too many people believe that cavities in baby teeth are of no concern because a child will lose these teeth anyway. However, cavities, infection or premature loss of baby teeth can cause damage to the permanent teeth.

The proper care of teeth is one of the most neglected health procedures at any age. Therefore, it is not surprising that many people pay little attention to a child's teeth even when gross abnormalities are present. This neglect should be corrected by serving good nutritious meals and by learning experiences in health (Chapter 3). Furthermore, every child should brush her teeth and vigorously rinse out the mouth with water after every meal or snack in the preschool. If cavities or toothaches are a problem, encourage the parents to take the child to the dentist.

Skin Rashes

To recognize different types of rashes is a very frustrating task. Children have many rashes and it is difficult to know at the beginning which ones are contagious and which are not. Often a rash that was of concern today may be gone tomorrow. Rashes associated with a fever, cough, runny nose, or a malaise (not feeling well) tend to be contagious—for example, scarlet fever, measles, German measles, and other viral rashes. Generally, rashes that look as though they have cloudy material in them (pus) and cause some itching are also contagious—for example, chickenpox, other viral diseases, and impetigo. Ringworm, the rash that gets its name from its appearance of raised bumps all in a ring anywhere on the body, is very contagious.

Thickened, roughened, darkened, reddened or oozing skin in the folds of the arms, legs, neck, and on the cheeks usually is not a contagious rash; it is usually allergic in nature. This rash (eczema) tends to cause itching, which produces scratching, irritability, discomfort, and more itching. Constant hard scratching may permit an infection to develop as in impetigo. All of the following have been known to cause severe itching in a child with eczema:

1. Changes in temperature.
2. Eating certain citrus fruits.
3. Sweating.
4. Wearing wool or silk clothing.
5. Using creams and oils on the skin.

Because the rash may become infected and may be confused with other infectious rashes, advise the child's parents to seek medical care when there is a dramatic change in the appearance of the rash. Changes in the condition of a child's skin may be kept to a minimum if you know what the child should avoid while under your care. Usually, the parents of such children are familiar with treatments that ease this problem and will discuss them with you at registration. Others, however, would welcome a chance to see if a new environment or different circumstances will give relief to their child.

Mild irritations of the skin are frequent. In these cases you may see redness or streaks on the skin from scratching. New, unwashed clothes, clothes made from synthetic fibers and the use of strong detergents to clean clothes may be a cause for the irritation of the skin of these children. Ask the parents if anything unusual or different has happened that may explain the skin reaction.

Children may have a very itchy cluster or streak of blisters on the skin not covered by clothes. Particularly if it is after a trip to a weedy or grassy area, you should think of poison ivy or poison oak as a cause. These children are not contagious to others. But the intense itching and general discomfort are reason enough to keep them at home.

A rash around the genital area and/or rectum may be due to scratching. The most common cause for this is pinworms (small white worms deposit eggs around the outside of the rectal opening during sleep and this produces severe itching). The itching leads to scratching, which leads to more irritation. Pinworms may affect as many as 10 to 30 percent of children in any preschool. They may also spread to the adults in the center. They are very difficult to eliminate because the pinworm eggs are spread when children do not wash their hands after using the toilet. The eggs even live under fingernails if scratching around the rectum is not followed by thorough handwashing. Medicine prescribed by a physician (often prescribed more than once) does get rid of them if all infected individuals are treated at the same time. You may notice that a child is scratching around the rectum during sleep or throughout any activity during the day. If this occurs you should tell the parents and suspect that pinworms are the cause.

Insect bites are frequent causes for rashes in young children. The scratching over one or more welts may be all you see. The scratching should be prevented because this often leads to an infection at the bite area.

An infestation with either lice or mites is to be suspected when a child continues to scratch his head, hands, wrists, back, or buttocks. An infestation with such insects is common and contagious. The insects are transferred through shared clothing, hairbrushes, and towels, and through close personal contact.

You may find lice or their eggs in or near the skin rash. But most often the lice are hiding in the seams of clothing or scurrying through the hair and out of sight. If seen they resemble a freckle or tiny blemish on the skin. The lice eggs look like dandruff but their stickiness keeps them attached to the hair whereas dandruff may be shed or pulled out. The use of an indirect light and parting of the hair are the best way to find the eggs. There may be sores in the head or lumps in the back of the neck (glands) because the scratching may have caused a skin infection.

Mites leave streaks like black threads ending in blisters around the ears, between the fingers, and on wrists and the buttocks. The insect burrows into the skin and dies, causing the itching and scratching.

Exclusion is a must if you suspect a child has either lice or mites. To be sure that no other children have become infected you should check everyone for suspicious rashes over the next two to three weeks. This is the time interval required for others to get an infestation if they are going to do so.

In general, to protect the health of all the children you should exclude anyone with any type of skin rash that has been present more than a day. Of course, if the rash is diagnosed by a health professional as being noncontagious you should not exclude the child.

Problems with Urination

Each child will establish his own patterns for urination just as he will for bowel elimination. However, urinary bladder control takes longer than regulation of bowels. It is accomplished by most two-year-old children. But the normal urinary pattern, the amount of urine produced and the frequency of urination, may change rapidly. This may be caused by a condition affecting the kidney, the bladder, or the total body, or by a condition in the child's environment.

Painful Urination Alicia told her teacher, "It burns when I pee," and she cried when she passed urine. Other indications of painful urination are the child holding his lower abdomen or squeezing his penis while voiding. He may refuse to pass urine until he cannot hold it any longer. Painful urination is associated with an infection of the urinary system (kidneys, bladder, or urinary tubes)

Care of the Child With Specific Signs, Symptoms, or Illnesses   145

or it may be due to some abnormality with which the child was born. It may be due to poor habits of personal hygiene, but more likely the reason for the problem may not be known. A urinary infection may also cause the child's urine to have a strong odor, to be dark in color or cloudy in appearance. Very high fever, shaking chills, stomach pain, and vomiting are often found with painful urination. Any child with painful urination needs an examination by a physician. He should be excluded from preschool until his condition is treated. Until care outside the preschool is offered the child should be given extra amounts of clear liquids and kept quiet.

Last week Eleanor seemed to be going to the bathroom frequently for two days. On the third day her teacher asked if anything was wrong. Eleanor's reply was that she had to urinate frequently. Earlier that day she wet her undergarments because she could not hold her urine until she was in the bathroom. The problem was called to the attention of Eleanor's mother at the end of the day. When Eleanor saw her physician a urinary infection was discovered and she received treatment.

Besides a urinary infection, frequent urination may be the result of an excessive intake of fluids while in the preschool.

Commonly, emotional stress may bring on frequent urination or wetting of undergarments. The tension may be created at home or in the preschool setting.

When you observe frequent urination mention it to the child's parents. Ask the parents if they think anything unusual has happened or if they also have frequent urination.

You may recognize some episodes in the preschool that cause the child to be tense. Also the parents may tell you that frequent urination occurred in the past under specific circumstances that are being duplicated now in the preschool setting. Make arrangements with the parents, your staff, and health professionals to correct the problem. However, parents are often reluctant to share incidents of family turmoil with you. Thus, simply suggest that the child have a medical evaluation if you see no apparent reason for the frequent urination.

Unusual Walking Patterns

In spite of the fact that everyone has her own unique walk, there are some characteristics that are abnormal in a walk. All of the following ways of walking are not normal:

1. Walking with toes turning in (pigeon toed).
2. Walking with the toes turned out.
3. Walking on toes or heels.
4. Walking on the inner or outer aspect of the feet.
5. Knees bumping together when walking.
6. Walking with the knees far apart or bowlegged.
7. Walking with a limp.
8. Walking similar to that of a duck, wobbling and waddling.
9. Walking with legs stiff, each leg in turn swinging forward in a small arc while dragging the toes on the ground, "scissor gait."
10. Dragging a foot or slapping the feet down while walking.

Some of the children with an abnormal gait will be under the care of a physician. This will be known at the time of registration. Others may be detected while under your care if you watch how all the children walk. But sometimes you will notice something wrong only after a child stumbles frequently or seems to be clumsy. Looking at his shoes to see how they are worn often suggests that something might be wrong with the way a child walks. Pain, corns, blisters, or calluses on the child's feet indicate an abnormal walk or shoes that do not fit properly. Improperly fitting shoes may be due to the quality of the shoes or to abnormalities in a child's bones or joints.

When you notice a child who has an abnormal gait mention it to the parents and your medical consultant. Frequently, parents will state that other members of the family had a similar problem and it was corrected with special shoes. Others will tell you that the child's walk is similar to that of an adult member of the family. In this situation, the parents probably do not think the walk is abnormal. They even may be offended if you suggest the child should have medical attention. Suggest that they speak with your medical consultant if they are indifferent, indignant, or unsure about your observations. Your skill and tact in presenting problems to the family will be supported by consultation with your medical advisor.

Child Neglect and Abuse

Silvester, who had bruises and bumps on his arms had been whipped by his mother the previous evening. His mother had been laid off by her employer that day. When Silvester knocked over his glass of milk at dinner that was all his mother could take. All of this became known when Silvester's mother came for him at the end of the day.

You are in a good position to be one of the first persons to recognize some difficulty between the child and the parents. You may learn of the family's relationship with one another in many different ways. Through periodic interviews you get to know how the family copes with all types of crises. The attitudes of parents toward their child become apparent when you report the child's progress or bouts with illness. How the children appear or what they say in preschool gives you insight into what happens at home, as was the case with Silvester. But what the family will not talk about may be just as important as what you observe or do discuss. Child abuse or neglect by parents or guardians usually occurs when several circumstances come together at the same time. These are not limited to any race, religious group, poor or rich families. These circumstances are:

1. A predisposition to abuse by the adults in a family.
2. The presence of a special child.
3. A crisis or a series of crises.

Credit: *Allan Brightman for Childrens Protective Services.*

The Predisposition to Abuse by Adults in a Family The predisposition to abuse is something that develops throughout an individual's life. Its development takes account of at least five factors. First, the adults who abuse children were often abused by their parents. If not abused, they were reared in such a way as to be expected to behave maturely and solve their own problems. That is, they were not allowed to be children or to learn how to be adults through examples from their parents. Second, the persons who abuse their children have often become isolated and are unable to trust and consult other people. They do not make friends easily and do not mix well in groups because they look to themselves for answers. Third, the parent who has abused a child does not have a give-and-take or warm relationship with the other parent. Not only are these parents unable to find relief from tensions in activities, or relationships with friends but are also unable to find relief in the relationship with a spouse. Fourth, a poor self-image or a feeling of inadequacy or worthlessness is another characteristic of parents who abuse their children. Fifth, parents who neglect or abuse their children have unrealistic expectations of children. These parents expect the child to do something for them. In many cases the role is reversed between child and parent. The adults expect the child to do what they wanted their parents to do for them. In other cases, the parents expect their children to behave at a level that is beyond their physical or intellectual level of development.

The Presence of a Special Child The abused or neglected child is usually a special child. This label is applied because the child is seen as different by the parents; that is, a child who does not perform as the parents expect. A special child may indeed be different; for example, he may be clumsy, extraintelligent, fussy and irritable, or hyperactive. Real or imagined, a family must deal with a special child.

A Crisis or a Series of Crises The crisis is the precipitating factor rather than the cause for abuse of a child. The crisis in the family may be a physical one: for example, the sink is clogged, there is no electricity or heat, there is no money for food today, the phone was disconnected or it is out of order. Or the crisis may be a personal one: such as the loss of a job, a divorce, death of a relative, a failure to progress in a job. When any of these factors occur at a certain psychological moment, neglect or abuse to a child may result.

A child who has had an encounter with physcial abuse may have bruises, burns, or pain in the arms or legs between one day and the next. The child may be fearful or evasive if you ask what happened. In other cases, the child will blurt out, "I was beaten," "I was tortured," "I was burned." The parents may be vague about the circumstances of the injury, they even may be angry about your asking what happened. For the sake of the child, any such episodes should be discussed tactfully with the parents or referred to your medical consultant.

You should be concerned about the child who repeatedly comes to the preschool center with an abnormal need for food. Mention this to the parent and ask if the child eats sufficiently at home. You may find that the parents are unable to give the child adequate food because of financial problems. Refer the parents to a social worker or agency for assistance. If you find the parents hostile and indignant about your inquiries, discuss this case with your social service consultant.

If you discover a child has not been getting appropriate medical care take it up with the parents. Some children who do not get medical examinations when requested to do so may be neglected due to overwhelming conflicts within the family. However, if children lag behind in their necessary immunizations they may be suffering from parental neglect. Where poverty or need and not neglect is an apparent cause, you should help the parents to find help from an appropriate social agency in the community.

Often the parents are relieved to share their problems with someone provided a good relationship has been established. Again your part in caring for the child's needs is of prime importance. Always seek help when needed from your medical advisor or the appropriate social service agency. Many states have legislation that requires reporting neglect of abuse of a child to the social service agency. The legislation also guarantees that you will not be sued for your action.

Poor Vision

Manuel enjoyed the time when everyone was allowed to look at picture books. However, he did not pay attention when his teacher used posters, projected slides, or movies. During this time he always wanted to be very close to the teacher. If he was not permitted to be in the front row he rubbed his eyes or squinted or he talked, squirmed, giggled, or wandered away during the presentation. The teacher spoke to the parents about it and with the help of the preschool's medical consultant an eye test was done. Manuel was found to have difficulty in seeing objects at a distance. Manuel's parents obtained glasses for him and now he enjoys activities which require both near and distant vision. He was nearsighted or myopic.

A major function of the eye is to focus light rays on the back of the eye (the retina). The eyeball may be either too short or too long. If the eyeball is too short the light rays focus behind the eye and the condition is farsighted vision. When the eyeball is too long, light rays focus in front of the retina and the condition is nearsighted vision. Over 90 percent of all vision defects in young children are due to farsightedness. This defect develops at an early stage. It requires glasses for correction.

Whenever Janice looked up from her activities her left eye turned outward. Every time Peter was tired his right eye appeared to turn in. Craig's eyes turned in almost all the time. All of these children exhibit eye muscle imbalance. The muscles of the eye move both eyes simultaneaously so that they are able to focus on an object at the same time. When this does not happen the condition is called an eye muscle imbalance, squint, strabismus, or crossed eyes. The significance of this abnormality is that double or blurred vision occurs. If the strabismus is not recognized and treated, the vision in the eye that does not focus is unconsciously suppressed. This repeated ignoring of images by one eye will lead to the gradual loss of vision or amblyopia in that eye. It may become permanent if not discovered and treated at an early age. Therefore, when you observe a child with a squint call it to the attention of the parents and urge them to seek advice from the child's physician.

Among preschool children approximately 5 out of 100 will be found to have some vision defect. Because the young child rarely states, "I can't see," the clues to recognition of poor vision are almost exclusively what you observe or find by screening (Chapter 5).

There are some characteristic appearances of the child's eyes that should make you suspicious of poor vision. These are:

1. Eyes that bounce or move up and down or from side to side (nystagmus).
2. Eyes that often appear bloodshot.
3. Reddened eyelid rims or watery eyes following visual concentration.
4. One or both eyelids droop.
5. One or both pupils (the center of the eye normally black in color) appears to be cloudy, gray, or white in color.

Both pupils should be the same size and react equally to

Care of the Child With Specific Signs, Symptoms, or Illnesses 151

light—small pupils in a bright light and large pupils in dim light. If you notice a difference in their size or response to light there could be an underlying visual problem.

Tasks or activities that require visual skills often produce signs of poor vision. Some illustrations follow. Nancy always put her head close to what she was doing. John seemed to drop anything he was carrying from one place to another just as he meant to put it down. Rochelle always turned her head to the left when she listened to the teacher. Jackson sat very stiffly whenever he needed to see anything across the room. Maxine moved her head back and forth when focusing on distant objects, for example, when the teacher asked her to identify pictures on cards held up in front of the room.

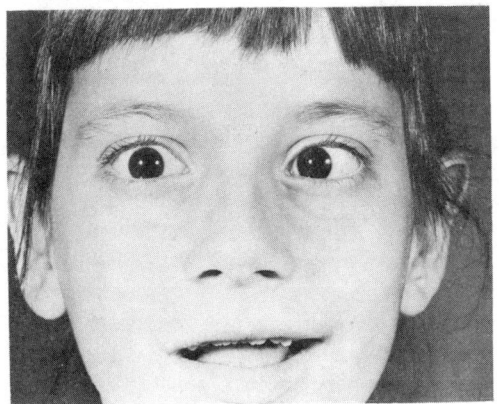

Credit: *National Society for the Prevention of Blindness, Inc.*

Geraldine always turned her head rather than her eyes while she played with her friends. Bob was thought to be clumsy before his glasses stopped him from bumping into everything and stumbling over steps and doorjambs. Jimmy became bored with any task that required his close attention for a long time.

Recurrent styes (an infection at the base of an eyelash) may result from repeated rubbing of the eyes with dirty hands. One reason for rubbing the eyes may be poor vision. The stye causes the eyelid to become red and swollen and drain pus. A stye can be very infectious to others through contaminated objects. Observe similar precautions as with pinkeye and exclude the child until the infection is cleared.

Your skilled observations to detect poor vision must be

supplemented by visual screening tests and by medical examination (Chapter 5). Therefore, share your observations with the child's parents and suggest a visual examination if this is not available within your preschool. You should be informed about any recommendation made, particularly if glasses are prescribed. All too frequently when glasses are the treatment you may find the child does not wear them as prescribed because they are broken, lost, or temporarily misplaced. A child who wears glasses also needs periodic reevaluation. You should assist the parents in following the medical advice given to them. Remember, good vision is most important throughout the entire lifetime and is a vital function in developing skills, reading being one example, which allow every person to achieve his greatest potential.

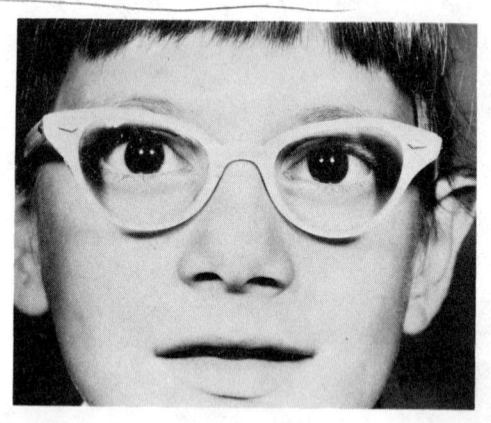

Credit: *National Society for the Prevention of Blindness, Inc.*

Speech Defects

Even though everyone uses speech, our understanding of what constitutes a speech defect in a child may be meager. To be able to identify a defect you should be familiar with the following:

1. Know what is the average or normal speaking ability for each age group in your preschool. It is a mistake to expect sounds, grammar, or word understanding beyond the developmental capabilities of a child. As a guideline, children between three and four years of age should demonstrate the following speech characteristics:
    (a) Understand and use pronouns I, you and me.
    (b) Understand and use some plurals.

Care of the Child With Specific Signs, Symptoms, or Illnesses   153

(c) Understand and use at least three prepositions—in, on, under.
(d) Follow directions that use three to four words.
(e) Use many verbs in speech.
(f) Ask "how," "where," and "what" questions.
(g) Have a vocabulary of around 1000 words of things that are around the child.
(h) Be understood 90 percent of the time.
(i) Pronounce 90 percent of the vowel sounds correctly.
(j) Have the ability to whisper.
(k) Say the following consonants (p, b, m, w, h, d, t, n).
(l) Carry on meaningful conversation.
(m) Pronounce the beginning of most words.

2. Be able to specifically identify the type and quality of speech that is heard. The terms "immature speech," "baby talk," or "difficult to understand" may have meaning to you but rarely do they have the same meaning to other people, particularly health professionals. Therefore, these terms are not useful descriptions.

An adequate description of a speech defect should include a comment on:

1. The vibration or resonance of sounds.
2. The voice.
3. The articulation or pronunciation.
4. The flow of natural speech.
5. Delay or reduction in the amount of speech.

Micky had a cold and when he talked all the sounds seemed to come through the throat. The "m's" and "n's" in his speech did not have any nasal quality nor did any of his speech. Jane talked the same way as Micky but she didn't have a cold. The teacher learned that Jane had an allergy that caused swelling of tissues in the nose and upper pharynx. Her speech was described as being hyponasal by her physician and speech therapist. The degree of vibration or resonance in the voice determines the amount of nasal quality present. The type of voice demonstrated by Micky and Jane may be temporary but if it persists there may be an associated hearing loss. Consequently, suggest that the parent obtain medical advice.

William sounded hoarse and Nicole had a husky and raspy

voice. The quality of William's voice returned to normal after his respiratory infection (laryngitis) was treated. The quality of Nicole's voice continued to be husky. She was said to have a growth on her vocal cords. Now that the growth has been removed her voice sounds clear. The child who is hard of hearing may have a high pitched squeaky voice or have a very loud or soft voice. Under any circumstances, mention any voice changes that you observe to the child's parents.

Virginia always said "wight" when she meant light, "lello" when she tried to say yellow, and "leh" when yes was what she meant. This type of defect is one of substitution. Harry always said "loo" and "boo" when he meant look and book. Omission is the type of defect Harry has. It is difficult to understand everything Linda says. She adds sounds in a word or has trouble pronouncing parts of words correctly. All of these articulation or pronounciation speech defects are the most common in young children. An appropriate definition of these problems should be made and a plan for their correction should be instituted. Ask each parent if they understand Virginia, Harry, and Linda. Tell the parents that both children and the adult staff have difficulty in understanding the children. You might suggest that each child have an evaluation by their physician.

A child may have a disturbance in the rate and rhythm of his speech so that stuttering, stammering, or jumbling results. Stuttering occurs when there is rapid repetition of syllables or words, a prolongation of sounds, or the inability to form certain sounds temporarily. Stuttering may be mild and occur occasionally or it may be severe and cause a distortion of the face with sputtering and very interrupted conversation. Stammering speech results when sounds are prolonged or there is searching for a particular sound. Jumbling speech means that the child speaks so rapidly that sounds or parts of words are omitted. Being ridiculed, teased, and ignored because of a speech defect does not help the affected child participate in the center's activities nor does it promote optimum development. Be alert to an early recognition of these defects so that therapy may be instituted at an early time also. On the other hand, a parent who is apprehensive about the child's speech may cause the child to become tense and therefore have speech difficulties. It is natural for a young child to hesitate or repeat words, especially when excited.

Larry did not talk very much the first week of preschool. When the teacher spoke with his mother she said, "Oh we believe he is too lazy to talk. There's really nothing wrong because, you know, he does everything I tell him. He never had to say much because he was the baby and everyone spoke for him. He gets everything he wants by pointing or using his own language." These clues are evidence of delayed speech. Because the family is not disturbed about Larry you should speak with your medical advisor; let her make suggestions about how to evaluate Larry.

Other health problems such as nosebleed, insulin reaction, diabetic coma, convulsions, and conditions that are the result of an injury are discussed in Chapter 8.

The conditions dealt with in this chapter and in Chapter 8, are the most common ones you might encounter. If other health problems occur, you may be able to take care of them according to your education in health or you may have to seek advice from a health professional. It will be helpful to keep a record of how to care for these conditions for future reference.

CONTENTS

7.1.0 COMMON BEHAVIORAL PROBLEMS
    Aggressiveness, Anger
    Temper Tantrums
    Balkiness, Contrariness
    Sex Play and Sexual Interest
    Nail Biting, Thumb Sucking
    Family Crises
    Jealousy
    Boredom; The "Know-It-All"
    Fears
    Timidness, Shyness
    Separations
    Learning Disability; The "Different" "Out-of-Step" Child
    Hyperactivity

CHAPTER 7

Behavioral Problems

Dealing with behavioral problems may cause concern and become time consuming for the preschool teacher. Yet the teacher often feels least comfortable about sorting out such problems in order to help deal with them. This hesitation is not unusual because it is shared frequently with the child's parents. Part of the difficulty is in not being able to determine if the behavior represents a harmless or temporary problem or if it needs special attention. Another factor is that behavioral characteristics may indicate a physical disturbance as well as point toward emotional and situational stresses. Therefore, do not exclude the possibility of a physical disturbance; let the health professional determine that.

The general rules necessary to care for behavioral problems do not differ from those required when a child is ill (Chapter 6). There are other special requirements, however.

First, you must know what can be expected developmentally of a child at different ages. The most common mistake is that adults misunderstand and misinterpret normal behavior such as curiosity, negativism, "sassiness," and striving for independence and thereby create a conflict between themselves and the child. Erroneously, this conflict is believed to be caused by the child's atypical behavior. Normal growth and development is the subject of many textbooks and is taught as a separate subject to preschool teachers, therefore it is not presented here.

Second, do not consider every behavioral deviation as emotional illness. Many characteristics observed are temporary and only need to be mentioned to the child's parents if they inhibit the child over several months or disrupt the classroom repeatedly.

Third, often the underlying causes for unusual behavior are conflicts, tensions or stresses in the child's home environment. You cannot be aware of all these circumstances that could cause difficulty but you must realize that the child's behavioral difficulties may not disappear unless the causes are known and are rectified. The best way to discover difficult home situations is through conferences with parents about the child's problems. Teacher-parent conferences are discussed in Chapter 5.

Fourth, there are no magic remedies to correct a child's behavioral problems. Patience, time, and trial with several individualized plans are the most useful remedies.

7.1.0 COMMON BEHAVIORAL PROBLEMS

A comprehensive understanding of and dealing with behavioral problems is a specialty beyond the scope of this book. Some accepted principles for temporary care of the most common problems follow.

Aggressiveness, Anger

John grabbed the red and orange paints from Jack. In turn, Jack ripped the partially colored picture from John's coloring book. Eunice bit Mary Jane because Eunice wanted to play alone with the building blocks. Ricki threw a ball at his teacher because he was not permitted to go outside to play at a particular time.

These situations demonstrate the lack of control each of these children have over their anger and aggressiveness. Children must learn that these urges must be controlled in a manner acceptable to society and they need guidance from adults in gaining such control. These children should be told firmly that this behavior is not acceptable. Then alternative activities should be presented to them. If Jack and John do not seem to play well together place them in separate play groups. If Eunice is unable to return to play permit her to help you with a task or allow her some quiet time to calm down.

Encourage each child to share with his or her playmates and to be tolerant of their individual personality traits. Divert any direct actions of hostility toward constructive games or activities. Praise a child when she is able to control anger or aggressiveness. These directions and attitudes strengthen a child's attempts to control her emotions.

Temper Tantrums

Iris jumped up and down, screamed, and then began to fling

toys in every direction because she did not want to come and eat lunch. Peaches cried and screamed then she held her breath until she was limp; suddenly she gasped for air and started screaming again. Peaches wanted the toy Minerva had.

Both Iris and Peaches had become frustrated and a temper tantrum was their release mechanism. In either situation the child should not provoke your anger. Instead, ignore them but permit them to come to you for comfort if that is what they might want. When they are calm tell them firmly that tantrums are not acceptable behavior.

Temper tantrums are encouraged if children are constantly reminded of restrictions about where they may go or what they may do.

In order to discourage new or repeated temper tantrums do not present new activities in a demanding or authoritative way nor give the child a choice that is different from your wishes. That is, do not say "You have to stop playing now and eat." It is better to say "We have 10 minutes more of play before lunch, so start to finish what you are doing." Neither should you say, "Are you ready for lunch?" while everyone is involved in outdoor games. Instead you should say, "Guess what? It's lunchtime. Who wants to help set the table and who wants to put the bats, balls, and toys away?" Select one or two children to help the volunteers and proceed to prepare for lunch.

Balkiness, Contrariness

Ethel refused to go outside until all her crayons, picture books, and pencils were in place in her drawer. Juan wanted to play with the trucks but he couldn't decide which ones to choose. Soon he started fussing with Julio because Julio wanted him to make a choice and move on. Edwina fussed when the teacher tried to help her put on her coat, hat, and rubbers.

All of these children need your patience, not your harsh admonishment or your taking over of the activity. The child is trying to decide things for himself but without much experience. You should support the child during this period by allowing time to linger indecisively or to slowly carry out the task alone. The intensity with which each child demonstrates this trait is variable but usually the duration is not long.

Sex Play and Sexual Interests

It is normal for a child to be interested in physical differences between boys and girls. Also masturbation or play with the sex organs is to be expected. The difficulty occurs when the child becomes preoccupied with masturbation or with exploring the bodies of other children. Correction and management of this activity should be handled calmly and quietly. Outrage, excitement, or a great show of dealing with this problem often creates anxiety and insecurity in the child. The cause of such acts is more important than the acts themselves. Cooperation between the preschool, the child's parents, and the medical team is essential in dealing with such emotionally charged events surrounding the child's sexual interests.

Nail Biting, Thumb Sucking

The tense, worrisome child is apt to bite his or her fingernails. The best way to handle this activity is to reduce the child's tensions. If you are unaware of specific tensions consult with the parents about some possible causes. Do not nag or punish the child for nail biting. This only creates a bigger problem and could increase the child's tensions.

The preschool child sucks on his thumb for comfort when tired, bored, facing a new situation, or is frustrated. Excessive thumb sucking usually indicates the child requires more comfort than she is getting. You should make the environment as warm and supportive as possible. For further assistance a discussion with the parent may help you identify deficiencies in the home that may be counteracted in the preschool setting.

Do not restrain the child from thumb sucking nor offer bribes of toys, food, or special activities. When this is done the child will probably accept the reward while continuing to suck his thumb.

Family Crises

Death, family turmoil, divorce, surgery, an accident at home, or a permanent separation from any family members are crises that may affect a child's emotional behavior. A child may become infantile or stop being toilet trained because of any of these circumstances. The child who has seen a family member die or a playmate injured may talk and play about injuries or death for some time. In another case, a child was very fearful of putting on a mask because she had to put one on for surgery. Anger and hatred directed to a parent departed because of divorce may be seen in a child's play with a doll or stuffed animal. It should be expected that any crises will leave an impression. Help the child to cope with the difficulty in a healthy way, realizing that it may take several months. Play is a very acceptable way of helping the child to cope with such crises.

Jealousy

Every child needs to feel that he or she is receiving equal affection, respect and attention from the teacher. When the child does not get this she will be jealous of one or more classmates. Jealously can take the form of bickering with the perceived rival or it may take the form of outright hostile acts toward others. The child may do silly or unacceptable things in order to get attention. If you arbitrate between jealous children, make every effort to demonstrate that each has an equal commitment from you. Instead of creating an unnatural situation by attempting to treat them equally, it would be better to give them something that you know they would appreciate individually. For example, let Eva help you set the table because she likes to do this and let Irene sit next to you when you read a story at storytime because she likes to be near you.

Boredom; The "Know-It-All"

The exceptionally intelligent child may appear disinterested or "fresh" and "have all the answers." This child may appear to have time for almost everything except what is expected at the moment. He may direct his extra energies into very bad habits or into classroom and playtime disruptions. Therefore, seek advice and consultation with the child's parents, if necessary, when the child exhibits this type of behavior. Punishment and rigid rules of discipline would be inappropriate and should be replaced by creative activities, additional tasks or leadership roles.

Fears

Preschool children may have a variety of fears because they are able to imagine all types of dangers that they have not previously faced. In each situation the child should be comforted and permitted to discuss the fear until she has overcome it. If the child has difficulty because of many fears then talk about your observations with the parents. This child needs help in developing independence and a suitable method for coping with the unknown.

Timidness, Shyness

Elmer is an only child who had not been exposed to many children before starting in preschool. He stood by while others grabbed his toys or he burst into tears when he was shoved aside. Melissa is a tiny girl who always has wide eyes and appears frightened of everyone's spontaneous, noisy activities in the school. When left alone she prefers to sit and watch while clutching her teddy bear or sucking on her thumb.

Credit: Allan Brightman for Childrens Protective Services.

Elmer should be encouraged to stand up for his rights to become confident and assertive. Melissa should be encouraged to join in the group and have both successful and frustrating experiences. This participation by Elmer and Melissa should be encouraged by you but not in a way to create a dependence on you. Do not always be eager to stand up for them and to act for them. You may try to pair them up with understanding and sympathetic playmates during certain activities.

If profound shyness persists talk with the parents so that a cooperative program may be found and used.

Common Behavioral Problems

Separations

Many children need the security of a parent, teacher, or playmate. Crying, tantrums, and negativism may all be part of the child's frustration in having to say goodbye to parents or to staff and friends at the preschool. The child should be assured that these separations are temporary.

Most conflicts occur when the child is left at the preschool by the parents at the beginning of the day. The child is afraid that the parent will disappear forever. He may have this fear because one parent has been temporarily away from home. The child is most fearful of parental separations when first entering preschool. At that time allow the parent to stay awhile with the child for as long as necessary. This usually does not last more than a few days. Occasionally a child may need the parent's presence for a longer time until the child is able to feel free to join in the group's activities.

Learning Disability; The "Different", "Out-of-Step" Child

Learning disability is a subject usually dealt with in much detail in a separate course in early childhood education programs. It is only briefly presented here.

A breakdown in the interaction of sensory messages or a garbling of them in the brain seems to produce what specialists call learning disabilities. Children with learning disabilities usually have average or above average intelligence; therefore, they are not mentally retarded. Neither are these children emotionally disturbed but they may become tense, depressed, or anxious because they are unable to learn as well as their classmates.

Many children with a learning disability unfortunately are not recognized until they reach school because the characteristics observed earlier are not good predictors of future problems. Also, these characteristics may be only mildly abnormal and may be therefore ignored. The need for some of these learning skills is not critically imporant before the child reaches school age. This should not stop the preschool worker from looking for learning abnormalities.

Children with the learning disabilities may have some of these signs but not necessarily all of them:

1. Hyperactivity, an inability to remain with a specific task very long.
2. Confusion in answering questions; the same answer is

given to a question even when the question changes. This happens because the child is unable to quickly change mental activities that require different thoughts.
3. Poor memory of what was seen.
4. Inability to discriminate between different but similar words or sounds.
5. Difficulty in coordinating hand movements with what the eyes see, as in hitting a ball, coloring, or using pencil and paper.
6. Difficulty in remembering the difference between left and right, up and down, over and under.
7. Inability to pick out one object from a group of objects.
8. Uncertainty in distinguishing familiar objects by feel or touch.
9. Inability to follow directions if more than one task is required, for example, go to the table, sit down, and then play with the blocks on the table.
10. Uncertainty in distinguishing between related symbols such as circles and ovals or squares and rectangles.

If the preschool teacher or the parents suspect that a child may have a learning disability they should not delay seeking help in the belief it will go away spontaneously. Always confer with the appropriate group of health professionals. The preschool environment can be structured to assist in helping with this problem and the child may be better integrated into the total group.

Hyperactivity

Currently the public is very concerned with what they believe to be hyperactive children. Unfortunately the term hyperactivity is used often too freely.

It is normal for children to be energetic, curious, enterprising, imaginative, and consequently busy and physically active. Therefore, you must learn to be tolerant of these characteristics and at the same time the child should be taught to control excessive physical energy.

Every child has their own normal range of activity that is influenced by various events. For example, it may be decreased during illness or increased with apprehension and anxiety. When groups of children are observed, quite naturally some will be more active than others. All such active children are not necessarily hyperactive. In the context of this publication, the term hyperactivity refers to the child who does not function properly and is observed to be overly energetic. Thus, a child who does not follow directions, constantly runs about, rarely finishes a meal, and has destructive behavior would be a hyperactive child. On the other hand there are overly energetic children who perform properly. The important factor is to determine how well a child performs.

You should document your observations about the frequency and the severity of hyperactivity and take into consideration how well specific activities were accomplished. If there appears to be a problem consult with your medical advisor before you label the child as being "hyperactive."

The child's problem may require the special skill of many professionals over a period of time, therefore do not think all hyperactive children should be on medication immediately. If medication is prescribed (ritalin, for example) the level of hyperactivity does not change quickly and often may be decreased without making the child's activity more productive.

The truly hyperactive child can create a difficult environment. To ease that tension Dr. B. Schmidt of Denver, Colorado, offers the following guidelines[1] to individuals who live with a hyperactive child: (1) accept the child's limitations, (2) provide outlets for release of the child's excess energy, (3) keep the home environment organized, (4) avoid fatigue in the child, (5) avoid large formal gatherings, (6) maintain firm discipline, (7) enforce discipline with nonphysical punishment, (8) stretch the child's attention span, (9) buffer the child against any overreaction from nonfamily members, and (10) periodically get away from it all.

It is important for the teacher to participate in the care of a child who is hyperactive. Accurate observations regarding changes in behavior and performance while a child is under medical care should be given to both the child's parents and physician. This activity should be consistent with your established policy to care for preschool children with special needs.

For reasons already stated, only the more common behavioral problems have been highlighted in this chapter. Yet you will want to develop experience in dealing with those problems that may be

[1]Barton, Schmidt, "Guidelines for Living with a Hyperactive Child," Letter to Editor, *Pediatrics*, Vol. 63, 387, 1977.

unique to your preschool setting and that were not discussed here. For any unfamiliar problems, summarize them and include the positive as well as negative approaches that were used to correct the problem. Your records of this may be a useful guide for handling similar problems in the future and it may serve as a teaching instrument.

CONTENTS

8.1.0 WHAT TO DO IN CASE OF AN ACCIDENT OR SUDDEN ILLNESS
    8.1.1 General Guidelines
    8.1.2 What General Principles for First Aid Should You Follow?
8.2.0 FIRST AID FOR SPECIFIC CONDITIONS AND INJURIES
    8.2.1 Wounds
    8.2.2 Common Injuries to Various Parts of the Body
    8.2.3 State of Shock
    8.2.4 Sprains, Broken Bones, Dislocations
    8.2.5 Burns
    8.2.6 Electrical Injuries
    8.2.7 Breathing Stoppage
    8.2.8 Other Emergencies
    8.2.9 Poisoning

CHAPTER 8

First Aid

Betty came running in from the back porch, clutching her throat. There were white stains around her mouth and on her dress. Did she swallow a chemical such as lye? What would you do?

While on the playground, a child fell off the swing. He lay on the ground motionless, unconscious. What would you do?

The purpose of this chapter is to guide preschool personnel in establishing policies for first aid and prepare them so they know what to do in case of an accident or other emergency.

While some accidents are unavoidable, many could be avoided by careful planning. The mother of a little girl similar to Betty who swallowed lye wrote a very touching article for her local newspaper. It was about how a container of leftover lye that changed the life of her little girl and the whole family. The teacher, the parent, and everyone in charge of young children must be prepared to render first aid in case of an accident or an emergency such as sudden illness. First aid courses are taught by the American National Red Cross and those who successfully complete the course are then certified. All teachers in preschools should be certified in first aid. In some communities first aid training is required for employment. Educators of preschool personnel should be first aid instructors, trained and certified by the Red Cross, so that they can teach first aid, especially as it pertains to the young child. The value of first aid training lies not only in the ability to administer first aid but also in accident prevention and safety awareness. First aid may mean the difference between permanent or temporary disability; it may mean faster recovery; and it may also save life.

The first aid principles in this chapter are applied specifically to the young child in a preschool setting or at home and are directed to all caretakers of children. First aid for accidents which occur elsewhere, such as snake bite or drowning, is not discussed here. First aid for sudden illness or signs of illness such as convulsions or fainting are dealt with in this chapter, but for care of the child who is ill refer to Chapter 6. This chapter supplements but does not replace the book *Standard First Aid and Personal Safety*, published by the Red Cross, which will be referred to as *Red Cross Manual* here. The psychological impact of a child's injury on a teacher is not dealt with in this chapter. Everyone should be reminded, however, that such events may have a psychologically traumatic effect on the individual in charge of that child. A teacher well prepared in first aid and safety not only will be better able to meet his or her responsibilities but guilt feelings will be lessened.

8.1.0 WHAT TO DO IN CASE OF AN ACCIDENT OR SUDDEN ILLNESS

The American National Red Cross defines first aid as the immediate care given to a person who has been injured or suddenly has been taken ill. This immediate care may include many things. It could be words of encouragement to the person in need of first aid and care for the injury itself. Immediate care also consists of seeking medical help, giving accurate information about the injury or illness to the proper authorities, arranging for transporation, and getting permission from parents for treatment of the child.

8.1.1 General Guidelines

Are you ready to do all the things that are a part of first aid? Careful preparation is necessary. Before considering procedures, let us discuss some planning steps.

1. *Who is to direct first aid activities?*
   One member of the staff and an alternate should be designated director of first aid and safety, and be held responsible for the coordination of all activities.

2. *Is everyone prepared?*
   The staff should be well educated in first aid, as mentioned earlier in this chapter. Only first aid procedures published by the American National Red Cross should be used. At least one person certified in first aid must be on the premises of the preschool at all times.

3. *Who handles an accident when it occurs?*
   The teacher in charge of the children at the time an accident occurs should administer first aid, unless the

What to Do in Case of an Accident or Sudden Illness   **171**

List of Important Phone Numbers to be Posted near the Telephone

1. Hospitals where emergency case is to go:

Name	Phone No.	Who to speak with

2. Physician who is medical advisor

Name	Phone No.

3. Members of health team who have agreed to help—a surgeon for example

Name	Phone No.

4. Fire Department _____
5. Police _____
6. Poison Control Center _____
7. Ambulance and/or Rescue Squad

Name	Phone No.

8. Taxicabs

Name	Phone No.

Name	Phone No.

Source. *E.H. Reinisch and R.E. Minear.*
Figure 8-1

facility has a different clearly stated policy.
4. *What emergency phone numbers are important?*
Have the following phone numbers listed near the telephone (Figure 8-1):
   (a) Hospitals to which you may bring any emergencies.
   (b) Physician who is your medical advisor.
   (c) Members of your health team who, by previous agreement, may be contacted for emergency purposes.
   (d) Fire department.
   (e) Police department.
   (f) Poison control center.
   (g) Ambulance and/or rescue squad.
   (h) Taxicab.
5. *What should you know about each child in case of an emergency?*
Have an easily accessible emergency file card (Figure 8-2) with the following information for every child (this card does not replace or duplicate the child's cumulative health record).
   (a) Home and business telephone numbers of parents or other person responsible for the child.
   (b) Was written permission obtained for emergency treatment? If not, what arrangements does parent want followed in case of need?
   (c) Name and phone number of child's physician.
   (d) Who will be responsible for payment for medical care?
   (e) What to do in case of emergency due to any special condition, such as diabetic shock or insect sting in allergic children.
   (f) Medication that the child is taking regularly.
   (g) When was the last tetanus injection given?
6. *How would you transport the child to medical help?*
Have a procedure for transporting a child to medical assistance in case of an emergency. This should be posted near the phone. Transportation by ambulance is preferable to private or school vehicle. However, if an ambulance is not used, include the persons who should drive, whose car to use, and who will accompany the driver. Where you will get funds for paying for an ambulance or taxicab should be noted also. There must be appropriate

Emergency File Card

Child's Name: _____
Child's Address: _____
In case of emergency call:

| Name (parent or guardian) | Work/home telephone no. |

| Name (any other person who has parents' permission to care for child in an emergency) | Work home telephone no. |

Written permission on file to give emergency care: yes ____ no ____
Family physician or other source of medical care:

| Name | Telephone no. |

Address
Who is responsible for payment of medical care (insurance or other)

Special medical conditions of the child:
_____
_____
_____

Medication the child takes regularly:
_____

Date of last tetanus injection _____

Source: *E.H. Reinisch and R.E. Minear.*

Figure 8-2

insurance and liability coverage if the preschool staff is involved in transportation of children.

7. *What reports do you file?*
Use an accident report in triplicate for every accident and emergency (Figure 8-3). Fill it out and if the child has to be treated at a medical facility, take on copy along.
Place a copy in the child's cumulative health record folder and give another copy to the preschool director or director of safety. Record every episode of injury, illness, or sign of illness in the cumulative health record. This is very important.

8. What *first aid supplies should be available?*
The following first aid supplies should be on hand:
   Adhesive compresses (bandaids)
   Butterfly bandages, 2, 3, and 4-inch sizes
   Gauze roller bandages, 1, 2, and 3-inches wide
   Sterile gauze pads, 3 inches by 3 inches
   Absorbent gauze
   Triangular bandages
   Scissors, tweezers, tourniquet
   Splints
   Blankets
   Syrup of ipecac
   Liquid green soap
   Stretcher
   Flashlight

Do not keep any first aid supplies or equipment that your staff is not authorized or trained to use. The preparation for first aid should be similar in the child's home.

8.1.2 What General Principles for First Aid Should You Follow?

Although each emergency situation is different, some general rules apply in most cases.

1. Keep calm. When a child is hurt or suddenly ill, you might get upset. You might even panic in a serious emergency. However, remember that you have had first aid training. Do the best you can. Be confident and reassure the child. Fear and panic on your part may worsen the child's condition.

ACCIDENT REPORT FORM
HAPPY NURSERY SCHOOL
SUNNYLAND, U.S.A.

ACCIDENT	1 Number	Date	Time	A.M.	P.M.

INJURED CHILD

2 Name   Age   Male   Female

3 Address

4 Parent or Guardian   Home Phone

5 Place of Employment   Phone

6 Name   Occupation

7 Name   Occupation

ACCIDENT

8 Location

9 Description

10 Person who gave description

11 Person in charge of children at time of accident

PROBABLE INJURY

12   Bruise   Sprain   Cut   Burn   Other

13 Part of: Leg   Foot   Arm   Back   Abdomen
    Body: Ankle   Hand   Elbow   Neck   Chest
                 Knee   Wrist   Shoulder   Head   Other

14 Description of Injury

15 Injured Child's Condition

16 Injured Child's Reaction

FIRST AID

17 Type of First Aid Given _____
18 By Whom _____
19 Child remained at school _____ Was taken to____
20 Who transported child _____ Means of Transportation____

Figure 8-3, p. 1

176 First Aid

PERSONS NOTIFIED OF ACCIDENT	21	
WITNESSES & COMMENTS	22	
PERSON FILLING OUT THIS REPORT	23	
		Signature of director _____
FOLLOWUP REPORT	24	Date: _____ Child's Condition _____ Followup made by phone _____ or _____. Person, his title or position, giving out information. Person making followup: _____

Source: *E.H. Reinisch and R.E. Minear.*
Figure 8-3, p. 2

2. **Find out what the problem is.** Gently question the child and try to find all injuries. If the child is unconscious or does not communicate clearly, ask others and look for clues. Do a systematic, gentle, and careful examination to determine the extent of the injuries.
3. **Plan what has to be done.** Do not leave the child, but enlist the help of other adults and even other children. Make arrangements for medical help if it seems necessary while first aid is being administered.
4. **Attend to the most important things first.** Do not act in haste, you might cause further injury. Handle or move an injured or sick child as little as possible. However, in case of fire, danger of explosion, presence of smoke or poisonous gases, the child has to be removed from danger immediately so that further injury would be prevented.
5. **If the child has to be transported to a medical facility, stay with him all the way to the emergency department.** If someone else has to accompany the child, make sure that they know exactly what happened and they have the accident report form and pertinent medical information (such as any special medical condition like allergy, or the name of child's physician) with them.
6. **Remember that your responsibility is to give first aid only, not to diagnose, not to treat, and not to give any drugs.** Remember to always call the parent when a child is hurt.

There are three emergencies when haste and immediate action is necessary.

1. Stoppage of breathing.
2. Severe bleeding.
3. Poisoning.

The procedure for handling accidents and other emergencies can be summarized as follows:

1. One person and an alternate will be in charge of first aid and safety.
2. At least one person certified in first aid must be present in the preschool at all times.

3. All preschool staff members should be certified in first aid by preemployment or in-service first aid education.
4. It should be determined ahead of time who will be in charge of first aid when an accident occurs.
5. First aid procedures established by the American National Red Cross should be used.
6. Establish a routine procedure in the event of an accident, and although hopefully it may never occur, of a missing child or a fatality.
7. A procedure for first aid in case of an emergency due to special health problems such as diabetes or allergies or insect stings should be established.
8. All necessary first aid supplies and equipment must be available.
9. All telephone numbers that may be required in an emergency and the child's emergency file card should be easily accessible.
10. Arrangements for emergency medical care should be made with a hospital, clinic, or other source of care.
11. Detailed guidelines for arranging transportation from the preschool in case of an emergency must be available and easily accessible.
12. A method for notifying parents and obtaining permission to offer care in case of an emergency must be established.
13. A procedure for action in case of fire, explosion, earthquake, or other disaster must be established.

8.2.0 FIRST AID FOR SPECIFIC CONDITIONS AND INJURIES

Children as well as adults encounter many scratches, bruises, and similar injuries. Even the apparently insignificant injuries or illnesses should receive first aid treatment and should be recorded in the child's cumulative health record. Even after an apparently minor episode the child should be watched for the appearance of any adverse symptoms while still at the preschool and parents should be told about the incident and also advised to watch for any symptoms that might indicate a more severe injury or illness. Some injuries or sudden illnesses do require medical attention and sometimes immediate action is urgent. Preschools as a rule have access to emergency medical care at a hospital, physician's office or health center within a relatively short distance. Transportation by ambulance or rescue squad is also usually available when necessary. Therefore, the first aid recommendations in this book do not include situations when medical care may not be available for a long time or when transporation over a great distance is necessary. Please refer to the *Red Cross Manual* in the following circumstances:

1. For greater detail.
2. For situations when medical care is not readily available.
3. When transportation is necessary over long distances.
4. For situations not covered in this chapter.

8.2.1 Wounds

While in the playground, Carlos is running too close to a chain-link fence. He slips under the fence and his calf is lacerated by the fence. Carlos cries and calls for the teacher, who saw the accident but could not warn Carlos in time.

What would you do? Would you walk with Carlos into the building and wash the wound with soap and water and bandage it? Or would you have Carlos lie down on the playground, take care of the wound there after the first aid kit was brought to you and then would you carry Carlos carefully on a stretcher into the building and have him transported to a hospital? Or, would you do the correct things that the teacher did?

The teacher left the children in charge of another teacher and had a first aid kit, blanket, and stretcher brought to her. She examined the wound; it was bleeding moderately. She held firmly several sterile gauze pads over the wound with her hand and applied a bandage. She then examined Carlos carefully and completely for further injuries. While doing so she talked to Carlos. He stopped crying, he watched what the teacher was doing with interest. In the meantime she called for the staff member in charge of first aid in the preschool. Carlos was placed on a stretcher, brought into the preschool and care for shock was given. The teacher filled out an accident report form and watched Carlos carefully. The director called the parent who would meet Carlos at the hospital and made arrangements for transportation to a hospital emergency room according to the school's policy. The accident form accompanied Carlos to the hospital. A copy of the accident form was placed in

180 First Aid

Carlos' cumulative health record and another copy was given to the preschool's director.

Tina falls on the playground and scrapes her knee. She gets up and comes to the teacher. Upon examination, the teacher finds a superficial abrasion (scraping) of the skin over the knee with dirt in the wound. Tina has no pain while moving the leg and walking.

What would you do? Would you wash the wound with soap and water, apply a disinfectant, and cover with a dressing and bandage? Then would you keep Tina in the preschool facility until her mother picks her up. Or, would you take Tina to the hospital for a tetanus injection after calling her parent? Or would you do what the teacher did? What the teacher did is correct because he was prepared.

The teacher and Tina went into the building. The teacher washed the wound with liquid green soap and rinsed it with water. Then he covered the wound with a sterile gauze pad and bandaged the knee. Tina stayed at school for the rest of the day but did not go outside to play. An accident form was filled out and the parent was told about the incident when she picked up Tina at the end of the day.

Carlos suffered a *laceration*. It is a jagged, irregular tear of soft tissue. Tina, on the other hand, suffered a scraping or *abrasion*, which is a superficial wound. This usually does not bleed much but is likely to get infected. Another type of wound is a cut or *incision* as may happen when injured with a knife or piece of glass. If it is deep, it may not only bleed severely but underlying structures such as tendons, nerves, and ligaments may be damaged. When a child is stabbed with a pencil or other sharp object or steps on a nail, the wound is deep. It is a *puncture wound* and there is danger of developing tetanus and other infection. The tetanus germs grow only in deep wounds. There is no danger of tetanus in an abrasion such as Tina had. Another type of wound is an *avulsion* which is a complete or partial tearing away of tissue. A bite that removes or nearly removes a piece of flesh or a finger detached accidentally by a sharp instrument are examples of avulsion wounds.

Lacerations, abrasions, incisions, punctures, and avulsions are examples of *open wounds*. *Closed wounds* are also frequent in young children. In these cases tissue injury and bleeding occur but the skin is not broken. The child who gets into a fight and has a black eye is a good example of a minor type of closed wound. Potentially serious closed wounds occur if the blow is particularly hard to a sensitive part of the body such as the head, eyes, ears, throat, abdomen, and genitals. For example, a child may get too close to playground equipment and suffer a hard blow to the abdomen. The child is likely to have a bruise but must be carefully watched because she might also suffer shock due to serious injury to an organ within the abdomen.

After any injury, a child may go into shock. This serious condition is discussed later in this chapter. But, since shock may also follow wounds, how to take care of it is always part of the first aid for wounds. Even after incurring simple wounds a child may become stunned or very quiet. The child may look pale, perspire a little, look dazed, or suddenly vomit. Refer to "state of shock" later in this chapter.

First Aid

The intent of first aid is to stop the bleeding, prevent infection, prevent shock, and procure medical care when necessary.

When a wound is not bleeding profusely, cleanse the wound with soap and water. Liquid green soap is easier to use than a cake of soap. Gently blot the wound dry with sterile gauze. Do not use absorbent cotton to cleanse or cover an open wound because cotton fibers adhere to the tissues and are difficult to remove. Cover with

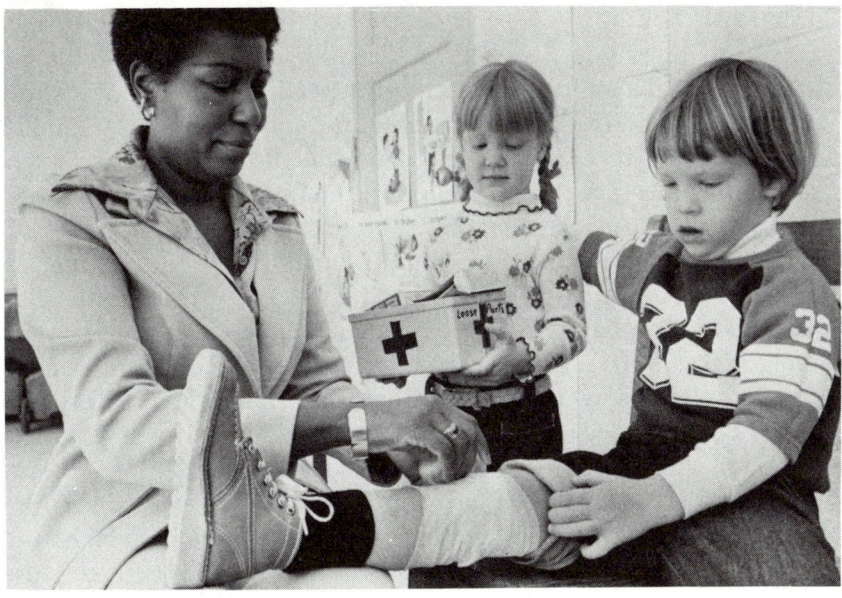

Credit: Marshall R. Hathaway

sterile gauze pads and hold them in place with a bandage. Light pressure applied by the bandage will control the bleeding. Keep the child in a lying down position and elevate the injured part if possible and if movement does not cause further injury or pain. He may stay in the preschool facility and subsequently, depending on his condition, may continue with normal activities.

When a wound is bleeding heavily, place several sterile gauze pads over the wound and apply pressure. If necessary, add more pads but never remove those already applied because it might renew the bleeding. Do not cleanse a profusely bleeding wound. When bleeding has stopped, apply gentle pressure by a bandage and proceed as above.

When a wound is bleeding very severely, do not waste time getting a dressing. This is one of the real emergencies in which a child may bleed to death within minutes if blood loss is severe. Use your bare hand to apply pressure to stop the bleeding. Have someone else get the first aid materials. Apply several pads of sterile gauze or a thick pad of other material if gauze is not available and apply pressure over it with the palm of your hand. If blood soaks through the pads, do not remove them but add more gauze and continue with the pressure of your hand. Elevate the injured part above the level of the child's heart except when the injured part is fractured. Maintain pressure on the wound. If direct pressure and elevation does not stop severe bleeding on the arm or leg then pressure on the supplying artery at a specific pressure point should be used in addition to direct pressure and elevation. It must be emphasized that the use of pressure points should be used only when absolutely necessary and should be maintained only as long as necessary because it stops circulation to the whole limb. Refer to the *Red Cross Manual* for proper use of pressure points. If even this procedure fails to stop severe bleeding then a tourniquet should be used. This is a dangerous procedure and is only used in a critical emergency. Refer again to the *Manual*. In a preschool situation, fortunately, this would be an unlikely occurrence. Medical attention should be obtained as quickly as possible, and care for shock should be given.

On a closed wound that is not serious, such as a bump on the head or a black eye, apply a cold compress to slow down bleeding in the tissues under the skin and to prevent swelling. When ice is used, do not apply it directly to the skin because localized freezing or frostbite might occur. Wrap the ice in a towel or some other material to prevent damage to the skin. In case of a serious closed wound, such as a severe blow to the abdomen, treat for shock, and get medical help.

When should you seek medical care for treatment of a wound? In all of the following instances: a severely bleeding wound, a wound that will require stitches for proper healing, a dirty wound that cannot be cleansed sufficiently by superficial washing, a deep wound where underlying tendons, nerves, or other tissues may be damaged, animal and human bites because of the possibility of infection including rabies in animal bites, a puncture wound because there is danger of tetanus as well as other infection (with possible injury to underlying tissues), a closed wound where underlying tissues may be damaged, and an infected wound. In the case of an infection it usually takes a day or so to show. The area around the wound will become red, swollen, and hot, it may be painful and red streaks may spread from the wound. If a child returns to the preschool facility with an infected wound, the parent should be notified and the wound should be seen by a physician.

8.2.2 Common Injuries to Various Parts of the Body

Head and Neck; Back

Michael fell to the ground from the top bar of the swing. He lay motionless as the teacher ran over to him. He stirred a little and seemed dazed, not quite conscious. What would you do? Would you pick him up and carry him inside? Would you leave him on the ground and get help? Would you be correctly prepared as was the teacher? The teacher stayed with Michael and sent a child to call another staff member. Another teacher took the children inside. What injuries could Michael have? He might have sustained a skull fracture. He might have injured his neck or back in the fall. In that case, moving the child may injure him even more. Without moving Michael's head, the teacher examined his head; there was a lump on the back of it. There was no fluid coming out of the ears or nose and the pupils of his eyes were equal in size. Michael still seemed only semiconscious. The teacher asked the other staff member to call the preschool director, the medical advisor, and then the parent. With the parent's consent, an ambulance was called to take the injured child to the emergency room of a hospital. While awaiting the ambulance's arrival, Michael was carefully observed and covered with a blanket to prevent chilling, which would contribute to shock. An accident report form was filled out.

A blow to the head by some object or as a result of a fall is not an uncommon event among children. The most dangerous result is a skull fracture or neck injury with brain or spinal cord damage.

There may or may not be symptoms immediately. If symptoms or signs of further damage are noticed they may appear slowly and quite some time after the injury occurred.

Any of the following may give you a clue that serious injury occurred: clear or bloody fluid oozing from ear, nose, or mouth; unconsciousness, which may persist, be temporary, or appear only later; headache, dizziness, convulsions; symptoms of shock; unequal size of pupils; speech difficulties; inability to move arms or legs; recurrent vomiting; loss of control over bowel and bladder function.

First Aid

Seek medical attention immediately. If neck or back fracture is suspected, do not move child unless there is danger of fire, explosion, or other serious life-threatening circumstances. Then move the child with greatest caution and according to *Red Cross Manual* directions. If there are breathing difficulties or bleeding, give immediate care for these. Give care for shock. Call an ambulance for transportation to a hospital emergency department. In case of head injury, control any bleeding with gentle direct pressure, bandage and care for shock, keep head and shoulders elevated, and call for proper transportation to an emergency room.

In Michael's case it was obvious that he was hurt and medical attention was needed. However, a blow to the head may not produce any immediate symptoms except perhaps a "lump," purplish discoloration, or swelling. It is possible that the blow causes slow bleeding inside the skull. In that situation only hours later various symptoms may appear such as headache, dizziness, drowsiness, blurred vision, vomiting, unconsciousness. Therefore, it is very important to inform parents whenever a child is hit on the head or hits the head in a fall. They then could watch for delayed symptoms indicating serious injury. It is a good precaution to have a witness when parents are told of the occurrence and even give a description of the event to them in writing.

The Eyes

It is not unusual for young children to have sand or dirt thrown or blown into their eyes. This may be quite painful. It is important for the child not to rub the eyes. Rinse the eyes with plenty of water. To rinse an eye with water place the child's head in such a position that water will flow from the inner (next to the nose) corner of the eye toward the outer one and hold the eyelids open while rinsing. The eye that is being rinsed should be lower than the other eye so that material would not enter the uninjured eye. Small, superficial materials in the eye can usually be removed from the surface of the eye. Immediate care of a physician is required when any object is embedded in the eye, penetrates the eye, or causes a scratch on the surface of the eye. Cover the injured eye gently with a dressing and hold it in place by a bandage. Whenever possible bandage both eyes because this will reduce movement of the eyeballs and reduce irritation. Take care not to put any pressure on the eye and seek immediate medical care.

If any harmful chemicals should enter the eye, immediately flush the eye with running water and continue to do so for 15 minutes. Time is very important; the sooner the chemical is diluted and removed the less damage will occur. Refer to chemical burns later in this chapter.

The Ears

Although the presence of a foreign object in the ear canal may not always cause injury, it may cause discomfort, pain, and may be the reason for an unexplained hearing impairment or earache (Chapter 6). Advise the child not to blow her nose forcibly or probe in the ear with the finger. If an object is discovered in the ear canal, unless very easily removed, medical attention will be required.

Discharge of fluid from the ear may follow a blow on the head and may be due to a skull fracture. Do not try to stop the flow. Administer first aid for suspected skull fracture as discussed above. In the absence of a suspected skull fracture discharge from the ear may be due to a ruptured eardrum caused by a middle ear infection or other conditions. In this case a small piece of gauze may be inserted loosely into the outer ear canal until medical attention is obtained.

The Nose

A nosebleed is not an uncommon occurrence in children. It may be caused by an injury such as a blow to the nose, a foreign object stuffed into the nose, by a disease such as a cold or a blood disease, by strenuous activity, dryness of atmosphere, or other factors. The nosebleed may frighten the child. Calmly have the child sit in a chair with the head forward to prevent aspiration or swallowing of the blood and nausea. Then press the bleeding nostril toward the midline or compress the nose with your index finger and thumb while the child is asked to breathe through the mouth. A cold compress may be placed over the child's nose and face. If the bleeding does not stop, a small piece of gauze can be inserted into the nostril and pressure applied as above. A piece of the gauze must be left protruding to allow removal later. If the bleeding still continues, seek medical help.

The Abdomen

Blows to a child's abdomen may result from accidents discussed earlier or from fights with other children. Whatever the cause, have the injured child rest on his back. Place a pillow gently and carefully under the knees to relax the muscles of the abdomen if it does not cause pain or discomfort. Administer care to prevent shock or to alleviate it if it occurs.

The Genital Organs

Kicks, blows, falling toilet seats, zippers and straddling accidents are some causes for injury to a child's genital organs. These injuries may cause a great deal of anxiety, much pain, swelling, and bleeding. Pressure should be applied to stop the bleeding. Use a cold compress to slow down swelling and have the child rest. Seek medical care when the injury is serious.

The Hand

Cuts, bruises, tears, punctures, and crushing blows are potentially serious injuries. Severe infection, or loss of a finger may cause impaired function in the future. The most important thing is to elevate the hand above the level of the heart while applying pressure to stop bleeding. If the injury is serious, get medical care as soon as possible. Cover the injured hand or finger with a sterile dressing, bandage it, and keep it elevated on a pillow or in a sling on the way to medical care.

8.2.3 State of Shock

Peter falls down a flight of stairs on the way to the preschool facility. He gets up, he cries, he is frightened but recovers shortly. His mother knew he fell down some steps but she did not get alarmed because nothing seemed to be broken. She was also reassured by Peter's quick recovery. As his mother leaves him at school, he complains about pain in the abdomen, he is very pale, his skin is cool, his hands sweat. The teacher lays him down on a cot. Peter is cold, he is shivering. The teacher feels his pulse. It is weak and fast. She covers him with a blanket and raises his feet a few inches by sliding a folded blanket under them. Peter says he is thirsty. He seems listless and reacts slowly when asked how he feels. The teacher tells the parent and consults the medical advisor by phone and is instructed to take Peter to the emergency department of the hospital. He evidently is suffering from shock caused by an injury resulting from the fall.

Shock is a very serious condition that can be fatal. It can be caused by an injury, especially burns, poisoning, fractures, and hemorrhage. The shock caused by injury is not to be confused with electrical shock or diabetic shock. Even though an injury may not seem serious in itself, the shock that may follow could be very dangerous. A person going into shock will have:

1. Pale or cyanotic face, in black people mucous membranes and lips are pale.
2. Cold and clammy skin.
3. Weak and rapid pulse.
4. Breathing that may be irregular.
5. Chills, thirst, and nausea.
6. Some degree of restlessness and anxiety.

First Aid

1. Keep the child lying down flat. Raise the feet 8 to 12 inches except when it might interfere with an injury. In case of nausea or unconsciousness turn head to the side.
2. Place a blanket under as well as over the child to keep him warm but not hot.
3. If the child is thirsty, moisten his lips. Do not give fluids if the child is nauseated, unconscious, has convulsions, has abdominal or head injuries, if the child may require

surgery, or if the ambulance will arrive in less than an hour.
4. Procure medical care as soon as possible.
5. Reassure and encourage the child.

8.2.4 Sprains, Broken Bones, Dislocations

Children are physically very active and it is not surprising that injuries to bones and joints do occur. Falling off a swing or other outdoor equipment, jumping off steps or chairs, twisting a limb while playing, being hit, and getting pushed are all activities that may cause a sprain, dislocation, or a broken bone. When a child is hurt, it is not important to know if the injury is a sprain,, break, or dislocation. What is important is to recognize that there is an injury, administer first aid, which includes immobilization, and decide if medical care is needed. Whenever in doubt if an injury is a sprain, dislocation, or fracture, suspect a fracture and handle it as such, with greatest care.

A *sprain* is an injury to tissue around a joint due to a movement beyond the normal limits of the joint; for example, twisting or excessive bending. When the end of a bone at a joint is pushed out of its normal position, the bone is *dislocated.* A *fracture* is a break in the bone. It might be only a crack, the two ends at the break might be pushed apart, or the bone could be broken in several places. When the ends of the bone are separated they could pierce through the skin.

Signs and symptoms for the three injuries are very similar or identical at times. Do not expect to be able to determine the type of injury. An X ray examination will do that. There will be pain especially when trying to move. But do not move or ask the child to move the injured part when a fracture is suspected. In addition, there might be swelling and discoloration of the skin; this usually appears later. When there is a dislocation, the joint will be deformed, that is, it will have an unusual shape. Compare it with the same joint on the other limb. When there is a fracture, the bone may be deformed at the place of the break. Give care for shock because it is often associated with fractures.

Susan jumped off the jungle gym and landed on her right arm and shoulder. She got up and as she started to walk toward the teacher, she was bent forward slightly. She held her right arm across the chest and supported it with her left arm. She complained of pain.

First Aid for Specific Conditions and Injuries

When questioned where it hurt, she motioned with her head toward the right shoulder region. She continued to hold her right arm. The teacher helped her sit down on a nearby bench and ran her fingers gently along the right collarbone from the shoulder toward the neck; part way down it really hurt. Susan cried when the bone was touched where there was a slight swelling. A fracture of the collarbone was suspected because of the way the child supported her arm and because of the location of the pain. The arm was supported by a sling and held in place by a tie around the chest. The usual arrangements were made for further medical care.

James was holding on to his mother's hand while he came up the steps to the preschool entrance. James stumbled and his mother kept him from falling by holding onto him by his hand. He was lifted by his hand to the next step where he continued up the remainder of the steps with his mother. Inside, James cried when his coat was removed by one of the preschool workers. Later, it was noted that he refused to bend his left arm and began to frown when he was required to use both arms in the usual activities that morning. He was found to have tenderness and pain at the left elbow. James was taken to his physician and his mother was told James had a dislocation of the head of the left radius, which is a bone in the forearm. The doctor explained that "pulled elbow" was common when a child is lifted or pulled by the hand or lower arm. The child should always be lifted by grasping him around the waist or under both arms.

First Aid

When an injury to a bone or a joint is suspected, do not move the child or the injured limb. You should observe the child, ask where it hurts, and examine the limb gently and carefully. Look for swelling and unusual shapes. If there is pain on any movement of the body, the child will usually avoid most activities, including walking. If there is an apparent mild ankle sprain and if the child does not want to walk, make the child lie down first. Then put a cold compress on the limb and elevate it. If pain is still present later, a medical examination is recommended. For example, it could happen that a person will walk on what is suspected to be a sprained ankle, but later is shown by X ray to be a fracture. After examining the injury, immobilize (eliminate movement) the injured limb. Any further movement may cause more injury.

Immobilization (Elimination of Movement) for Bone and Joint Injuries

It is important to prevent a broken or dislocated bone and a sprained joint from moving. Immobilization will prevent further damage; it will diminish pain and reduce the possibility of bringing on shock. Immobilization is accomplished by the use of splints. However, in some instances, such as that of a broken collar bone or shoulder, a sling and bandages are used. A splint is a piece of stiff material that is tied to the suspected fractured part. It must be long enough to reach beyond the joints on either side of the injury. The joints on either side of the suspected break must be immobilized so that the injured part may not be moved by the child or during transportation. The splint should be padded to prevent pressure damage to the skin and underlying tissues, to provide comfort, to conform to the injured part, and to give more support. It should be tied securely but without obstructing circulation both above and below the suspected fracture, and near the joints above and below the fracture. Splints may be made from pieces of wood, or improvised from rolled blankets, magazines, newspapers, or other objects. See Figure 8-4 for an example of immobilization of the lower leg. Refer to the *Red Cross Manual*, Chapter 14 on immobilization.

Fracture of the Collarbone

This type of fracture is not uncommon in children. It is relatively easy to recognize because of the pain in the region of the collarbone. The shoulder level will be lower in comparison with the uninjured side. The child will usually try to support the arm on the side of the break with the uninjured arm. This tends to reduce the pain. See Figure 8-5, for immobilization of broken collarbone.

Suspected Fracture of the Neck or Back

A fracture of the neck or back is extremely dangerous because the slightest movement may cause an injury to the spinal cord or the nerves coming from it. If such an injury is suspected, do not move the child. You must get immediate help, call a physician and an ambulance crew. Refer to the *Red Cross Manual*.

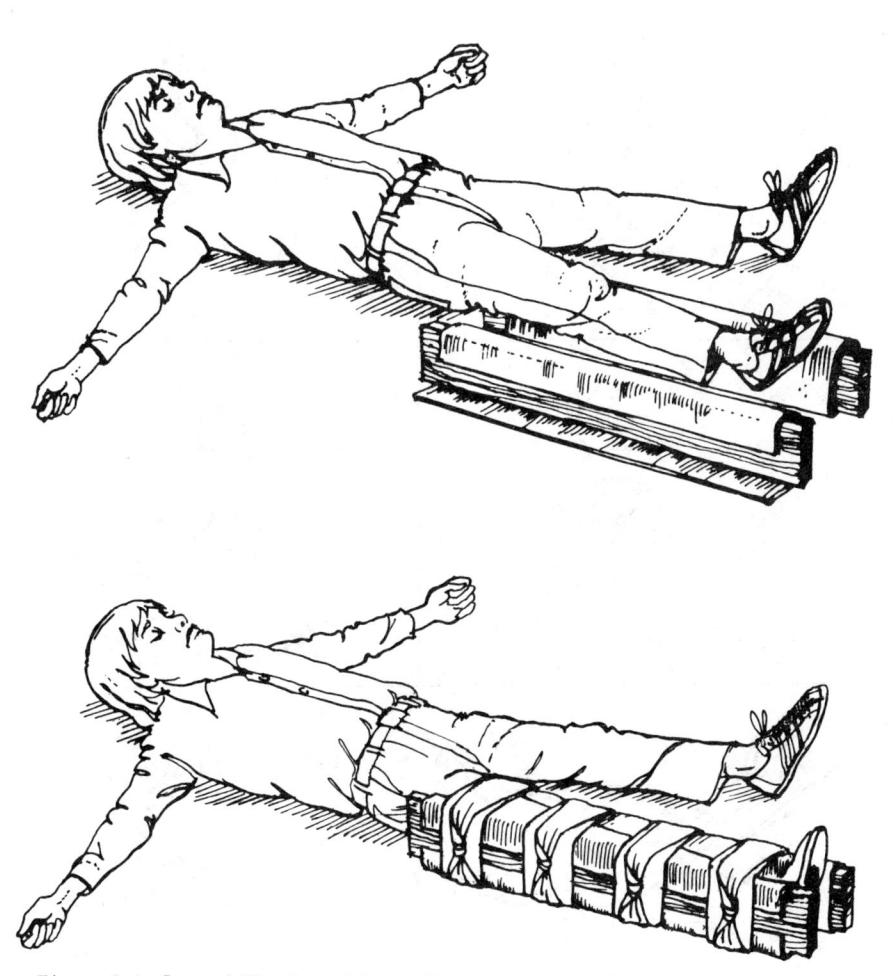

First Aid for Specific Conditions and Injuries 191

Figure 8-4 Immobilization of lower leg.

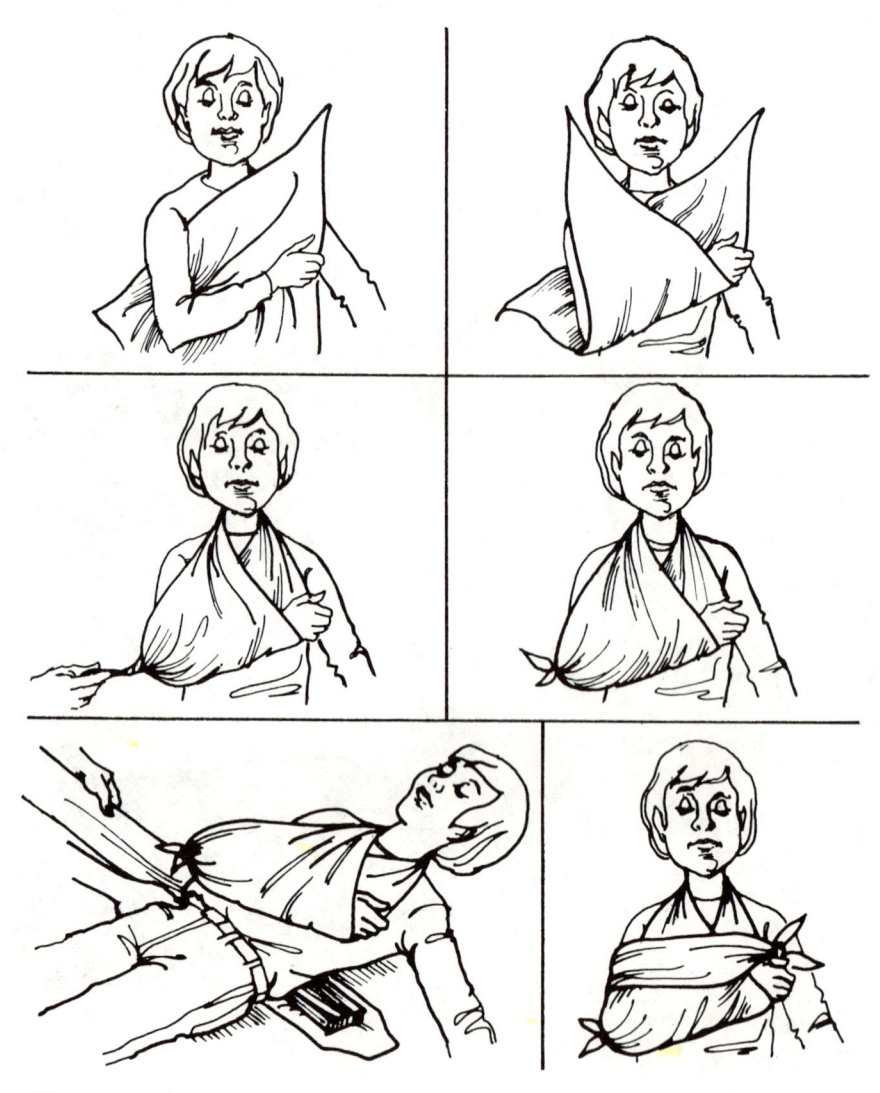

Figure 8-5 Immobilization of collarbone.

8.2.5 Burns

Burns can be caused by heat, chemicals, and electric current.

Heat Burns

Children might be exposed to open fire, scalding liquids, or touch a very hot object. Burns may be very dangerous. If 10 percent or more of a child's body surface is burned or in the case of any third-degree burns, medical treatment is *mandatory*. Remember that a child's body surface is much smaller than that of an adult and a small burn is more dangerous to a child than to an adult. For example the surface area of a child of 20 pounds is 0.4 square meters while that of a person weighing 132 pounds is 1.7 square meters. A first-degree burn causes redness, swelling, and pain. A second-degree burn is deeper, has an uneven, mottled, or red appearance and later blisters will form. If the top layer of the flesh is gone then the surface may appear shiny. This is a more serious level of a second-degree burn. In a third-degree burn tissue will be destroyed and the burned area may be white or charred (black).

If the burn is mild or moderate (first and second-degree) and the skin is not broken, submerge the burned part in cold water. If this is not possible, apply a cold, clean, wet cloth. When pain eases, dry very gently and cover with a sterile dressing. Use no ointment, antiseptic, or any other medication. Elevate the burned part.

If the burn is severe (a more serious second-degree burn, in which the skin is broken, and a third-degree burn), do not chill or submerge the child in cold water because you may hasten shock. Cover the burned areas with thick, dry, sterile dressing; then, if needed, with cold, dry applications. Elevate if possible. Do not touch the burned area; use no ointments or antiseptics. Treat for shock and arrange for immediate transportation to an emergency department of a hospital.

If the child's clothes are on fire, stop the child from running, force the child down on the floor and smother the flames by rolling the child in a blanket, coat, or on the ground. If the child has been scalded, take off any clothes that have been soaked with the hot liquid or pour cold water on it, whichever is faster. Proceed with first aid as described above.

Chemical Burns

If a chemical is spilled on a child's skin, remove any clothing that has the chemical on it. Wash the skin immediately with running water for at least 5 minutes and seek medical help. If a chemical comes in contact with a child's eyes, rinse immediately with running water for at least 15 minutes. Turn the child's head to one side and flush in the direction away from the corner of the eye next to the nose. Alkaline chemicals, such as drain cleaner or strong cleaning preparations, are especially dangerous. Rinse for 15 minutes. Any pieces of the chemical on the surface of the eye should be gently removed if flushing does not do it. After the rinsing bandage both eyes and seek medical aid promptly.

8.2.6 Electrical Injuries

Children might come in contact with electrical current in several ways. They could push a metal object like a hairpin into an electric outlet. They might touch a damaged electric cord that is attached to a functioning light fixture or other electrical appliance. They could chew on an electrical wire that contains live electrical current. The electric current might cause a burn, unconsciousness, stoppage of breathing and heartbeat, or it might be fatal.

First Aid

The most important thing is to break the contact between the child and the electrical current. If possible, the plug or connector to the electrical source should be pulled out of the socket; if this is impossible disconnect the main electrical switch. If the current cannot be disconnected, pull the child away. To do this you must use a very long dry stick, rope, rubber, or cloth. Be certain that your hands are dry, that you stand on dry ground, and that you do not directly touch the child. If breathing has stopped give mouth to mouth/nose respiration at once. If the heartbeat also has stopped, give cardiopulmonary resuscitation. (Refer to the *Red Cross Manual*.) Give first aid for burns. Treat for shock. Get immediate medical care.

8.2.7 Breathing Stoppage

Cessation of breathing is a life-threatening emergency and requires

First Aid for Specific Conditions and Injuries 195

immediate action. You have about four to six minutes or less in which to restore breathing and the heart beat. There will be permanent brain damage if breathing does not begin between four to six minutes after breathing and the heartbeat has stopped. Under these conditions the person will probably not regain consciousness even if breathing is restored.

The cause for stoppage of breathing may be an obstruction in the air passageway. Such blockage could be caused by a foreign object that was swallowed or blood and secretions that collect from an injury to the face or throat. There may be swelling that is due to damage after the swallowing of a corrosive substance. Constriction as in croup (Chapter 6) or acute asthma also may cause breathing to stop. Breathing may be suspended for many other reasons. For example, it may be due to lack of oxygen in the air as in gas poisoning, a plastic bag may have been pulled over the head, a child may have been locked in a refrigerator, or it may be due to electric shock, poisoning, or drowning. Whatever the reason, immediate action is necessary. A child who has stopped breathing will be unconscious; there will be no movements of the chest or stomach in order to bring air in and out of the chest; the lips will become blue; the pupils will dilate.

First Aid

Have someone else call for a physician or ambulance while you immediately give first aid.

Artificial respiration is breathing for a person who cannot breath for himself. When a child stops breathing, start artificial respiration immediately. Use the mouth-to-mouth method (see below). For small children when your mouth can cover the child's mouth and nose, the mouth-to-nose methods should be used (see below). If there is an injury to the face, a different method may have to be used. In this case, refer to the *Red Cross Manual.*

Artificial respiration should be continued until the child resumes breathing or until care is taken over by medical personnel. If the child is transported by ambulance, she should be given continuous artificial respiration even while being transferred to a stretcher.

Treat for shock and get medical care as soon as possible even if breathing has been restored.

Mouth-to-Mouth Method of Artificial Respiration

Step 1. Lay the child on his back on a firm surface. Kneel next to the head. Establish if the child is really unresponsive and not just in a deep sleep by shaking the child gently and speaking very loudly.

Step 2. Gently tilt the head back by placing one hand under the neck close to the head and raise the neck slightly. Place your other hand on the child's forehead and keep the head in this position (Figure 8-6). At this time check if there is any spontaneous breathing. Put your ear close to the child's mouth, look if the chest or abdomen rise and fall, and listen and feel if any air is being exhaled. Do this for approximately five seconds.

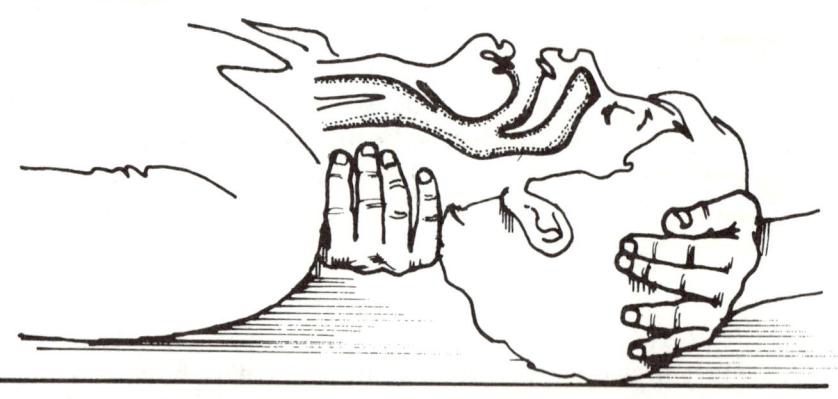

Figure 8-6 Tilt head back.

Step 3. Take a breath, open your mouth and place it firmly over the child's mouth to form a tight seal. Pinch the nostrils with the hand that was placed on the child's forehead or you can seal the nostrils by leaning against them with your cheek. Blow in four breaths in quick succession without waiting for the air to come out of the lungs between the breaths.

Step 4. Blow air gently into the mouth. Watch the child's chest rise and stop blowing. Lift your head, turn it to the side and listen to the air being exhaled.

Step 5. Step 4 should be repeated 16 to 18 times a minute which means one breath every 3 to 4 seconds. You may ask someone else to time you to help you keep the proper rate of artificial respiration.

First Aid for Specific Conditions and Injuries 197

Step 6. Once the child takes a breath again, stop the artificial respiration but watch if she continues to breathe. The child may breathe for awhile and stop again. Resume artificial respiration immediately should breathing stop.

Step 7. Be alert to some of the reasons why you may fail to get quick or good results with artificial respiration: improper head tilt, failure to pinch the nose, incomplete seal around the mouth, foreign body obstruction of the airway.

Mouth-to-Mouth-and-Nose Method of Artificial Respiration
If the child is small, you may use the mouth-to-mouth-and-nose method. Follow all the steps given for mouth-to-mouth respiration but substitute the following procedure for step 3.

Keep the child's head tilted back and keep one hand on the child's forehead. Place your mouth over both the mouth and the nose. Blow only air from your cheeks gently into the nose and mouth like blowing out a candle. Watch the child's chest rise.

8.2.8 Other Emergencies

Fainting
This condition is partial or complete loss of consciousness and is caused by a temporary reduced blood supply to the brain. This may happen either very suddenly (without warning signs) or there may be some clues. One may suspect that a child is going to faint because of appearance. Some indications are paleness, sweating, dizziness, or vomiting.

First Aid
If fainting is sudden, the child will fall. Try to aid the falling child to prevent harm from the fall. Leave him lying down. Turn the child's head to the side so that he does not choke on or aspirate vomitus. Loosen any tight clothing and check if the child injured himself when he fell. Do not administer any liquids. Usually the child will regain consciousness within a short time. Then keep the child separated from the other children, so that he may rest and you may observe the child. Fainting spells should be recorded; parents and medical advisor should be notified. The cause of the fainting might be a serious illness. If the child does not regain consciousness, watch his breathing, check for clues for poisoning (see next section),

and get the child to medical care. When you suspect that a child is about to faint, have him sit and bend the head down between the knees, or lay the child down flat and proceed to loosen his clothing, protect the child's airway from being blocked and provide assistance should the child become unconscious.

Convulsions

A child who has convulsions will become unconscious, and have jerky movements of the body due to alternate muscle contraction and relaxation that cannot be stopped. The onset is usually sudden; the body will become rigid before the convulsions appear. During the convulsion, the child may soil her pants with urine and feces. The causes of convulsions are many and varied. They may be due to poisoning, epilepsy, brain damage, food poisoning, reaction to medication, drug intake or they may occur during any infectious disease when high fever is present. An infection of the nervous system (meningitis) may be a cause of convulsions also.

First Aid

First aid consists of preventing children from hurting themselves during convulsions. Keep the child lying down. Clear away any object that may be nearby so she will not hit herself. The child might bite her tongue during a convulsion. A padded tongue depressor or similar object may be placed between the teeth if it is easily inserted. However, if force is necessary, do not attempt it because instead of being helped the child might be injured. Do not give any fluids; do not hold the child down or restrain him; do not throw water on him. After the convulsions stop, let the child rest; usually she will go to sleep. The child will have no memory of the events during the convulsion. Notify the parent when a child has a convulsion.

Choking

Choking due to objects that have been swallowed occurs in young children, especially those under the age of four. They may swallow wads of paper, beads, parts of toys, buttons, pencil erasers, and improperly chewed food. The object may permit limited breathing or obstruct the air passage completely because of its size or shape.

Suspect a foreign object in the air passage if the child is choking, forcefully coughing, and wheezing in between coughs

First Aid for Specific Conditions and Injuries 199

when breathing in, or may be coughing only weakly and making wheezing sounds when trying to breathe in. The above signs occur in partial airway obstruction. If the air passage is obstructed completely the child will not be able to speak or breathe and if not relieved of the obstruction will turn blue and become unconscious.

First Aid

If the child is coughing and successfully breathing, encourage the child in his effort and do not interfere. First aid procedures should be started only when the child has extreme difficulty in breathing. Then proper action is urgent.

When the child is conscious and complete obstruction of the airway is recognized because she will not be able to speak, cough, or breathe, as described above, start the following sequence of procedures:

1. *Back Blows.* Bend the child face down over your forearm. In rapid succession strike the child between the shoulder blades four times with hard blows with the heel of your hand. The head must be level with or preferably lower than the chest. If the back blows are not successful in bringing up the foreign object proceed with the following procedure.

2. *Abdominal Thrust.* With the child in a standing or sitting position, stand behind her and place your arms around her waist. Place the thumb side of the fist on her abdomen slightly above the navel and below the rib cage. With the other hand grab the fist and press into the abdomen with a quick upward push four times. If the child is small and the rescuer large perform a one-handed thrust using the fist only, to prevent injury. The abdominal thrust technique is shown in Figure 8-7. After the foreign object has been dislodged perform artificial respiration if breathing is not resumed. If the foreign object was not dislodged repeat the back blows and the abdominal thrust.

If the child is unconscious have someone call for medical help and immediately proceed with the mouth-to-mouth method of artificial respiration. If the air you are blowing in is not entering into the child's lungs (you will feel resistance) and you have checked your procedure according to step 7, mouth-to-mouth method, start the following sequence of procedures.

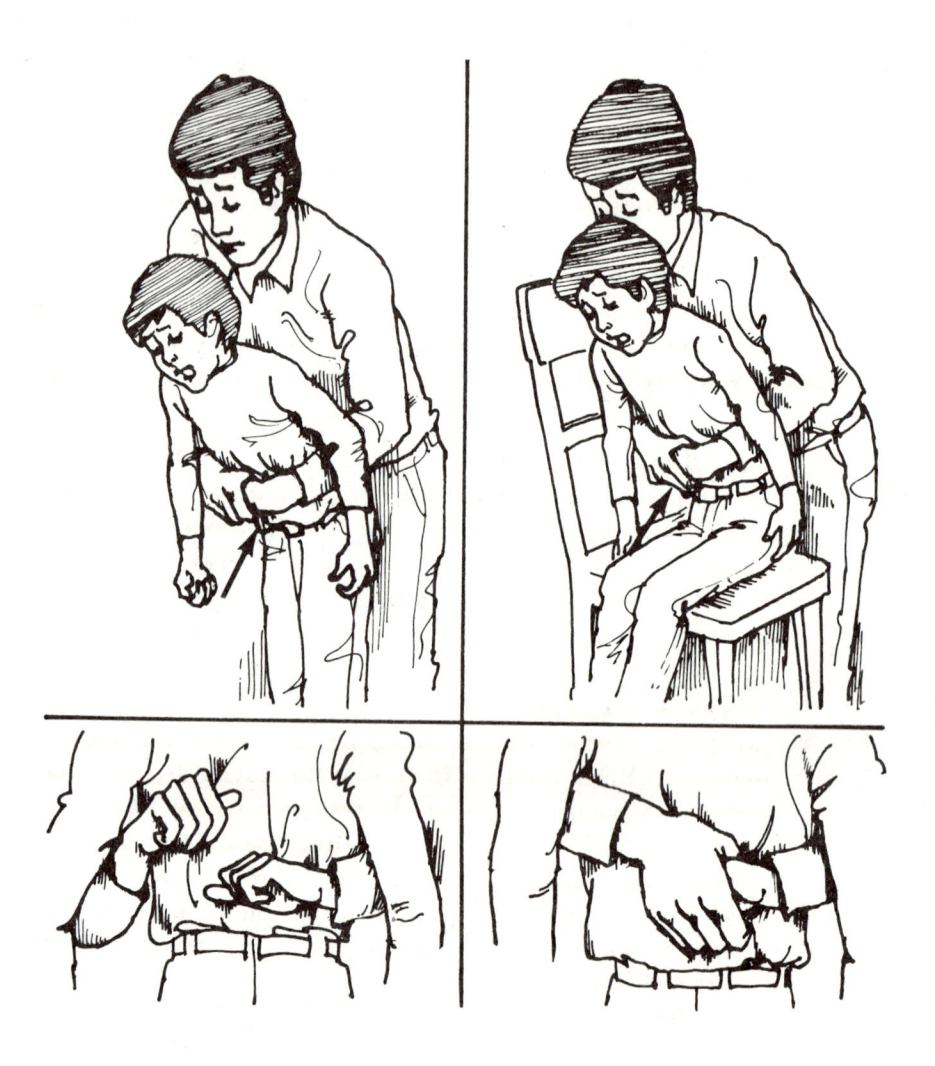

Figure 8-7 Abdominal thrust.

1. *Back Blows.* Kneel next to the child and roll him onto his side facing you with the chest leaning against your knee and thigh. In rapid succession strike the child between the shoulder blades four times with hard blows with the heel of your hand. If the back blows are not successful in bringing up the foreign object use the following procedure.

2. *Abdominal Thrust.* With the child lying on his back kneel next to him and place the heel of one hand on his abdomen slightly above the navel and below the rib cage. If the child is small or the rescuer is large, perform a single-handed thrust because a two-handed thrust might cause injury. With the one hand placed on the abdomen as described above push into the abdomen with a quick upward motion toward the chest four times. In the two-handed thrust, the other hand is placed on top of the hand on the abdomen and the quick upward motion is done with both hands. If this procedure does not dislodge the foreign object repeat back blows and abdominal thrust procedures. A manual removal of the foreign object may not be possible in the small mouth of a young child. But continue with your efforts. The muscles will relax as the child becomes more deprived of oxygen and the procedures that were previously unsuccessful may become successful.

Whenever a child recovers after having received artificial respiration, cardiopulmonary resuscitation, or first aid for removal of a foreign body obstruction of the airway, he must receive medical attention and be carefully watched.

Demonstrating the abdominal thrust on a person may cause serious internal injuries. Therefore, only show positioning of the hands without performing the actual thrust when you teach or practice it.

Emergencies Due to Diabetes

If one of the children in your preschool has diabetes, it is essential that you have a conference with both the parents and child at the time of admission. At this time, ascertain that either a parent or the physician can be reached in case of emergency. Information about the child and the diabetes usually is best obtained from the parents since they know how their child reacts during a crisis of either extreme, high or low blood sugar. No two children manifest the signs and symptoms of high or low sugar exactly the same way.

Diabetes is rare in the very young child, but it does happen.

In this disease, the body is unable to metabolize ingested carbohydrates properly. There is a deficiency of insulin, a substance secreted by a gland in the abdomen, the pancreas. The young child is almost always required to take insulin injections. A medical regime of insulin, diet, and a predictable, consistent pattern of exercise is set up and should be followed as closely as possible. This should take into consideration the educational and social needs of the child and should be planned to allow the child participation in all activities whenever possible. When the disease is successfully managed, the child with diabetes can have a full, productive and happy life. However, emergency situations can arise and anyone who spends time with the child should be aware of the indications of trouble and be able to take appropriate action.

First aid
Insulin or Hypoglycemic (Low Blood Sugar) Reaction
This is sometimes referred to as insulin shock. The signs and symptoms are caused by either a very rapid drop in blood sugar level or a drop to a very low level. This is due to either too much insulin, not enough food, delayed eating time, or an unusual amount of physical activity.

The insulin reaction occurs suddenly—over a short period of time, even minutes. It is most likely to occur before lunch if the child is on a quick acting insulin, or in midafternoon if on the intermediate type. Ascertain from the parents when the child is most likely to run into trouble. The child may feel weak, be pale and sweaty, complain of a headache, blurred vision, hunger, trembling, or feeling "strange." If the child shows sudden drowsiness, inability to concentrate, wandering attention span, or sudden, dramatic behavior change, consider low blood sugar as the cause for the abnormal behavior. Not all these signs and symptoms occur in any given child. *Immediately* give something sweet. *Do not delay* as the hypoglycemic reaction can progress to unconsciousness or convulsions. You will not harm the child if she is *not* in insulin reaction. Give anything sweet (sweetened juice, regular soda, hard candy, jelly beans, Coke or Karo syrup), but not chocolate as it slows down the rate of absorption. Stay with the child while she ingests what is administered. Follow this with a light snack such as milk and crackers, peanut butter, and crackers with milk, plain cookies and milk. She should be much better in 5 to 15 minutes. If the child is semiconscious or choking, *do not force anything by mouth*. Take the child immediately to the nurse, if there is one in your preschool, or to another source of medical care. Let the parent know of the problem (time, duration, and severity, for example). Do *not* routinely send the child home from school. In most cases, after a short rest, the child will continue his daily activities.

One word of caution concerning naps. If nap time comes before meals, snacks, or after exercise, check the child frequently during sleep. If he is extremely difficult to arouse, he may have unrecognized low blood sugar and it should be treated promptly.

The other acute emergency for the diabetic child is *hyperglycemia (high blood sugar) or ketoacidosis*. It develops very gradually. You may notice a great increase in thirst, hunger, and frequent need to urinate, lethargy, or apparent illness. Ketoacidosis can be particularly precipitated by vomiting, missed insulin injection, improper diet, fever, infection (particularly flu), or severe emotional stress. Keep the child warm, resting, and give unsweetened fluids if he is conscious and not vomiting, get prompt medical help and notify the parent.

The American Diabetes Association has published informative material for school personnel and for babysitters (Figure 8-8 and 8-9).

Frostbite

It is unlikely that you will encounter frostbite in a preschool situation. However, on a very cold day, children might arrive at the preschool with a frostbitten finger, ear, cheek, or other part of the body. When the child comes in, you may notice that the frostbitten part is very pale, almost white; it looks as though made of wax. The child may not feel anything; he may not even know he has frostbite or he may have pain in the frostbitten part.

First Aid

Bring the child into a warm room and if possible, submerge the frostbitten part in a basin of warm, not hot water. First, test the water by placing some of it on your skin just above the wrist on the forearm. It should feel warm, not hot. Then rapidly increase the temperature to between 102° and 105°F if tolerated by the child.

WHAT SCHOOL PERSONNEL SHOULD KNOW ABOUT THE STUDENT WITH DIABETES

Prepared by American Diabetes Association, Committee on Diabetes in Youth
Endorsed by the National Education Association, Department of School Nurses

GENERAL INFORMATION

All school personnel (teachers, nurses, principal, lunchroom workers, playground and hall supervisors, bus drivers, counselors, etc.) *must* be informed that a student has diabetes. It is imperative all personnel understand the fundamentals of the disease and its care.

Diabetes is NOT an infectious disease. It results from failure of the pancreas to make a sufficient amount of insulin. Without insulin food cannot be used properly. Diabetes currently cannot be cured but can be controlled. Treatment consists of daily injections of insulin and a prescribed food plan. Children with diabetes can participate in all school activities and should not be considered different from other students. It is essential school personnel have conferences with parents early in each school year to obtain more specific information about the individual child and his specific needs. Communication and cooperation between parents and school personnel can help the diabetic child have a happy and well adjusted school experience.

INSULIN REACTIONS

Insulin reactions occur when the amount of sugar in the blood is too low. This is caused by an imbalance of insulin, too much exercise, or too little food. Under these circumstances the body sends out numerous warning signs. If these signs are recognized early, reactions may be promptly terminated by giving some form of sugar. If a reaction is not treated, unconsciousness and convulsions may result. The child may recognize many of the following warning signs of low blood sugar and should be encouraged to report them.

WARNING SIGNS OF INSULIN REACTIONS

Excessive Hunger	Blurred Vision	Poor Coordination
Perspiration	Irritability	Abdominal Pain
Pallor	Crying	or Nausea
Headache	Confusion	Inappropriate
Dizziness	Inability to Concentrate	Actions/Responses
Nervousness or Trembling	Drowsiness or Fatigue	

TREATMENT

At the first sign of any of the above warning signs:

Give sugar immediately in one of the following forms:

   a. Sugar—5 small cubes, 2 packets, or 2 teaspoons
   b. Fruit juice—1/2 to 2/3's cup
   c. Carbonated beverage—*(Not diet or sugarless soda pop)*—6 ounces
   d. Candy—1/4 to 1/3 candy bar

The student experiencing a reaction may need coaxing to eat. If improvement does not occur within 15-20 minutes, repeat the feeding. If the child does not improve after administration of the second feeding containing sugar, the parents or physician should be called. When the child improves, he should be given a small feeding of 1/2 sandwich and a glass of milk. He should then resume normal school activities and the parents advised of the incident.

(over)

Figure 8-8, p. 1

First Aid for Specific Conditions and Injuries 205

DIET — Children with diabetes follow a prescribed diet and may select their foods from the school lunch menu or bring their own lunch. Lunchroom managers should be made aware of the child's dietary needs, which may include midmorning and midafternoon snacks to help avoid insulin reactions. Adequate time should be provided for finishing meals.

URINE TESTING — The amount of sugar in the urine of a child with diabetes reflects the level of sugar in the blood. Testing the urine for sugar several times a day serves as an effective guide to proper diabetes control. Urine tests for sugar should be made before meals, and time should be allowed before lunch for the diabetic child to perform this test if requested.

GENERAL ADVICE — The child with diabetes should be carefully observed in class, particularly before lunch. It is best not to schedule physical education just before lunch; and if possible the child should not be assigned to a late lunch period. Many children require nourishment before strenuous exercise. Teachers and nurses should have sugar available at all times. The child with diabetes should also carry a sugar supply and be permitted to treat a reaction when it occurs.

Diabetic coma, a serious complication of the disease, results from uncontrolled diabetes. This does *NOT* come on suddenly and generally need not be a concern to school personnel.

THE FOLLOWING INFORMATION SHOULD BE OBTAINED FROM PARENTS WHEN CONFERENCE IS HELD AT THE BEGINNING OF THE SCHOOL TERM.

Child's Name _____ Date _____

Parent's Name _____ Address _____ Phone _____

Alternate person to call in emergency _____ Relationship _____ Phone _____

Physician's Name _____ Address _____ Phone _____

Signs and symptoms the child usually exhibits preceding insulin reaction: _____

Time of day reaction most likely to occur: _____
Most effective treatment (sweets most readily accepted): _____
Kind of morning or afternoon snack: _____

Suggested "treats" for in-school parties: _____

SUBSTITUTE AND/OR SPECIAL TEACHERS SHOULD HAVE ACCESS TO THE ABOVE INFORMATION.

This material may be reprinted for the child's cumulative school record. For additional information or copies of this card, contact: American Diabetes Association, 1 West 48th Street, New York, New York 10020

Figure 8-8, p. 2

A child with diabetes checks his urine during the day to find out about his sugar level. There are various methods to use. The parents will show you the method they use.

NOTES FOR TODAY:

Test urine at:

_____   _____   _____

and record below:

_____   _____   _____

Snacks or meals:
Serve _____

_____
_____ at _____ o'clock

Serve _____

_____
_____ at _____ o'clock

Serve _____

_____
_____ at _____ o'clock

Parents are at:
_____ Phone _____

Physician:
_____ Phone _____

▲ American Diabetes Association, Inc.

Figure 8-8, p. 3

First Aid for Specific Conditions and Injuries **207**

To the Babysitter:

_____ has diabetes.

Diabetes means that this child's pancreas does not make enough insulin. Without insulin, food cannot be used properly. A child with diabetes must take daily injections of insulin and must balance his food and exercise.

An insulin reaction may occur if the blood sugar gets too low—especially before meals or after exercise.

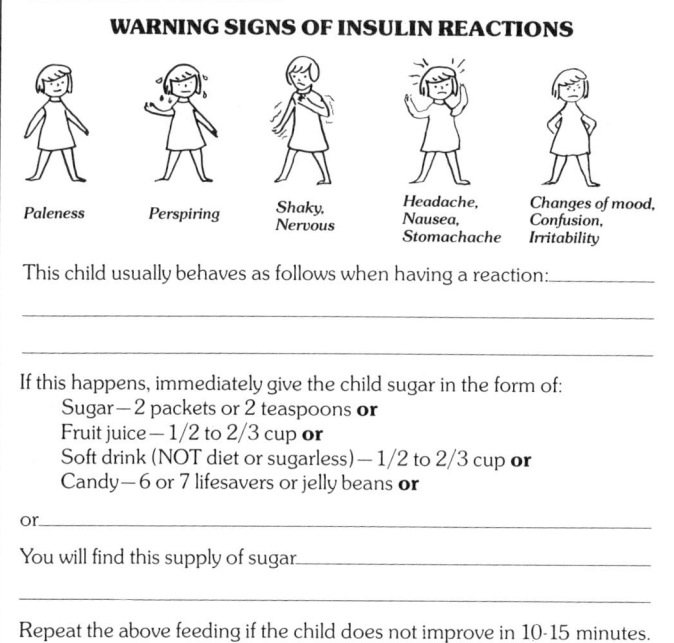

WARNING SIGNS OF INSULIN REACTIONS

| Paleness | Perspiring | Shaky, Nervous | Headache, Nausea, Stomachache | Changes of mood, Confusion, Irritability |

This child usually behaves as follows when having a reaction: _____
_____

If this happens, immediately give the child sugar in the form of:
- Sugar—2 packets or 2 teaspoons **or**
- Fruit juice—1/2 to 2/3 cup **or**
- Soft drink (NOT diet or sugarless)—1/2 to 2/3 cup **or**
- Candy—6 or 7 lifesavers or jelly beans **or**

or_____

You will find this supply of sugar_____
_____

Repeat the above feeding if the child does not improve in 10-15 minutes.

Follow with a milk and cookie or sandwich snack.

If the child does not improve after eating the snack, the parents or physician should be called.

Figure 8-9

Maintain that temperature by carefully adding warm water. If the frostbitten part cannot be immersed in water (a cheek or nose, for example) cover it gently with a warm cloth or hold your hand over it to warm it. Do not apply pressure. As soon as the skin of the frostbitten part appears flushed discontine the warming procedures. If the part was immersed in water, blot it gently dry with sterile material or a clean cloth. Do not apply additional heat. Handle the frostbitten part gently, do not rub or massage it. Tell the parent about the frostbite and seek medical advice when necessary.

Insect Stings

Usually insect stings cause only slight discomfort that can be relieved by application of cold cloths or a soothing lotion to the site of the sting.

On rare occasions, stings from bees, wasps, and ants may cause a severe reaction and even death. The signs and symptoms of such a reaction may include marked swelling at the site of the sting, sweating, nausea, shock, and difficulty in breathing.

First Aid

Administer artificial respiration when required. Place a constricting band above the site of the sting if it is on the arm or leg. The band should not be so tight that it will stop the pulse in the affected limb. It should be loose enough so that one could slip a finger under it. The purpose of the constricting band is to slow down the absorption of the poison into the blood circulation. Position the affected part below the heart level. Apply cold cloths or ice wrapped in cloths to the sting site.

Do not wait for symptoms to appear but procure medical care *immediately* if the child with the insect bite is known to be allergic to insect bites, has hay fever or asthma, or is highly sensitive to other substances.

8.2.9 Poisoning

A four-year-old child found a rodent-killer preparation under the kitchen sink and ate it. A five-year-old child found a can of weed killer in the garage and fed it to his three-year-old brother. A one-and-a-half-year-old child consumed furniture polish stored in a soft drink bottle. A one year old drank lighter fluid left in the backyard. Many children, but especially the three to four year olds, swallow large numbers of aspirin pills. Others take any pill found in the trash, in drawers, purses, or bottles that do not have safety closures. A two-year-old girl swallowed lye that was left on the porch. Because of that one unfortunate moment when lye was within her reach, she will face numerous operations and, if she survives, lifelong disability. Some of the above examples are given by the U.S. Product Safety Commission. Any hospital emergency room has numerous additional examples. The saddest cases are the personal testimonies of parents with children who were injured by poisons. Most of the accidents could be prevented. Refer to Chapter 9 on how to prevent accidental poisoning in your preschool.

Accidental poisoning happens wherever children have access to substances that are poisonous to them when swallowed, breathed, or touched. Ninety percent of all accidental poisonings occur to children under five years old. The preschool is very similar to a home. It may contain cleaning supplies, drain cleaners, paints, glue, probably some drugs and pesticides, insecticides, and rodent killers. The most frequent causes of poisoning are drugs (especially aspirin), household cleaners, insect sprays, kerosene, furniture polish, and pesticides. Poisoning is one of the three instances when proper action is very urgent. The other two are stoppage of breathing and severe bleeding.

Recognition of Poisoning

What are the signs and symptoms of poisoning? Suppose you do not know that a child had ingested some poisonous substance, what would make you suspect it? Clues are given in the following illustration.

After a period of free playtime a three-year-old girl was found coughing and gagging while sitting on the floor in the corner of the playroom. Her teacher's purse was beside her and the contents were strewn about. The child smelled of lighter fluid and the lighter fluid container was lying on the floor in a pool of fluid. It was difficult to know how much the child might have swallowed. The girl continued to cough and spit up while she was being cleaned. She seemed to become agitated and irritable and wanted to vomit. In spite of this she was given sips of milk to drink. The child's mother was called and also the emergency room of the city hospital. Then the girl was offered some more milk, which she drank. Following this she was taken to the hospital for medical care because she was suffering from the effects of petroleum products in the lighter fluid. The possible development of pneumonia and some depression of brain function in the girl were the concerns of the health professionals.

Remember that poisoning may not have occurred in the preschool center. The child may have swallowed something at home before coming to school. For example, shortly after arriving in the preschool, Jeff, a three year old, complained of being nauseated and dizzy. He was excused to go and lie down. When he was lying down the teacher noticed he was breathing fast. She also found Jeff was sweating and felt hot. Jeff requested some water and took sips of it. Then suddenly he vomited and there was some blood in what he vomited. The teacher called his mother to learn if Jeff had been ill during the night. Jeff's mother was on the way to the phone to call the preschool center. Apparently, she just found several aspirin tablets under Jeff's pillow. Jeff's mother then quickly looked for the aspirin bottle that is normally in the bathroom. When she finally found it under Jeff's night table she became very worried. Jeff was taken to the hospital for tests and observation. The health professionals did not know when Jeff took the aspirin tablets, probably at bedtime the night before. Jeff's mother felt that the bottle of 25 tablets was about half full but she could not be certain. The symptoms will vary depending on the poison and the amount of exposure the child had. He may become suddenly ill, have cramping abdominal pains, or vomit, have breathing difficulties, and a very slow or very rapid pulse. The pupils of the child's eyes may be very small or very large. He may be restless, drowsy, unconscious, or suddenly have convulsions. Look for clues that may help you to find the cause of his illness. Ask the child what happened. He may tell you himself if he swallowed some unusual substance. Ask other children what they have seen. Smell the ill child's breath. Look for stains or burns around the mouth or on the clothes. Look for a container from which the child may have taken something. Look into the child's clothes, pockets, or personal belongings for powders, tablets, or capsules.

If you suspect that a child has swallowed a poison follow the directions described below:

First Aid for the Conscious Child.

1. Give the child a glass of water or milk to drink to dilute

the poison. Discontinue this if the child becomes nauseated. If the child is having convulsions give nothing to drink.
2. Save the label or the container of the substance swallowed if it is available to identify the poison. If the child vomited save the vomited material.
3. Call the poison control center or a physician for medical advice.
4. If the child becomes unconscious, keep the airway open. If necessary administer artificial respiration or cardiopulmonary resuscitation when required. Call an ambulance or rescue squad immediately. Then continue with first aid for the unconscious victim as described below.
5. Notify the parent.

What Not to Do
Do not give the child vinegar or lemon juice to neutralize the poison. Do not give any oil.

If the Poison Control Center or Physician Cannot Be Reached
Induce vomiting only if:
1. The child swallowed an overdose of drugs or medications.
2. If you are certain that the substance swallowed was not a strong acid, alkali, or petroleum product. Arrange for transportation of the victim to a medical facility as soon as possible.

How to Induce Vomiting
Induce vomiting only on the advice and instructions of a physician or poison control center or under the conditions described above. Give the child one tablespoon of syrup of ipecac. If this substance is not available induce vomiting by tickling the back of the child's throat with your finger or the blunt end of a fork or spoon.

How to Recognize If Strong Acids, Alkalis, or Petroleum Products Were Swallowed
There may be burns around the child's mouth or a kerosene, gasoline, or similar odor. Some examples of these substances are toilet bowl and drain cleaner, ammonia, lye, bleach, sulfuric acid,

furniture polish, kerosene, gasoline, turpentine, oven cleaner, and cleaning fluids.

Special Considerations for Strong Alkalis

When liquid corrosive poisons, especially strong alkalis, such as drain cleaner or oven cleaner, are swallowed, the damage to the tissues of the mouth, throat, and esophagus is immediate. Diluting does not remedy the damage already done but will weaken the poison. However, it might induce vomiting. This only produces more damage. Therefore, in this case wise dilution, as tolerated without causing excessive nausea leading to vomiting, should be employed.

Special Considerations for Petroleum Products

Some petroleum products such as those containing pesticides are extremely poisonous when swallowed. In this case, the poison control center or a physician may advise the induction of vomiting.

Instruction on Labels

The information on labels of the containers of poisonous substances are frequently revised. Thus American Red Cross advises that one should follow the guidance of a poison control center or physician. If this is not available then follow the recommendations of the American Red Cross as described here and as published.[1]

First Aid for the Unconscious Child

1. Maintain an open airway.
2. Call for an ambulance or rescue squad immediately.
3. Administer artificial respiration or cardiopulmonary respiration if needed.
4. Save the container of the suspected poison.
5. Save a sample of vomited material if the patient has vomited.
6. Do not give any fluids or anything else by mouth to an unconscious child.
7. Do not induce vomiting. If the child is vomiting roll him on his side to drain the vomited material out of the mouth.

[1]*First Aid for Poisoning,* The American National Red Cross, 1977

First Aid for Specific Conditions and Injuries 213

8. Ask another staff member to notify the hospital to which the child is being taken.
9. Ask another staff member to notify the parent.

First Aid for the Child Having Convulsions

1. Call for an ambulance or rescue squad immediately.
2. Position the child so that she will not injure herself by hitting against anything.
3. Loosen any tight clothing around neck or waist.
4. Observe if the airway is staying open. If there is an obstruction of the airway attempt to correct it by proper head positioning. If necessary give artificial respiration and cardiopulmonary resuscitation.
5. Do not force any object between the teeth.
6. Do not give fluids.
7. Do not induce vomiting. If the child is vomiting turn her on her side to drain the vomited material from the mouth. After the convulsion keep the head turned to the side to drain the fluids.
8. Have someone notify the parent.

Because first aid procedures are constantly changing, update your information by contacting the American Red Cross yearly.

The importance of recording every injury, illness or any event affecting the child's health in the child's cumulative record cannot be emphasized strongly enough. This is a vital part of the preschool's health program.

CONTENTS

9.1.0 FACTORS THAT CONTRIBUTE TO ACCIDENTS
9.2.0 PRINCIPLES OF ACCIDENT PREVENTION
9.3.0 ACCIDENT PREVENTION IN THE PRESCHOOL
    9.3.1 Official Inspections
    9.3.2 Room-by-Room Check
    9.3.3 Poisoning Prevention
    9.3.4 Disaster Preparedness
    9.3.5 Safety and Accident Prevention Education
9.4.0 LEGAL CONSIDERATIONS

Credit: Marshall R. Hathaway

CHAPTER 9

Accident Prevention and Safety

An accident is an unexpected, unplanned event that could result in injury, disability, even death. On the other hand, safety could mean health, or life not harmed, damaged, or threatened. To insure that safety exists the following are required:

1. Awareness of hazards or sources of danger.
2. Information and knowledge.
3. Planning and preparation.

Even when you know and attempt to carry out the principles of safety, accidents are still apt to occur. But many accidents happen under circumstances in which safety precautions are not observed. So that this may not be said of your preschool setting, you should be aware of what has been found to threaten the safety of the young child. Information about hazards to a child may be found in data of the National Safety Council, the National Center for Health Statistics and the Administration for Children, Youth and Families (HEW).

Accidents cause more deaths and disability in children less than five years of age than does any disease. The types of accidents occurring frequently involve motor vehicles, drowning, playground equipment, ingestion of drugs and poisons, and burns. We will not concern ourselves with motor vehicle accidents and drownings because these accidents are not likely to occur in a preschool setting.

Playground Equipment

The National Safety Council reported that in 1973 playground equipment was involved in 100,000 injuries, which required some kind of medical attention. Children aged two to nine years were the largest group involved. The most frequent injuries were wounds to

215

the area above the neck. Swings and swing sets were most frequently the types of equipment involved in the accident. Often the legs supporting swings came away from the ground because children would swing or climb on the top bar and offset the balance of the equipment. Pushing, shoving, or standing too close to moving playground apparatus preceded many of the accidents.

Credit: Marshall R. Hathaway

Ingestions (Poisonings)

National Safety Council statistics for 1973 indicated that children less than five years old accounted for the major number of patients treated in emergency rooms for poisonings.

Death May Occur After Ingestions

The materials commonly involved are aspirin and similar drugs taken to reduce pain and fever, household cleaning products, and insecticides.

Burns

Frequent causes of burns among young children are floor heaters, hot liquids and vapors, stoves, and electric appliances. Flammability of wearing apparel is a serious contributor to burn injuries. Clothing fires can occur when children are near open fires, stoves and heaters, or play with matches.

9.1.0 FACTORS THAT CONTRIBUTE TO ACCIDENTS

There are many factors that contribute to accidents. For a better understanding, these factors may be grouped according to common causes for accidents. Such causes are:

1. Characteristics of children.
2. The environment.
3. Human nature.

Characteristics of Children

Children are inquisitive, adventurous, and active. When they see something, they will reach for it and taste it or at least put it to their mouth. By the time they are two or older, they not only walk and run but they can climb and open doors. They can use a stool or chair to climb higher and reach shelves or cabinet handles. Pushing over furniture or pulling over objects just at their reach are activities of the growing and exploring child. Children constantly imitate grownups. They cannot read yet, so labels on containers do not mean anything. But they are attracted by colorful packages. This means they will taste and swallow just about anything. The natural behavior of children, as we see, can be a hazard in itself. This hazard, of course, cannot be removed by us. Since we cannot change the natural behavior of children, we must supervise them and make the environment as safe as possible while we educate them in accident prevention. Children also have a great potential to develop natural skills; they learn to run, climb, jump, slide, and use outdoor play equipment. The teacher should guide, encourage, challenge, and coach them to develop the motor skills and competencies to cope with the world around them. It may seem that in this book we neglect to emphasize this. The encouragement, challenging, and guidance needed to expedite the development of motor skills is the subject of other publications and should be stressed throughout early childhood education. Our focus is on accident prevention and protection in general.

Environment

The environment has many sources of danger. We can control many hazards but we cannot make the environment totally safe. The environmental hazards are (1) the structures that are used, such as chairs, playground equipment, stairs, carts, tricycles, and baseball bats; (2) activities of other children such as shoving, pushing, hitting, and running; (3) materials appropriate for adult use but not for children such as electrical appliances, cleaning and polishing substances, and lighter fluids; (4) substances that are hazardous to everyone but particularly to children such as poisons, lye, pesticides, insecticides, and poisonous outdoor plants.

Human Nature

Human nature is another source of danger that contributes to accidents. We are not machines that are constant and predictable; we react differently under stress than under normal conditions. We are forgetful, absentminded, and even careless at times. Our judgment may be wrong and often we do not recognize some hazards. How many people, for instance, are aware that furniture polish can be very dangerous when swallowed by a small child? There are many dangerous substances around us, but it is the human factor, that is, the way we as adults handle these substances, that can make the difference between safety and accident. Every preschool organization uses glue and paints in working with children. Some of these products are especially made safe for children, others may be harmful. If the teacher is called away to answer the phone, it only takes a second for a child to swallow some glue. The child who has watched the teacher take aspirin, will imitate the teacher and grab the medicine bottle during the time the teacher goes to get a glass of water. The hazard caused by human factors must be controlled by education, planning, and practice.

9.2.0 PRINCIPLES OF ACCIDENT PREVENTION

There are four basic principles in accident prevention according to *School Safety Policies*, a publication by the American Association for Health, Physical Education and Recreation. First, one must recognize the source of danger or hazard. Second, do away with the hazard if possible. Third, keep the source of danger under control, if it cannot be removed. Fourth, do not add new hazards.

9.3.0 ACCIDENT PREVENTION IN THE PRESCHOOL

Every preschool must comply with the state safety standards for buildings and grounds to receive or renew the license to operate. It is important to maintain these standards, which are only minimal requirements, and to strive beyond these to attain the best possible safety.

9.3.1 Official Inspections

An official inspection of the building by the appropriate authorities is concerned in general with safe and appropriate construction and space arrangements. The health department inspects the facility to determine if it complies with accepted sanitary conditions and practices. The fire department checks to be certain that there is adequate fire prevention and there are fire disaster procedures which are understood by all staff and practiced at regular intervals (fire drills).

The best way to apply the principles of accident prevention is to participate in the official inspections of the facility performed by the regulatory agencies and also to conduct a room-by-room safety check tour at designated intervals. The preschool staff person in charge of first aid and safety and other preschool staff, if possible, should accompany the inspector. This will contribute to their understanding of rules and regulations and will explain why any existing conditions are to be corrected. To keep a record of the inspections, use a form typified by Figure 9-1.

```
                    Official Safety Inspections

Type of Inspection: _____ Date_____
Performed by (agency): _____
Official in Charge (name and title): _____
Day Care Staff Present (names): _____
Recommendations: _____
Result (approval, nonapproval, other): _____
```

Source. *E.H. Reinisch and R.E. Minear.*
Figure 9-1

9.3.2 Room-by-Room Inspection

The room-by-room safety check tour should be conducted by the safety director and other staff members as well as the housekeeping staff. Set a regular time to repeat the tour, for instance, on the first day of each month and keep a record of all observations. The tour itself can serve as inservice training in safety if properly planned. At the time of the inspection tour any accidents that may have occurred in the previous month may be reviewed. An open discussion should identify the cause of each and what additional preventive measures need to be taken.

Look at everything from the child's point of view and height. Actually get on your knees and position your head to the average child's level; then look around. You will be surprised at what you see but especially at what you do not see, particularly on top of counters. You will understand why a child will reach and pull down partially visible things.

Safety Checklist for Building and Grounds

Electric Wiring: check if any cords are damaged_____; are unused outlets covered_____; too many appliances connected to an outlet_____.

Fire Prevention: proper disposal and storage of flammable material_____; proper disposal of trash_____; location of fire extinguishers_____.

Floors, Walls, Ceilings: any slippery floors, damaged tiles, or other hazard_____; evidence of wall or ceiling damage_____.

Windows: all windows secure_____.

Dangerous objects: any plastic bags, matches, sharp objects, or other hazardous objects within reach of children_____; empty refrigerators or chests_____.

Poisonous Substances: are paints, cleaning agents, medicine and other dangerous substances stored under lock_____.

Stairs: check for lighting_____, and slippery conditions_____.

Kitchen: any heavy objects on counters that could be pulled down_____; children do not have free access to kitchen_____; any danger in case children do enter unsupervised_____.

Bathroom, Toilet: presence of any dangerous objects, medicine, scissors, other_____.

Classroom: check for hazardous objects, toys_____; proper maintenance of equipment_____.

Playground: is equipment in proper condition_____; are weekly maintenance checks and repairs performed_____; is ground in safe condition_____.

Source. *E.H. Reinisch and R.E. Minear.*

Figure 9-2

A checklist similar to Figure 9-2 can be used for the systematic tour that should include all of the following:

1. *Electrical Wiring.* Look for frayed or old cracked cords. Are too many electrical appliances connected to one outlet? Unused outlets should be covered. Do you know where the fuse box is, what size fuses to use, and where they are stored? You should never use any substitute for a fuse. Do you know where and how to disconnect the main power switch and whether or not you have a circuit breaker? Seek help from your electric company or an electrician if you do not know the answers to the above questions. Your fire department will check electrical hazards. These could cause electrical shocks and burns to children or they could be the cause of fires. All electrical wall outlets should be above children's reach or be covered with an outlet cover.

2. *Fire Prevention.* Make sure that your fire department has made a recent inspection. Go with them when they inspect your facility. Dispose of all trash promptly. Keep matches, paint thinner and other flammable materials under lock and away from intense heat. There should be no smoking in the preschool but this may be difficult to enforce. Have fire extinguishers in strategic locations. All staff should know where they are and how to use them.

3. *Floors, Walls, Ceilings and Heating Equipment.* Check floors in the whole center. You must immediately tack down loose carpeting, replace damaged or missing tiles and correct any slippery conditions. Look at all walls and ceilings for any indication of cracking or bulging. These conditions must be corrected. Radiators or other heating devices must be covered to protect children from burns. There should be no floor registers that could burn feet.

4. *Windows and Clear Glass Panels.* Make sure that children are prevented from opening windows. It is so easy for children to fall out of windows or crash through a window pane when they try to open or close windows. Do not use heavy curtain rods that can be brought down on a person if the curtains or drapes are forcefully pulled. Clear glass panels between rooms or between a room and the outside are serious hazards to children. Severe injuries have been received by children and adults who ran into

clear glass panels because they did not know they were there. Paint the panels or decorate them so that they can be seen.

5. *Hazards That Can Cause Suffocation.* Discard all plastic bags. A plastic bag pulled over a child's head can cause suffocation in minutes. This type of accident is not limited to the very young child. Even older children imitate adult use of plastic bags or play with large plastic trash bags or bags covering dry-cleaned garments. If possible, remove all chests, trunks, empty refrigerators, and freezers. If they cannot be removed, the doors, lids, or covers must be permanently secured or removed. In spite of frequent warnings and regulations, children still die when they use these containers for hiding places.

To prevent suffocation due to obstruction of the air passages by foreign objects, do not keep buttons, beads, and similar objects in the preschool. Be sure to have safe, sturdy toys. Do not serve foods that require much chewing to the children such as raw carrots, unchopped meats, or fruits with pits and nuts. Their teeth are not as well developed as in adults. When children are eating, they must be sitting down. Provide a quiet environment for meals. Teach children not to put objects other than food in their mouth.

6. *Stairs.* Check all stairways inside and outside of the center. You should be certain that the stairs have sufficient lighting, that the banisters can be reached, are sturdy and without points or splinters, and that the surface of the stairs is level, not rotten or slippery. Have a soft carpet tacked down at the bottom of the stairs; it will cushion a fall.

7. *Kitchen.* Clear counters of heavy objects, electrical appliances and containers of hot liquids. A child might pull them down on himself or another child. Children should not have access to electrical appliances. If a gas stove is used, the knobs should be out of reach of the children. Handles of pots and pans should be turned away from the edge of the stove to keep them also out of reach. A partially visible pot containing boiling liquid or a protruding pot handle are always dangerous to a young

child. Keep a container of salt near the stove; it will smother a small fire. Have a fire extinguisher in an accessible location or install sprinklers over the stove in the ceiling. Do not keep any substances such as paints, glue, kerosene, or furniture polish under the sink. Keep all hazardous substances in a locked storage room or in a place inaccessible to children. The kitchen should not be used by children unless they are closely supervised by the staff.

8. *Storage Room, Cellar, Attic.* Keep all doors that lead to storage areas locked at all times. However, check these areas, because a child could enter them in an unguarded moment. Dispose of trash, leftover paints, and other incompletely used substances. Do not forget to disconnect power tools and cover sharp, pointed, rough or otherwise hazardous objects.

9. *Bathroom, Toilet.* Make certain that doors cannot be locked from the inside. Some preschool acitivities are conducted in homes with bathrooms primarily designed for all members of a family. Child safety may not be the most important consideration in these circumstances. Do not keep medicines, cosmetics, or sharp objects, such as razors or scissors, in a medicine cabinet accessible to children. Electrical appliances should not be kept in the bathroom, since electrical shock may occur when a person touches a wet surface and an appliance that is plugged into an electrical outlet at the same time. Drinking containers should be made of plastic so they will not break when dropped on the sink or floor.

10. *Classroom.* Heavy objects should not be placed on tables or counters because a child might pull them down. Tall, free-standing, heavily loaded bookcases, file cabinets, and upright pianos may be toppled and cause very serious, even fatal, accidents. Material used for play such as paint or glue, should be of the nontoxic type and always used under continuous supervision, without exception. Read labels on the containers of all materials used in the classroom. If you are in doubt whether they might be harmful, call your local poison control center. If poison control information is not available then use these

substances with caution and assume that they are hazardous when swallowed. Keep the floors clear of toys, food particles, or liquid substances to prevent stumbling, slipping, or sliding falls.

Toys used in preschool activities must be safe for the child. The U.S. Consumer Product Safety Commission, under the Federal Hazardous Substances Act, has the authority to ban from sale hazardous toys and other articles intended for use by children. Until recently, many toys were banned each year. However, the commission found that it could not possibly check all toys. Therefore, instead of banning some toys, the commission now publishes recommendations on how to choose safe toys. You should follow the commission's general principles for selecting toys for your program. That is, (1) choose toys for the proper age level; (2) look for safety labels such as "nontoxic," "flame retardant/flame resistant"; and (3) watch for sharp or pointed edges, or small parts that could be loosened or removed and then swallowed. The U.S. Consumer Product Safety Commission has many pamphlets containing important safety information that every preschool facility should have. It is of utmost importance to check toys regularly and repair them promptly when damaged. Soiled toys should be either cleansed or washed, if possible, or discarded if cleansing is not possible. Electrical toys should never be used by children in preschool.

11. *Playground Area.*[1] Playground equipment should be chosen carefully for the proper age level. Check it for safe construction and be sure that all items are carefully installed and anchored before being used. Then conduct weekly checks for any defects, that is, loosening of parts, rusting, wear that would produce splinters, rough edges, or jagged points. Children should be taught how to use equipment safely and they should be supervised at all times in the playground area.

---

[1]Write to the U.S. Consumer Products Safety Commission for information concerning proper playground equipment.

Credit: Marshall R. Hathaway

9.3.3 Poisoning Prevention

Statistics about numbers of individuals poisoned, examples of types of poisoning, and methods of prevention have already been presented in Chapter 8. Following are some additional measures and summary of poisoning prevention procedures. The subject cannot be overemphasized.

Read labels on all household cleaning agents, cosmetics, and drugs. Reading these labels will help you to realize how dangerous some of these substances are to children when they are swallowed or when they come in contact with skin, eyes, or other body surfaces. Keep all of these potentially dangerous substances under lock or in inaccessible places. While using any of these substances, do not get distracted by a phone call or other event. It only takes a second to swallow a poison. Keep all substances in their original containers. Never transfer any toxic substance to a container used for food or drink. Discard the poisonous substances in a safe way; that is, flush drugs down the toilet. Children can retrieve discarded things from trash containers, if not at your preschool then anywhere else, before they reach the town dump. Certain drugs and other products are required by law to be sold in safety packagings. This type of container is not a guarantee that they cannot be opened by children. The packaging, according to the law, must be sufficiently difficult so that it cannot be opened by 80 percent of children under five. It may be more difficult to open by some children but not by all. Do not remove drugs from the safety container while they are in your preschool.

Do not take drugs yourself in front of children. Do not coax children to take a drug prescribed by a physician by calling it "candy." If medication must be administered to a child while in preschool, do not do this in front of the other children. Use pesticides only when absolutely necessary. Read all labels first before using pesticides; some pesticides should not be used at all where children are present. Never use ant cups. Remember that cleanliness and proper storage of food goes a long way toward keeping ants and roaches away.

Accident research is showing some interesting relationships. It seems that accidents occur more frequently when a child is hungry and tired, when in a new environment or when a new person is caring for him. Also a child is able to sense tension that may exist among grownups around him; at that time extra vigilance is

Accident Prevention in the Preschool **227**

necessary according to findings of accident research.

9.3.4 Disaster Preparedness

Develop a plan of action for disaster events such as a fire, an explosion, an earthquake, or flooding. Rehearse evacuation procedures at regularly scheduled disaster preparedness meetings. The following information should be known to every adult in the preschool and should be posted:

1. *Telephone numbers of the fire department and the heating unit service company.* Keep these numbers listed near the telephone.
2. *The main shutoff valve or switch for electricity, gas heating unit, and water.* Keep a diagram noting their location on your wall (Figure 9-3).
3. *All exits.* Keep a master diagram on the wall in all rooms (Figure 9-4). They must be clearly marked and free of obstacles at all times. Often teachers plan activities in doorways or leave furniture or play materials in the exits. This should be forbidden.
4. *Alternate evacuation routes* depending on the location of the fire.
5. *The closest fire alarm box.* Keep a master diagram or blueprint on the wall in your office.
6. *A flashlight on the premises* in an accessible location.

Location of Safety Control

1. Main water shutoff valve _____
2. Electric current circuit breaker _____
3. Heating unit shutoff switch _____
4. Fire extinguishers

Note: A diagram of the day care facility with the location of the safety controls is helpful.

Source: E.H. Reinisch and R.E. Minear.
Figure 9-3

If a fire breaks out follow these directions:

1. Get the children out of the building before you do

228 Accident Prevention and Safety

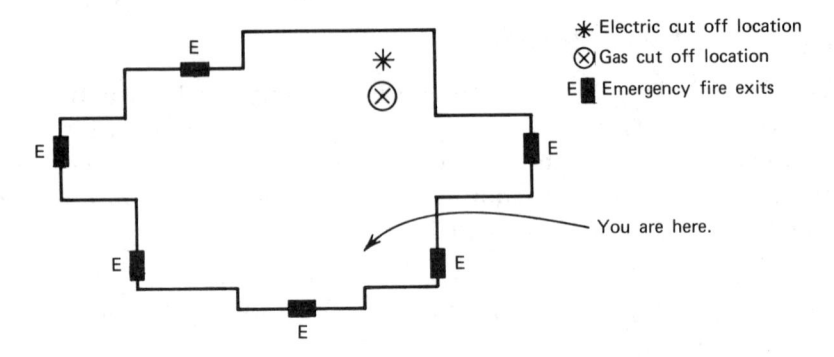

✱ Electric cut off location
⊗ Gas cut off location
E ▮ Emergency fire exits

You are here.

Floor Plan of the Center

Emergency Evacuation Plan

Keep one posted in each room.

Evacuation Routes:

A. Where to go when leaving this room
   Go down the stairs outside of this room and go outside by the door at the foot of the stairs. Get clear of the building and stay with your leader.

B. Who is the leader for this room?
   Miss Gray
   Miss Smith

C. Who are the center's group leaders?
   Mr. Guerra
   Ms. James
   Mrs. White
   Miss Appleby

Source. *E.H. Reinisch and R.E. Minear.*
Figure 9-4

anything else. Do not delay; if you count the number of children each day (as you should) you can match this with the number of children evacuated.
2. Call the fire department and do not hang up; they may want to verify the location of the call.
3. If you use an alarm box, pull the alarm and have someone stay there so that the fire department may be directed to the fire.
4. Do not go back into a burning building for pets, belongings, or any valuable objects.
5. Lower the children through a window, if you are trapped on the second floor; there will be only an 8- to 10-foot drop. Lower yourself from the windowsill rather than jumping.
6. Feel a closed door during a fire before you open it. If it is warm, do not open it.
7. Avoid entering a smoke-filled stairwell.
8. If trapped in a room, stay with your head low and close to the floor because hot air and poisonous gas tend to rise.

In case of a heating unit explosion, turn the shutoff switch if possible. In case of a water pipe break, turn off the main water valve.

In case of an earthquake keep children indoors, under tables, in door frames or other sturdy structures. Keep them away from windows, chimneys, or any objects that might fall.

Children should be assured that teachers will stay with them during any disaster. They should be cautioned not to panic and run away but to stay with the teacher. Parents should also be assured that the children will be cared for by the teachers until parents can call for them.

9.3.5 Safety and Accident Prevention Education

Safety and accident prevention is not something that can be simply established once and then forgotten. It is a concept that everyone has to understand and be aware of constantly. That is the purpose of the safety and accident prevention education program. Offered to preschool personnel, parents, and even young children, it can be very effective. All of the staff including housekeeping, food service, and maintenance personnel should be given training. All new employees should have a complete orientation to the facility and the safety program. The children should learn about safety and accident prevention in a variety of experiences. For example, the U.S. Department of Health, Education and Welfare has prepared a *Guide for Teaching Poison Prevention in Kindergartens and Primary Grades*.[2] This excellent publication can be adapted to the preschool child. The guide's teaching objectives [are:]

"1. To assure a safe school environment for pupils
2. To provide pupils with experiences which will:
   a. Help them recognize situations which involve potential poisoning hazards
   b. Begin to develop a sense of responsibility on the part of every boy and girl for the safety of himself and others in relationship to the use of potentially poisonous substances, especially in the home
   c. Develop the pupils' understanding of the need to ask before tasting, and to form the habit of following this procedure.
3. Through interest of pupils, reach parents with lifesaving information on prevention of poisoning in the home."

This guide contains a variety of suggested activities that help children attain the objectives of accidental poisoning prevention. For example, games, dramatic plays, discussion, stories, and other activities are presented. There are also suggestions for involving parents. Activities for a Poison Prevention Week are suggested.

A list of resources for the teacher is in the guide as well. A similar approach can be used for the prevention of accidents other than poisoning.[3] For instance, children may be involved in some phases of the teacher's first aid refresher course. They might participate in the techniques of bandaging and application of splints. While they are doing this you should discuss the dangers of falls or improper use of playground equipment. A preschool could sponsor a first aid course for parents. There are films on accident prevention and safety that may be used for this purpose. You could have a joint program for parents and the early childhood education teachers. Community

---

[2]*Teaching Poison Prevention in Kindergartens and Primary Grades*, Superintendent of Documents, U.S. Government Printing Office, Washington, D.C., 20402.

[3]American National Red Cross, Health and Safety Course for Primary Grades, 1975.

resources should be used for education in accident prevention and safety. As an example, in one community, Springfield, Mass., the fire department organized an educational safety program for babysitters and then published a booklet from its experience. This type of safety program applies not only to child caretakers but to personnel of any preschool. It is an excellent example of how you could utilize community organizations in accident prevention and safety education.

Rules that apply to children's activities should be used as a part of their education for safety. It is important to have definite rules for children's behavior. Have as few and as simple rules as possible but enforce them strictly and be sure the reason for each is understood. A sample of such rules might be:

1. Sit down to eat.
2. Do not run with objects in your mouth (a brush, pencil, or stick).
3. Use playground equipment as instructed.

```
                        Record of
                   Safety Education Activities

First Aid Refresher Course          Date: from_____ to_____
Number of total hours_____ Number of sessions_____
Conducted by: teacher_____ (certified instructor -
or other_____)
Sponsoring organization _____
Number of participants_____. List names on separate sheet.
Contents:_____ Comments: _____

Disaster Preparation Procedure      Date: _____
                                    Duration: _____
Conducted by:
Number of participants_____. List names on separate sheet.
Description: _____

Safety Check of Building and Grounds   Date: _____
                                       Duration: _____
Conducted by: _____
Number of participants_____. List names on separate sheet.
Description: _____
```

Source. *E.H. Reinisch and R.E. Minear.*
Figure 9-5

4. No shoving or pushing in the playground.
5. Keep a safe distance from moving playground equipment (swings, seesaws, or merry-go-round).
6. Keep out of the kitchen.
7. Do not put anything in your mouth except the food served to you.

The previously mentioned participation of staff in official inspections, disaster preparedness, and safety check tours is also important education for all preschool staff.

Records of safety and accident prevention education program activities should be kept (Figure 9-5).

9.4.0 LEGAL CONSIDERATIONS

Most states have laws that mandate certain health and safety measures in preschools. When measures are mandated it means that they are required. Some measures, on the other hand, may be permitted but are not required. The difference between permission and requirement is illustrated in the following example. According to one state's rules and regulations, a director of a preschool may agree to give medication to children when other arrangements cannot be made. This activity is not required of the director. However, if she agrees to do so, it is mandatory that written permission of a parent be received.

State laws form a legal foundation for the school health and safety program. The responsibility for safety and health rests with the preschool's administration and staff. A teacher could be held liable for damages that a child incurred due to an accident while under supervision. This is so only if it could be proven that the teacher was negligent or at fault in the performance of his duties. The teacher must know the laws. Ignorance of a law will not protect a teacher or administrator from liability in case of an accident that happened because the law was not obeyed.

Young children are protected by law because of their age; they are defined as minors. They cannot take care of themselves. Even if children disobey a rule and are at fault, they will not be held liable. Should a parent sign a waiver that frees the teacher from responsibility, the law will still protect the child, and the teacher can be held liable. A waiver is an act of intentionally giving up or relinquishing a right, such as the right of a child to be protected by law. If legally challenged, a teacher must show that she met responsibilities.

How does the school's director and each individual teacher meet their responsibilities? All laws pertaining to preschools must be obeyed. Every teacher must know the laws and keep up with changes in the laws, which may take place every year. The school must have a good health and safety program.

All teachers should be certified in first aid. In some communities this is a requirement for employment and this policy is highly recommended. The school should have clear first aid, accident prevention, and safety policies, as set forth in chapter 8 and 9. There should be rules for safe behavior of children.

Record keeping is very important. Every accident should be accurately and fully recorded. The school's administration should be notified and receive a copy of all accident reports. Parents should be notified of all unusual occurrences in writing as well as being told. Written permission should be obtained for field trips, special medical tests, and other unusual events. If a child is given medication while in the preschool, written instructions from the physician and parents' permission must be obtained.

Every preschool organization should have a legal advisor who may be consulted when health and safety policies are being formulated and whenever legal advice is required.

Every preschool and every teacher should carry liability insurance. Teachers accepting a position in a preschool should know the insurance arrangements of their employer.

GLOSSARY

Abdomen. The body cavity between the chest and pelvis.

Abrasion. A wound caused by scraping or rubbing away a portion of the skin surface.

Acute illness. Has a rapid onset, severe symptoms, and a short course.

Allergen. A substance that produces an allergic reaction.

Allergy. An unusual reaction of sensitive individuals to specific substances. A nonsensitive individual will not react in any unusual manner when exposed to these substances.

Amblyopia. Decreased vision in an eye due to causes external to the eye.

Amino acids. The basic building blocks of protein. The essential amino acids must be supplied to humans by animal or plant nutrients. Nonessential amino acids are made in the body.

Anemia. A condition in which there is less than normal amount of red blood cells or hemoglobin, the oxygen carrying substance in these cells.

Antibiotic. A chemical substance that kills or inhibits the growth of microorganisms. It is used in the treatment of infectious diseases.

Antibody. A substance produced in the body in response to a sensitizing material called an antigen. The antibody protects an individual from disease (provides immunity).

Antidote. A substance that counteracts a poison or its effects.

Artificial respiration. The maintenance of breathing by artificial means when a person cannot breathe without aid.

Asthma. A condition of difficult breathing due to contraction of muscles surrounding the small bronchial tubes leading to small air spaces in the lungs. Asthma is usually an allergic condition.

Audiometer. An instrument used for measuring hearing.

Calorie. A unit to measure energy.

Carbohydrates. Sugars and starches, they are the main source of energy in our food.

Cardiopulmonary resuscitation (CPR). A combination of artificial respiration and artificial circulation. It is an emergency procedure when the heartbeat stops.

Catarrh. Inflammation of mucous membranes.

Chickenpox. An acute viral communicable disease causing itchy vesicles (tiny blisters) on the skin and mucous membranes.

Chronic illness. Lasting a long time, not acute.

Color blindness. Inherited inability to recognize, distinguish or perceive one or more colors.

Communicable disease. A disease caused by an infectious agent that can be transmitted directly or indirectly from man or animal to a susceptible individual.

Congenital. Present at birth.

Conjunctivitis. An inflammation of the mucous membrane covering the eye.

Constipation. A condition in which there is a lack of regular or soft bowel movements.

Convalescent period. The time interval during which an individual is recovering from a disease.

Convulsion. Repeated involuntary muscle contractions and relaxations lasting several minutes or longer with loss of consciousness and at times also loss of bowel and bladder control.

Cough. Forceful expulsion of air from lungs to remove irritants in the lungs or lower airway.

Cover test. A screening test for crossed eyes (strabismus).

Croup. A type of breathing difficulty characterized by a raspy noise during inspiration and a barking sound on expiration. Croup can be caused by an infection, swelling, or foreign body in the voice box or throat.

Cystic fibrosis. An inherited disease that affects mucus secreting glands. Respiratory and pancreatic abnormalities are the most frequently observed.

Dehydration. A shortage of fluid in the body due to excessive loss or insufficient intake of water. It causes disturbance in body function.

Dental cavities. The breakdown and loss of the enamel and subsequent damage to the core of the tooth.

Diabetes. An inherited disease in which the body does not make proper use of sugar.

Diabetic coma. Loss of consciousness due to severe diabetes that has not been treated or has not been adequately controlled.

Digestion. The process of changing food that has been eaten into substances that can be absorbed and incorporated into the body.

Diphtheria. An acute communicable disease usually involving the tonsils, throat, and larynx. It causes grayish membranes to form in the throat and may cause heart damage.

Dislocation. The displacement of a bone from its normal joint position.

Dysentery. Inflammation of the intestinal lining that can be caused by a variety of infectious agents. It is characterized by diarrhea and other symptoms.

Eczema. An acute or chronic inflammation of the skin, usually itchy, not contagious.

Enzymes. Complex chemical substances that initiate or speed up chemical reactions in the body.

Epistaxis. Nosebleed.

Etiology. The study of the causes of disease.

Farsightedness. A defect in vision due to light rays coming into focus behind the eye instead of on the retina. Farsighted persons see faraway objects well but close objects are blurry.

Fatty acids. The part of the fat that determines its nutritional characteristics. Fatty acids are classified as saturated, unsaturated, and polyunsaturated. Polyunsaturated and unsaturated fatty acids are nutritionally better than saturated ones.

Febrile. Feverish.

Fever. An elevation of body temperature above normal. Fever in a child is a temperature of 101° or greater as measured by a thermometer.

Fungi (singular: fungus). Types of organisms. Some are microorganisms that can cause infections.

Gamma globulin. A protein in the blood that gives immunity to certain infections.

German measles (rubella). A viral communicable disease particularly dangerous in pregnant women because of the damage it may cause to the unborn child very early in pregnancy.

Health assessment. An evaluation or measurement of an individual's health by the use of many methods.

Health history. A record of all past events that affected an individual's health, such as illnesses, operations, and injuries.

Health professionals. Physicians, nurses, physician's assistants, pediatric nurse practitioners, physical therapists, and other professionals whose primary task is to supervise and take care of the health of individuals.

Hemophilia. An inherited defect in the blood-clotting mechanism so that blood will not clot in the normal length of time causing abnormal bleeding.

Hydrocarbons. Petroleum products that are poisonous when ingested.

Immune. Protected from a disease.

Immunization. The process of making an individual immune.

Impetigo. A communicable skin disease marked by lesions that contain pus.

Incubation period. The time between exposure to an infectious agent and appearance of the first symptoms of the disease in question.

Infection. The entry and multiplication of an infectious agent into the body. Not synonymous with infectious disease. An infection does not necessarily manifest signs or symptoms, but when it progresses into an infectious disease then signs and symptoms appear.

Infectious agent. An organism, most often a microorganism, capable of producing an infection or infectious disease.

Infectious disease. A disease of man or animal resulting from an infection.

Infectious hepatitis. A communicable viral disease affecting the liver and often causing jaundice.

Infestation. The presence and reproduction of arthropods, a group of animals such as lice and fleas, on the body surface or in the clothing.

Insulin reaction. An emergency situation that occurs when the blood sugar is too low due to an excess of insulin in the body.

Jaundice. Yellow color of the skin and the whites of the eyes due to an excess of bilirubin (a bile pigment) in the blood.

Junk foods. Foods that are very high in carbohydrate content and produce energy when eaten but without providing nutrients.

Glossary 239

Laceration. An irregular, jagged tear in the skin and underlying tissues.

Laryngitis. An inflammation of the larynx or voice box.

Larynx. The organ of voice.

Lead poisoning. A disease caused by the intake of the metal lead into the body. It affects the functioning of the nervous system.

Learning disability. A defect in the ability to perform tasks expected of most individuals at a particular developmental age.

Manual thrusts. A rapid series of thrusts to the upper abdomen or chest that force air from the lungs. It is an emergency procedure when a foreign body obstructs the airway.

Measles. A highly communicable disease caused by a virus.

Meningitis. An inflammation of the membranes surrounding the brain and spinal cord.

Metabolism. The process that utilizes the nutrients that have been absorbed into the body; it is the sum of all chemical and physical changes that take place within the body.

Microorganism. Small living body not visible to the naked eye. Examples are bacteria and viruses.

Minerals. Solid elements occurring in nature. Some minerals are important in our diet.

Minimum daily (nutritional) requirements. The minimum amounts of nutrients needed daily to provide energy and promote growth. They vary with the age and weight of an individual.

Mite. A small type of organism. Some mites are parasites and cause skin irritations such as scabies.

Mumps. A communicable viral disease affecting primarily the parotid gland (a salivary gland located in front and below the ear lobe).

Myopia. Nearsightedness. It occurs when light rays focus in front of instead of on the retina. Nearsighted persons see nearby objects well but not those that are far away.

Nausea. The urge to vomit.

Neurological disorder. Any condition that affects the nervous system so that it does not function properly.

Nutrients. Carbohydrates, fats, proteins, water, vitamins, and minerals that provide energy and promote growth.

Nystagmus. Constant, involuntary, rapid movement of the eyeballs.

Obesity. Overweight due to an increase in the amount of fat in the body.

Paroxysm. Sudden recurrence of symptoms of a disease.

Pasteurization. The heating of a fluid at a specified temperature and for a specified time to destroy undesirable bacteria without significantly changing the composition of the fluid.

Period of communicability. The interval of time during the course of a communicable disease when the disease can be transmitted to another person.

Perception. Being aware of sensory stimulation.

Pertussis (whooping cough). A communicable bacterial disease causing repeated spells of a "whooping" cough.

Pharynx. Throat.

Pinworm. A small parasite causing an infection of the intestines and rectum.

Pneumonia. Inflammation of the lungs.

Poison ivy. A plant that causes an inflammation of the skin when a person comes in contact with it.

Poison oak. A plant that causes an inflammation of the skin when a person comes in contact with it.

Poliomyelitis. An acute viral disease that affects the nervous system. Paralysis may occur.

Prematurity. A child born before the normal time or a child less developed than normal even though born after the normal length of time.

Prodromal period. Initial stage of a disease when the first symptoms appear.

Proteins. Nutrients that are the major source of nitrogen. Composed of smaller units called amino acids, some of which are essential.

Pus. A liquid, usually yellow, which is the result of an inflammation.

Resonance. A quality of sound due to vibration.

Retina. The inner layer of the eye where receptors for light rays are located.

Scabies. A highly communicable skin disease caused by a mite, a small parasite.

Scarlet fever. An acute communicable disease caused by an infection with the bacterium called streptococcus. It produces a sore throat and a fine granular skin rash particularly in the skin folds.

Semantics. The meaning given to words.

Sickle cell anemia. An inherited abnormality of the chemical structure of substances in the red blood cells. It causes the red blood cells to be sickle or crescent shaped and not to function properly.

Signs of a disease. The objective evidence of an illness that another person may observe, in contrast to symptoms that are subjective.

Snellen chart. A chart used to test visual acuity.

Sputum. The material that is expelled by coughing.

Strabismus, squint, or crossed eyes. A condition that causes one or both eyes to turn in toward the nose or out away from the nose or up or down. This prevents both eyes from looking at the same object at the same time.

Strep throat. An infection of the throat caused by the bacterium called streptococcus. If not treated with appropriate antibiotics serious after effects may result.

Stye. An infection at the base of an eyelash.

Susceptible. A person who presumable does not have enough resistance to a particular disease-producing agent to prevent contracting a disease when exposed to the agent.

Symptoms. Characteristics of a disease that are subjective, that is only apparent to the patient. Note: Sometimes the term symptom is used to include both characteristics that are subjective as well as the objective ones, called signs.

Syphilis. A sexually transmitted infectious disease.

Tooth enamel. The hard white substance that covers the exposed surface of teeth.

Tuberculosis. An infectious bacterial disease that most frequently affects the lungs and lymph glands.

Tuberculin test. A skin test used to determine the presence or absence of a tuberculous infection.

Vaccination. The process of making an individual immune.

Visual acuity. The relative ability to see clearly at a specified distance.

Vomitus. The material brought out by vomiting.

BIBLIOGRAPHY

American Academy of Pediatrics, *Report of the Committee on Infectious Diseases,* Evanston, IL., 1977.
American Academy of Pediatrics, *Recommendations for Day Care Centers for Infants and Children,* Evanston, IL., 1973.
American Association for Health, Physical Education and Recreation, *School Safety Policies,* Washington, D.C., 1968.
American Academy of Orthopaedic Surgeons, *Emergency Care and Transportation of the Sick and Injured,* George Banta Co., Wisconsin, 1977.
American National Red Cross, *Advanced First Aid and Emergency Care,* Doubleday and Co., New York, 1973.
American National Red Cross, *First Aid for Foreign Body Obstruction of the Airway,* 1976.
American National Red Cross, *First Aid for Poisoning,* 1977.
American National Red Cross, *Standard First Aid and Personal Safety,* Doubleday and Co., New York, 1973.
Bailey, E. N. et al., "Screening in Pediatric Practice," *Pediatric Clinics of North America,* 21, 123-165, 1974.
Benenson, A.S., *Control of Communicable Diseases in Man,* American Public health Association, Washington, D.C., 1975.
Bete, Channing L. Co., Inc., *About Speech and Hearing Problems,* Greenfield, Mass. 1973.
Black's Law Dictionary, West Publishing Co., St. Paul, Minn. 1968.
Brown, M.S., "Approaches to Hearing Testing of Children in the Office—Coments on Present Status," *Clinical Pediatrics,* 7, 639-646, 1975.
Calderone, M. S., "Sex Education and the Very Young Child," *PTA Magazine,* 61, 16-18, 1966.
Commonwealth of Massachusetts, Office for Children, *Standards for the Licensure of Approval of Group Day Care Centers* (Regulations of the Office for Children, Chapter VII), Boston, 1976.
Cooley, D. G., ed., *Family Medical Guide,* Better Homes and Gardens, Meredith Corp., New York, 1973.
Eisner, V. and A. Oglesby, "Health Assessment of School Children—Physical Examinations," *J. School Health,* 41, 239-242, 1971.
Eisner, V. and A. Oglesby, "Health Assessment of School Children—Screening Tests," *J. School Health,* 41, 344-346, 1971.
Eisner, V. and A. Oglesby, "Health Assessment of School Children—Vision," *J. School Health,* 41, 408-410, 1971.
Eisner, V. and A. Oglesby, "Health Assessment of School Children—Hearing," *J. School Health,* 41, 495-497, 1971.
Eisner, V. and A. Oglesby, "Health Assessment of School Children—Selecting Screening Tests," *J. School Health,* 42, 21-24, 1972.
Eisner, V. and A. Oglesby, "Health Assessment of School Children—Height and Weight," *J. School Health,* 42, 164-165, 1972.

Bibliography

Frankenburg, W. K. and J. B. Dodds, *Denver Developmental Screening Test Manual*, University of Colorado Medical Center, 1967.

Gallahue, D. L., *Motor Development and Movement Experiences for Young Children (3-7)*, Wiley, New York, 1976.

General Mills Inc., *Meal Planning for Young Children*, Nutrition Department, 1974.

Goodwin, M. T. and G. Pollen, *Creative Food Experiences for Children*, Center for Science in the Public Interest, Washington, D.C., 1974.

Green, M. I., *A Sigh of Relief—The First-Aid Handbook for Childhood Emergencies*, Bantam Books, 1977.

Hess, R. D. and D. H. Croft, *Teachers of Young Children*, Houghton Mifflin, Boston, MA., 1972.

Jelliffe, D. B. and E. F. P. Jelliffe, "A Bookshelf of Nutrition Programs for Preschool Children"—*American Journal of Public Health*, 62, 469-475, 1972.

Kalt, B. R. and R. Bass, *The Mother's Guide to Child Safety*, Grosset and Dunlap, New York, 1971.

Leeper, S. H. et al., *Good Schools for Young Children*, Macmillan, 1974.

McWilliams, M., *Nutrition for the Growing Years*, Wiley, New York, 1975.

Masland, M. W., "Speech and Hearing Checklist," Volta Reviews, *Journal of the Alexander Graham Bell Association for the Deaf*, 1970.

Mayer, J., *Health*, D. Van Nostrand, New York, 1974.

Metropolitan Life Insurance Co., Health and Welfare Division, *Day Care—What and Why*, 1976.

Metropolitan Life Insurance Co., Health and Welfare Division, *Looking for Health*, 1976.

Metropolitan Life Insurance Co., Health and Welfare Division, *Memo to Parents about Immunization*, 1976.

Metropolitan Life Insurance Co., Health and Welfare Division, *Panic/or Plan?*, 1977.

Metropolitan Life Insurance Co., Health and Welfare Division, *The Personal Health Record*, 1972.

National Bureau of Standards, Toy Safety, C 13.20/2:72-76, 1977.

National Committee on School Health Policies, *Suggested School Health Policies*, American Medical Association, Chicago, IL., 1966.

National Dairy Council, *Health Education Materials*, Chicago, (yearly).

National Dairy Council, *Food Before Six*, A Feeding Guide for Parents of Young Children, Chicago, IL., 1968.

National Safety Council, *Directory of Home Safety Films*, No. 1101-169, Chicago, IL., 1973.

National Safety Council, *Falls*, Safety Education Data Sheet No. 5, 1973.

National Safety Council, *Flammability of Wearing Apparel*, Safety Education Data Sheet No. 90, revised, 1975.

National Safety Council, "*A New Look at Poisonous Plants.*" reprinted from *Family Safety Magazine*, Chicago, IL., 1972.

National Safety Council, *Play Areas*, Safety Education Data Sheet No. 29, 1967.

National Safety Council, *Playground Apparatus*, Safety Education Data Sheet No. 69, 1973.

Bibliography 245

National Safety Council, *Solid and Liquid Poisons*, Safety Education Data Sheet No. 21, 1974.

National Safety Council, *Toy and Play Equipment*, Safety Education Data Sheet No. 4, 1976.

National Society for the Prevention of Blindness, Inc., *A Guide for Eye Inspection and Testing Visual Acuity of Preschool Age Children*, No. P200A, 1973.

National Society for the Prevention of Blindness, Inc., *Your Child's Sight— How You can Help*, No. G108, 1975.

National Society for the Prevention of Blindness, Inc., *Crossed Eyes: A Needless Handicap*, No. G106, 1974.

National Society for the Prevention of Blindness, Inc., *Preschool Vision Screening*, No. P253, 1973.

National Society for the Prevention of Blindness, Inc., *Signs of Possible Eye Trouble in Children*, No. G102, 1975.

Oberteuffer, D. et al., *School Health Education*, Harper & Row, New York, 1954.

Pollock, M. B., and D. Oberteuffer, *Health Science and the Young Child*, Harper & Row, New York, 1974.

Sandell, P., *Teaching Dental Health to Elementary School Children*, American Association for Health, Physical Education and Recreation, The Classroom Teacher Series in Health Education, No. 1, Washington, D.C., 1967.

Shriners Burns Institute, *Common Questions About Fire and Burns*, Boston, 1974.

Springfield Fire Department, *Baby Tender Care Safety Program, Baby Sitters Program*, Springfield, MA., 1975.

State of Connecticut, State Department of Health, *General Statutes Relating to Child Day Care Centers*, 1974.

State of Vermont, Agency of Human Services, *Regulations for Day Care*, 1973.

Stare, F.J. and M. McWilliams, *Living Nutrition*, Wiley, New York, 1973.

Stein, M. et al., "Beyond Benevolence—The Mental Health Role of the Preschool Teacher," *Young Children*, 30, 358-372, 1975.

U.S. Consumer Product Safety Commission, *Poisonous Household Products*, Fact Sheet No. 21, 1974.

U.S. Consumer Product Safety Commission, *Toys*, Fact Sheet No. 47, 1974.

U.S. Department of Agriculture, *Food Buying Guide for Child Care Centers*, FNS-108, Washington, D.C., 1974.

U.S. Department of Agriculture, Food and Nutrition Service, *Planning Guide for Food Service in Child Care Centers*, A98.9; 64-2, Washington, D.C., 1976.

U.S. Department of Health, Education and Welfare, Bureau of Product Safety, *Teaching Poison Prevention in Kindergarten and Primary Grades*, DHEW Publication No. (FDA), 72-7017, 1972.

U.S. Department of Health, Education and Welfare, Bureau of Product Safety, *Toy Safety*, DHEW Publication No. (FDA), 73-7009, 1972.

U.S. Department of Health, Education and Welfare, Center for Disease Control, *The Flake and His Secret Plan*, DHEW Publication No. (CDC) 75-8264, 1975.

U.S. Department of Health, Education and Welfare, Center for Disease Control, *Increased Lead Absorption and Lead Poisoning in Young Children*, a statement by the Center for Disease Control, 1975.

U.S. Department of Health, Education and Welfare, Center for Disease Control,

Lead Paint Poisoning in Children—A Problem in Your Community? DHEW Publication No. (CDC) 77-8293, revised, 1977.

U.S. Department of Health, Education and Welfare, Office of Child Development, Day Care Series 7, *Administration*, DHEW Publication No. (OCD) 72-70, 1971.

U.S. Department of Health, Education and Welfare, Office of Child Development, *Films Suitable for Head Start and Other Child Development Programs*, DHEW Publication No. (OHD) 75-1039, 1975.

U.S. Department of Health, Education and Welfare, Office of Child Development, *A Handicapped Child in Your Home*, DHEW Publication No. (OCD) 73-29, 1973.

U.S. Department of Health, Education and Welfare, Office of Child Development, *Health Services: A Guide for Project Directors and Health Personnel*, Day Care Series 6, DHEW Publication No. (OCD) 73-12, 1973.

U.S. Department of Health, Education and Welfare, Office of Child Development, Day Care Series 3, *Serving Preschool Children*, DHEW Publication No. (OCD) 76-31057, 1975.

U.S. Department of Health, Education and Welfare, Office of Child Development, Day Care Series 5, *Staff Training*, DHEW Publication No. (OCD) 73-23, 1971.

U.S. Department of Health, Education and Welfare, Office of Child Development, *Teach Children Fire Will Burn*, DHEW Publication (OCD) 471-1969, 1973.

U.S. Department of Health, Education and Welfare, Office of Child Development, *Your Child from 1 to 6*. DHEW Publication No. (OCD) 73-26, 1973.

U.S. Department of Health, Education and Welfare, Office of Child Development, *Your Child from 3 to 4*, HEW Publication No. (OCD) 72-57, 1972.

Warner-Chilcott, Division of Warner-Lambert Co., *Your Precious Ears*, 153-34, Morris Plains, N.J., 1973.

Wheatley, G.M. and G.T. Hallock, *Health Observation of School Children*, McGraw-Hill, New York, 1965.

Willgoose, C.E., *Health Education in the Elementary School*, Saunders, Philadelphia, 1974.

Winick, M. P., *Films for Early Childhood—A Selected Annotated Bibliography*, Early Childhood Education Council of New York City, 1973.

FILMS

Before We Are Six (Screening Vision of Children), National Society for the Prevention of Blindness.
Child Beater, Children's Memorial Hospital.
Child Safety Is No Accident, Modern Talking Picture Service.
The Child Watchers, Time-Life Films.
Crossroads at 4 (Amblyopia), National Society for the Prevention Blindness.
Denver Developmental Screening Test, National Audio Visual Center.
Early Recognition of Learning Disabilities, M-1890, National Medical Audiovisual Center.
The Eyes Have It (Eye Safety), National Society for the Prevention Blindness.
Getting Ready for the Dentist, New York University.
Guiding Behavior, New York University.
The Hyperactive Child, CIBA Pharmaceutical Co.
If These Were Your Children, Metropolitan Life Insurance Co.
Introduction to Speech Disorders, Wayne State University.
Jenny Is A Good Thing (Nutrition), New York University.
Johnny's New World (Detection and Treatment of Children's Eye Problems), National Society for the Prevention of Blindness.
Lead Poisoning: The Hidden Epidemic, Long Island Film Studios.
Looking at Children (Observation to determine whether health problems exist), Metropolitan Life Insurance Co.
My Children Are Safe!, Acadia Mutual Life Insurance Co.
Right From the Start (Immunization), Public Affairs Commission.
Sickle Cell Anemia, Lee Creative Communications.
Teachers, Parents, Children, Sterling Films.
Testing Vision in the Preschool Child, M-2789-X, National Medical Audiovisual Center.
Testing Hearing in the Preschool Child, M-2790-X, National Medical Audiovisual Center.
The Things a Teacher Sees, International Film Bureau.
Time of Growing, Metropolitan Life Insurance Co.
Visual Perception and Failure to Learn, Churchill Films.

GUIDE TO SOURCES OF SELECTED PUBLICATIONS AND FILMS

Acadia Mutual Life, 51 Louisiana Ave., N.W., Washington, D.C., 20001
Alexander Graham Bell Association for the Deaf, 3417 Volta Place, N.W., Washington, D.C. 20007
American Association for Health, Physical Education and Recreation, 1201 Sixteenth St., N.W., Washington, D.C. 20036
American Optometric Association, 7000 Chippewa, St. Louis, MO 63119
American Public Health Association, 1015 Eighteenth St., N.W., Washington, D.C. 20036
Association Sterling Films, 600 Grand Avenue, Richfield, NJ 07657
Center for Science in the Public Interest, 1779 Church St., Washington, D.C. 20036
Children's Memorial Hospital, 2300 Children's Plaza, Chicago, IL 60614
Churchill Films, 662 North Robertson Boulevard, Los Angeles, CA 90069
CIBA Pharmaceutical Co., 300 Elizabeth Avenue, Somerset, NJ 07071
Early Childhood Education Council of New York City, 196 Bleecker St., New York, N.Y., 10012
General Mills Inc., P.O. Box 1113, Minneapolis, MN 55440
International Film Bureau, Inc., 332 South Michigan Avenue, Chicago, Il 60604
Lee Creative Communications, Inc., P.O. Box 1367, Rochester, NY 14603
Long Island Film Studios, P.O. Box P, Brightwaters, NY 11718
Metropolitan Life Insurance Co., One Madison Avenue, New York, NY 10010
Modern Talking Picture Service, Inc., 2323 New Hyde Park Road, New Hyde Park, NY 11040
National Audiovisual Center, National Archives and Records Service, Washington, D.C. 20409
National Medical Audiovisual Center, Station K, Atlanta, GA 30324
National Safety Council, 425 No. Michigan Avenue, Chicago, IL 60611
National Society for the Prevention of Blindness, Inc., 79 Madison Avenue, New York, NY 10016
New York University Film Library, 26 Washington Place, New York, NY 10003
Public Affairs Commission, 22 East 38th St., New York, NY 10016
Shriners Burns Institute, 51 Blossom St., Boston, MA 02114
Time-Life Films, 43 West 16th St., New York, NY 10011
Wayne State University, 5448 Cass St., Detroit, MI 48202

INDEX

Figures are designated by numbers in *italics*.

Abdomen:
  injury to, 186
  pain in, 129, 133
Abdominal thrust, *200*, 201
Accident or sudden illness, 170-178, 217-218
  emergency phone numbers in,*172*, *173*
  record keeping of, *174*, *175*, 225
  what to do in cases, of 170, *171*, 172, *174*, *175*, *176*, 177-178
  see also under specific accident or illness
Accident prevention and safety, 215-216, 218-219, *219*, 220, *221-224*
  education in, 43, 229-231
  emergency phone numbers in, 172, *173*
  program of, 8, 36-37, 58
Aches and pains, 81
Activities, variety of, 36-37, 58
Acute illness, record of, *130*
Administration and administrative responsibility, 8, 55
Administration for children, youth and families, 53, 215
Admission information and procedure, 17, 56
Advisory committee, 44
Aggressiveness, 158
Aides, 2. See also Teachers and assistant teachers
Allen picture cards, 112
Allergies, 178
American Academy of Pediatrics, 55
American Association for Health, Physical Education and Recreation, 218
American Diabetes Association, 206
American Red Cross, *see* Red Cross
Amino acids, *see* Proteins
Anger, 158
Antibiotics, 80

Antibodies, 89, 91
Artificial respiration, 196, *196*, 197
Assistant teachers, *see* Teachers and Assistant Teachers
Asthma, 137
Avulsion, 180

Back blows, 201
Back injuries, 183-184, 190, *191*
Bacteria, 79, 84
Balkiness, 159-160
"Basic Four" food groups, 71, 74
"Basic Seven" food groups, 71-74
Bathrooms and toilets, 223
Before We are Six (film), 113
Behavioral problems 157-158. See also *under specific problem*
Bites, animal and human, 183. See also Insect bites
Bleeding, severe, 177, 182 (HASTE AND IMMEDIATE ACTION NECESSARY)
Booster dose, 92
Boredom, 161
Breathing, stoppage of, need for immediate action, 177, 194-197
Bronchitis, 82, 86
Buildings and grounds, inspection of, 55, 58, 220
  safety check list for, *200*
  see also Playground equipment
Burns, 193-194, 216

Calcium, 70, 72
Calories, 65, 67, 73
Carbohydrates, 64, 65, 67, 73
Carriers, intermediate, 54
Chickenpox, 83, 85-87
Child and children:
  adult relationships, 17, 74

251

growth and development, course in, 39.
    See also Development
  health, course in, 39
  neglect and abuse, 24, 25, 26, 56,
    146-149
  specialized care for, 24
  see also Handicapped child
Children's Protective Services, 24
Chloride, 70
Choking, 198, 199
Cholesterol, 66
Colds, see Common cold
Collarbone fracture, 190, 192
Common cold, 82, 83, 84, 87, 95
Communicable diseases, 100
Community agencies, 43
Conjunctivitis, 82. See also Pinkeye
Consultants, 53, 56. See also Medical consultants and specialists
Contrariness, 160
Convulsions, 135, 198
Coordination difficulties, 164
Cots and blankets, 58
Cough, 133, 142
Cramps, 133
Crossed eyes, 105, 112
Croup, 136
Crying, 163
Curiosity, 157

Dehydration, 134
Dental cavities and examinations, 141-142
Dentist, 56
Denver Developmental Screening Test, 120, 121
Development, 108, 125
  disorders of, screening for, 119, 120, 121
Diabetes:
  emergencies due to, 201-203
  first aid in, 178
  information on, 204-207
  insulin reactions in, 204
  record in, 206
Diptheria, 80, 83, 91, 92
Disaster preparation, 227, 227, 231
  in case of fire, 227-228, 229
  see also under specific disaster

Discipline and punishment, 59
Diseases, food-borne, 96-99. See also Communicable diseases; Infectious diseases; Rashes, viral; and under specific disease
Dislocations (bones), 188-192. See also under specific bone
Dysentery, 83

Earache, ear infection and injuries, 86, 137, 185
Earthquake, procedure for action in event of, 178
Eating habits, irregular, 62. See also Food; Nutrients
Electric wiring, 221
Emergency care, course in, 43-44
Emergency evacuation plan, 228
Emergency file card, 178
Emergency medical care, 178
Emotional stress and conflicts, 70, 105
Encephalitis, 86
Equipment, 58. See also Playground equipment
Evacuation, 228
Explosion, procedure in event of, 178
Eyes:
  crossed, 105, 112
  injuries to, 185
  inspection and testing of, 113, 230
  watery, 80
  see also under Vision

Fainting, 197-198
Family crises, 160-161
Fatality, procedure in event of, 176
Fatigue, 8. See also Malaise
Fats, 64, 65-66, 67-68
Fever, 80, 81, 134-135, 142
Field trips, 233
Fire, procedure in event of, 57, 178, 227 227-228, 229, 229
Fire prevention, 221
First aid, 169-170, 171, 172, 173, 174, 175, 176, 177-178
  guidelines for, 170, 171, 172, 173, 174, 175, 176, 177-178
  refresher courses in, 43, 44

supplies for, 174, 178
see also under specific accident, emergency or injury
Food:
  cultural and ethnic customs concerning, 61
  faulty intake of, 75
  groups, 71-74
  and health, *see* Nutrients
  poisoning, 83, 96-99, 132
  sanitation, 96
  serving of, 74-76
  see also "Junk foods"; Snacks and snacking
Frostbite, 203, 208
Fungus, 79

Goodenough Draw-A-Person test, 122
Growth charts, *116-117*
Growth and development, course in, 39. See also Development; Physical growth
Guide for Eye Inspection and Testing, 113
Guide for Teaching Poison Prevention, 230

Handicapped child, 24, 56
Hand injuries, 186
Head injuries, *183-184*
Head start programs, 2
Health assessments, 103-107, 124-125
Health evaluation, periodic, 8, 24, 28, *30-31*
  preadmission, 8, 9-10, 108
Health examinations, preadmission, 108
Health histories, 56, 107-108
Health observations, daily, *20, 21, 23*, 108-111
  periodic, 43
Health problems, care and follow-up of, 24, 32
Health professionals, 1-2, 56
Health program, 8-9, *49*, 56
  administration of, 44, *45*, 46, 52-53
  budget guide for, *49*
  financial management of, 46

parent's agreement with, 20
record keeping of, 46
Health record, 8, 28-29, *30-31*, 33, 46, 48
  cumulative, 28, 33, 57
  see also Dental cavities and examinations
Health review, periodic, 28
Health and safety measures, legal considerations for, 233-234
Health services, contracts for, 44, *45*
Health supervision, continuous, 8, 18, 56-57
Health team, 3, 39, 104
Hearing examination and test, 45, 56, 111-112, *113*, 113-114
Hearing loss, 138-140
Hepatitis, 83. *See also* Infectious hepatitis
Hostile acts, 161
Hyperactivity, 163

Immobilization, elimination of movement, 190, *191-192*
Immunity:
  active, 79-80, 89-90, *91*
  of newborn, 90
  passive, 91-92
Immunization, 79-80, 90, *91, 93*, 100
  preadmission, 56
  in pregnant women, 94
  record, 15, 57
Impetigo, 142
Independence, 157
Infectious diseases, 79-100. *See also under specific disease*
Infectious hepatitis, 82, 85, 94. *See also* Hepatitis
Infectious mononucleosis, 87
Infectious agent, process, reservoir and transmision, 81-84
Influenza, 79, 82, 85
Ingestions, *see* Poisoning
Injuries, 183-186. *See also under specific part of body*
Insect bites, 143, 178
In-service education and training, 43-44, 59. *See also* Staff, education of
Inspections, official, 219
  room-by-room, 219, 220

Index

Insurance, 233
Iodine, 71
Iron, 71, 72
Isolation room, 56, 137

Jealousy, 161
"Junk foods," 62, 72, 75

Kitchen, 57, 58, 222-223
"Know-it-all" child, 161

Lacerations, 180-181
Laws, rules and regulations, 53-56
Lead poisoning and detection, immediate treatment essential, 58, 115, 118
Learning difficulties, 163-164
Leg, immobilization of, 190, *191*, 192
Legal considerations and adviser, 232-233
Liability insurance, 233
Lice, infestation with, 143-144
Licensing, 55
Limp (gait), 105
Lockjaw, *see* Tetanus

Magnesium, 70
Malaise, 142
Meals and snacks, 57. *See also* Nutrients; Nutrition
Measles, 79, 80, 81, 82-84, 85-86, 87
Medical consultants and specialists, 1-2, 8, 53. *See also* Pediatrician
Medical evaluation, comprehensive, 10
Medical examinations, 122-124
Medical tests, 233
  special, *see* Special procedures
Medication, administration of, 56, 129
Meningitis, 82, 108
Menus, 57, 76
Metabolism, 63-64
Microorganisms, 79, 81, 84
Minerals, 67, 70-71, 73
Missing child, procedure in event of, 178
Mites, infestation with, 143-144
Mumps, 80, 82, 83

Nail biting, 160

Nasal drip, 80, 81, 142. *See also* Runny nose
National Center for Health Statistics, 115, 215
National Safety Council, 215, 216
Neck fracture, suspected, 190
Negativism, 157. *See also* Separations
Neglect, *see* Child and children, neglect and abuse
Nosebleeds, 133, 186
Nose, injuries to, 186. *See also* Nasal drip
Nursery school, *see* Preschool environment
Nurses, 2, 9, 56. *See also* Teachers and assistant teachers
Nutrients, 64-66. *See also* Carbohydrates; Fats; Food, groups; Minerals; Proteins; *and* Vitamins
Nutrition:
  and food service, 33-34, *35*, 36, 55, 57-58
  learning experiences associated with, 33, 36
  program, abnormalities associated with, 57

Obesity, 76
Observations, *see* Health observations

Parent:
  communications and conferences with, 8, 51, *52*, 57
  involvement of, 59
  notification of, in illness, 37
  preadmission interview with, 10-17, 18, *19-20*, 56
Pediatrician, 8, 55
Penicillin, 80
Permission forms, *19, 20*
Personal hygiene, 83, 96
Personnel, 39, 55. *See also* Staff
Pertussis, 92. *See also* Whooping cough
Phosphorus, 71
Physical growth, screening for, 114, *115-116*
Physician and physician assistants, 1, 2
  emergency arrangements for, 56
  instructions from, *see* Special procedures

Index

see also Pediatrician; Teachers and assistant teachers
Pinkeye, 82, 84, 140-141
Pinworms, 73, 143
Planning committee, 8
Playground equipment, 215-216
  inspection of, 224
Pneumonia, 79, 82, 86
Poison Control Center, 211, 212
Poisoning:
  haste and immediate attention necessary, 177, 208, 213
  after ingestion of fever, and pain-reducing drugs, 216
  first aid for:
    child with convulsions, 213
    conscious child in, 211-213
    unconscious child, 212-213
  how to induce vomiting in, 211
  recognition of ingested matter in, 209-213
  special consideration for alkalis and petroleum products, 212
  see also Food poisoning; Poison prevention
Poison ivy and poison oak, 143
Poison prevention, 226-227, 230
Poison Prevention Week, 230
Poliomyelitis, 82, 87
Poor vision, 149-151
Preadmission examination, see Health examinations, preadmission
Preadmission health evaluation, 8, 9, 10, 108
Preadmission interview, see Parent
Preschool directors, 2. See also Teachers and assistant teachers
Preschool environment, 2. See also Playground equipment
Preschool health program, see Health program
Preschool Vision Screening (guide), 113
Proteins, 64, 66, 68, 73
Punishment, 59

Rashes, 81, 85-86
  viral, 142, 144

Recommendations for Preschools, 55
Record keeping and records, 8, 46, 233
  administrative, 51
  individual, 48
  release of, 48, 50
Red Cross, 43, 169, 213
Red Cross Manual, 170, 195
Regulations, see Laws, rules and regulations
Responsible adults on the premises, need for, 57
Ringworm, 79, 82, 83, 142
Rubella, 80, 81-82, 84
  See also German measles
Rules and regulations, 53-56
Runny nose, 133. See also Nasal drip

Safety and safety measures:
  education in, 229-231, *231*, 232
  legal considerations for, 282
  location of controls for, *227*
  official inspections of, *219*
Screening:
  for hearing, 111-112
  for physical growth, 114-115
  for vision, 112-113
  see also Testing
Separations, 163
Sex play and sexual interest, 169
Shyness, 162
Shock, 181. See also State of shock
Smallpox, 82, 90
Snacks and snacking, 47, 74
Snellen chart, 112
Social worker, 9, 56
Sodium, 70
Sore throat, 80, 81, 133, 135
Special procedures, 233
  parent's permission for, 27
  physician's instructions for, 27
Special programs, 24, 56
Speech defects and problems, 105, 151-154
Sprains, 188-190
Staff, education of:
  in child health and first aid, 8, 39, 43-44, 57, 158
  emotional difficulties of, 39
  first aid certification of, 158

256 Index

health evaluation and supervision of, 8, 37, *38*
health program for, 8, 17
health requirement and rules for, 55, 59
preeducation and posteducation tests for, 43
records of, 48
See also Personnel
Standard First Aid and Personal Safety (course), 170
Staphylococcus, 82
Starches, 65, 73
State of shock, 181, 187-188
Stomach pain, 129, 133
Storage rooms, 223
Strabismus, 105, 112
Strycar miniature toy test, 112
Student teachers, 2. See also Teachers and assistant teachers
Styes, 151
Sudden illness, see Accident and sudden illness
Sugars, 65
Sulphur, 70

Teachers and assistant teachers, 2-3
and child health assessment, 103-107
evaluation of, *40-43*
Temper tantrums, 158-159. See also Separations
Testing, parental permission for, 111. See also Screening

Tetanus, 80, 82, 84, 85, 87, 91, 92
Throat infection, 84
Thumb sucking, 160
Timidness, 162
Toilets, 223
Toothache, 141-142
Toys, 224
Tuberculin test and tuberculosis, 79, 95, 118-119

U.S. Consumer Product Safety Commission, 224
U.S. Department of Agriculture, 71
U.S. Department of Health, Education and Welfare, 23
Urination, problems with, 144-145

Vaccination, 90, 91
Viral rashes, 142-144
Visual Acuity of Preschool Age Children (guide), 113
Vision examination and test, 43, 57
Vision, poor, 149-151
Vitamins, 66-67, 68-70, 72, 73-74
Volunteers, 2, *42*
Vomiting, 63, 132-133
how to induce, 211

Walking patterns, unusual, 145-146
Water, 65, 67
Whooping cough, 79, 80, 82, 85, 87, 88
Wounds, 179-183